Century of Voices

Detroit Women Writers

Anthology

1900-2000

by

The Detroit Women Writers

C/O Friends of the Detroit Public Library
5201 Woodward Avenue
Detroit, Michigan, 48202

Cover and Book Design: Carolyn Vosburg Hall
Desktop type set on Mac Performa computer
Cover font: Bankenscript, Avant Garde
Text font: 10 pt and 9 pt Palatino

Printed by Book Crafters, Chelsea, MI
Publisher: Detroit Women Writers
Back cover photo: Elizabeth Kane Buzzelli

Library of Congress Catalog Card number: 99-072575
ISBN number 0-9670318-0-X

Grant from The Metro Book & Authors

About this Book

This book is for readers, for aspiring writers, for teachers, for anyone who loves the printed word and the thought behind it. Eighty-seven writers present works for you to enjoy, agree with, reject, or wonder about.

This representative collection by Detroit Women Writers members, a group that spreads across Michigan and beyond to Florida, Canada and even Japan, presents published works by nearly one-fifth of the all-time 500 members. These short works — each less than 1500 words or abridged — show the broad range of experience, skills, interests, and market opportunities over the years. The women focus more on home than war, more on aesthetics than business, and more on nature than the nation. Women write about what they know best and see every day.

In the book, material is arranged by theme with each selection, whether fiction, poetry, essay, drama, or article, flowing into or contrasting with the next. The first section, Century of Change, contrasts older and current members' writing styles and describes changing group workshop techniques. The second, Coming To Order, tells of organizational changes and cultural attitudes from suffragettes to feminists over the years. The third, The Middle Years, pictures the members through their meetings and activities. The fourth, Expanding Our Scope, shows the group's influence through conferences, seminars, readings, teaching classes, and other community involvement. The fifth, What Women Write, touches on the broad range of subject matter to illustrate the enormous body of work produced by the group. A final section includes the appendix and lists all 500 members and year joined.

A consistent style in punctuation and usage has been imposed on these pieces to make for easier reading. Text will vary in minor ways from original publication.

The Editors: Corinne Abatt
Elizabeth Kane Buzzelli
Carolyn Vosburg Hall
Marion Tuttle Marzolf
Doris Scharfenberg

Acknowledgments

By nature, writers are confident/insecure, productive/lazy, clear/obfuscating, all bound up in complex voices aiming to construct models and paradigms for our readers' enjoyment and reflection. Still, you will find writing strength and sheer magic here in *Century of Voices.*

Our stated purpose, since Detroit Women Writers was founded on June 5, 1900, has been to encourage creative writing of the highest professional standard, and to serve as a creative workshop for published writers. Over these last 100 years, that goal has not wavered, but persevered and matured. We celebrate here in *Century of Voices* that standard of excellence in its many permutations: fiction, essay, journalism, scholarly writing, playwriting, poetry, and more.

Thanks to all Detroit Women Writers members for the gift of their talent and time, and especially the five editors for their focused endurance in this vast undertaking: Corinne Abatt, Elizabeth Kane Buzzelli, Carolyn Vosburg Hall, Marion Tuttle Marzolf, and Doris Scharfenberg. In addition, the list of contributing Detroit Women Writers members includes: contributing editors — Gladys Leithauser, Elaine Watson and Jeanne Duran; copy editors (in addition to Abatt, Buzzelli, Hall, and Marzolf) — Carol Chadwick and Kathleen Ripley Leo; marketing —Vivian DeGain and Ruth Cain; and committee members — Louise Heck-Rabi, Marilyn Lyman, Victoria Diaz, Bettie Cannon, and Virginia Parker, chair of the year 2000 celebration.

Thanks to Jenny Nolan, The Detroit Free Press librarian for her assistance on historic matters.

Appreciation goes to the Detroit Public Library's Burton Collection for making available historic material.

Deepest appreciation goes to the Metro Book & Authors for believing in this project and providing seed money to make it happen.

Happy Reading!

Kathleen Ripley Leo, DWW president 1997-1999

Table of Contents

Section One: Century of Change

Section Two: Coming To Order

Section Three: The Middle Years

Section Four: Expanding Scope

Section Five: What Women Write

Appendix

Acknowledgments:
"First Light," by Gloria Whelan, an excerpt from a story of the same name appearing in *Playing With Shadows*, a collection by Gloria Whelen, copyright 1988. Reprinted by permission of the author and the University of Illinois.

"Last of the Big Breakfast Eaters," by Jeanne Duran, published in the Detroit Free Press, copyright 1962. Reprinted by permission of the author and the Detroit Free Press.

"December — All Mixed Up," by Cynthia King is chapter five from the book, *The Year Of Mr. Nobody*, by Cynthia King, Harper and Row, copyright 1978. This portion reprinted by permission of the author.

All other works printed by permission of the author or heirs.

Section One

* * * * * * * * *

Century of Change

HOW WOMEN WRITE POEMS
by Judith Goren
Passages North Anthology, 1990

Judith Goren, a DWW member since 1970, is a poet whose work has appeared in The Centennial Review, Passages North, Green River Review, and The Bridge. Her most recent of two published collections of poems was Traveling From The Heart, 1994.

A woman told me
that poems walk into her kitchen
while she is loading the dishwasher
or rolling dough for a quiche.
She pencils them on her white Formica table,
and later sponges them off,
squeezing melted words into the sink.

I know another woman
whose poems arrive on horseback,
gallop up behind her, grab her
by the throat and demand to live,
and one who holds lines all day
under her tongue, like unmelted
mints, until her babies are in bed
and the last dish is washed.
Then words roll out
neat as a package of Lifesavers.

A woman poet told me she has days
when, as she writes a line,
another tumbles after it
and then another, like a row
of irrepressible clowns
falling over sideways one by one.

But mine are another story.
All day I sit in my house
with the doors and windows wide,
waiting for the wind to blow something in.
Nothing has come this summer but flies,
and my tables are heavy with dust.

CENTURY OF CHANGE:

FROM SHAKESPEARE'S COTTAGE

On June 5, 1900, 13 Detroit women started what would eventually become Detroit Women Writers. Though most of the original 13 were members of the Woman's International Press Union, their written work included not journalism alone but poetry, fiction, non-fiction, librettos, and plays.

A condescending description in the 1909-10 Detroit Federation of Women's Clubs Directory states:

> There are two features in which this club differs from the others (writers' groups), namely: the meetings are held in the evening; and, second, the work of the members is taken up as a relaxation rather than literary labor. No topics requiring deep study, solid reading or diligent research through libraries or encyclopedias are given out, but everything is made practical, tending to daily uplift of thought, giving to each other the benefit of literary experiences.

The members were, however, serious and ambitious writers. One, Hattie C. Sleeper, ran the successful Michigan Clipping Bureau; both Lucy Leggett and Mrs. Franc Nichols served as vice principal of the Sprague Correspondence School of Journalism; many published novels, non-fiction books, articles, and poetry.

While it is not clear whether the members of the group workshopped their pieces when they first met at the clipping bureau in the Buhl block of downtown Detroit, by 1909 workshopping was a part of every meeting.

In 1909, Lester Bather, Cass Tech senior and son of member, Della H. Bather of Trumbull Avenue, designed and built a wood and cardboard miniature of Shakespeare's cottage for the group. The cottage was the designated place for manuscripts when the women gathered. "The doors and windows swing invitingly open. Even the door knocker reaches out appealingly." (1919 newspaper article: "Detroit Women Writers' Club").

In 1912, when Louise Breitenbach joined the group, she read her first story 12 times before it was "approved." Later, Breitenbach, needing something to read, began a serial: *Alma Of Hadley Hall*. Successive books took Alma on through college.

Many of the women writing at the time were publishing nationally.

By the 1920s, the meetings opened with the critics half hour. Manuscripts were drawn from Shakespeare's cottage, read, and critiqued.

A piece in *The Bulletin of the Detroit Women Writers' Club* of January, 1924, recapped January topics assigned to the members. On Tuesday, January 8, the Poetry Group was to write, " . . .two stanzas on "My Day Is Done." First and last lines of first stanza and last line of last stanza carry the refrain. Also six lines all ending in the same rhyme, any subject.

On January 22 the subject was "Windows." The Short Story Group wrote on:

1. A dialogue between two women in love with the same man.
2. A dialogue between two men in love with the same woman.
3. A brief character sketch, or short story, relying mainly on conversation to display character.

By the end of the century, Shakespeare's cottage has disappeared along with assigned writing topics. Workshopping is still a part of most meetings, with 20 minutes (or as time permits) allotted each reader. Usually ten minutes of this time is used for reading and ten minutes for critiquing. Marketing suggestions form part of the critique.

In the 1980s, splinter workshops were started again (in earlier years separate groups had formed from time to time), when Julia Grice began a fiction group. Soon other splinter workshops popped up until, here at the end of the century, there are playwriting groups, poetry groups, fiction groups, and eclectic groups where anything can be read. The splinter groups meet in member's homes. They have not become a part of the regularly scheduled meetings.

Differences between the work of early DWW members and later members tend not to be substantive. Subject matter — diverse and varied — remains much the same. Topics include home, family, love, grief, and fear. The writing muse, herself, has always been a source of worship and anger. In first president, Alice Elinor Bartlett's, 1905 "Among the Birches," we are given the hyperbolic, "Oh, ladies of the forest in gowns of silvery white" as poetic muse. By 1949, Myrtle Reynolds Adams is protesting against too much fact in her poem:

Slight Protest to Now

Give back my magic sun, My singing star ,, my fountains
of delight. My glimmering forests where the fancies run.
And mystic roads that lead beyond the night.

Here, at the end of the century, our poets find it possible to rail openly against a recalcitrant bitch/goddess/god muse. Judith Goren, in her poem, "How Women Write Poems, " complains:

All day I sit in my house
with the doors and windows wide,
waiting for the wind to blow something in.
Nothing has come this summer but flies,
and my tables are heavy with dust.

And poet Mary Jo Firth Gillett confesses her addiction to the "Word," set following with no indent to accommodate the line breaks: Not just a syllable, a ululation, click, roll, slur, trill. I want the whole damn thing, the roller-coaster ride of consonant, vowel, accent and innuendo.

What has changed over the century, however, are the people who write and the depths to which familiar subjects are explored.

Because Detroit has always been a melting pot within a melting pot, it was inevitable that the immigrant and unheard voices, stilled so long by poverty and custom, would begin to be heard once the second generation was educated. Linda Nemec Foster, in her poem, "Dancing with My Sister" (1995), celebrates 'crazy Polish weddings in Cleveland,' The Beer Barrel Polka, and offers a touching counter-look at the tarnished American Dream:

We glow because we came from the same burnt-out dream of
second-generation immigrants and learned to smile
at the closed mouth of loss and dance, dance, dance.

Poet, Kathleen Ripley Leo, sees another version of this life with an open-eyed look at her grandfather in "The Old Ways (vi)":

Once he made her sit
in the middle of the room while he yelled
about something in their language. She cupped
her chin like the yolk, her other hand
picked at her skirt, but she did not wince.

Naomi Long Madgett, writes of the black experience. In "Boy on a Bicycle," we see the child:

Where is he going, young black boy
in a city full of clouds and shadows,
pedaling two wheels up a hill in the rain?

Another obvious difference between 1900 and 1999 is the freedom to explore subjects the earlier women, in more constricted times, didn't enjoy. Compare the content of the 1891 *A Work Of Love* by E. Cora DePuy and Julia Grice's jarring *Jagged Light.* Compare Della Thompson Lutes 1936 comic memoir of her father with the clear piece by Vivian De Gain in which her father's drunkenness is spoken of openly.

It's been a tumultuous century of war, cruelty, change, progress, and growth. Yet, despite all the years between the early women and the women writing today, much has remained the same. We write of our lives, of our families, of our hurts, of loves, of losses. We write about emotion, about being women.

If there were still a Shakespeare's cottage to draw work from and read, it isn't too far fetched to imagine our first president, Alice Elinor Bartlett, reading to a circle of today's DWW members and being given considered and considerate criticism. We might tell her to drop a few of her more florid phrases, but beneath the words and fashionable style we would understand her need to express herself and make her life and her intelligence count. Beneath all the superficial differences, the passion for writing still burns.

Elizabeth Kane Buzzelli, co-editor

WHEN THE PARSON COMES TO TEA

by Alice Elinor Bartlett

Birch Leaves, the Franklin Press, Detroit, Michigan, 1905

Alice Elinor (Bowen) Bartlett, (pseudonym: Birch Arnold), the new group's first president, was a columnist for the Detroit Journal as well as a novelist, poet, and librettist for at least one comic opera. Her books included: Until Day Breaks, 1877, A New Aristocracy, 1891, Spirit of the Inland Seas, 1901, and The Mystery Of the Monogram, 1904.

They've got a bran' new parson,
Since conference, come to town,
And they say he isn't married,
And they say his name is Brown,
And mam has gone to scrubbin',
And sis is taffyin' me,
And dad is studyin' scripter,
'Fore the parson comes to tea.

You'd think we lived like heathen
The way the soap and sand
Is polishin' up the chair seats
And makin' things look grand.
You'd swear that sis's an angel
If you could only see
The way she smiles and twitters
'Fore the parson comes to tea.

The butt'ry's full of gimcracks,
We're livin' tho' on bread,
An' when I steal a cookie
I get whacked upon the head,
For mam is mighty savin',
An' she often says to me:
"Just wait, my little sonny,
'Till the parson comes to tea."

Sis wears her hair in papers,
And she's got a bran' new gown,
An' I'll bet you she's expectin'
To capture Mr. Brown.
Fer she's sayin' prunes an' prisms
As perlite as she can be,

So she won't be makin' blunders
When the parson comes to tea.

I see her lookin' sideways
At "sonny" now and then.
An' she an' mam were sayin'
"Some boys are little men;"
An' I know they're growin' anxious
'Bout what they'll do with me,
Fer "sonny" isn't in it
When the parson comes to tea.

An' dad'Il fix the woodpile
When the supper table's set,
An' send me out to whack it
With the dull old ax, you bet.
An' Sis'll be triumphant
Because the way is free
To show her airs and graces,
When the parson comes to tea.

But there's a satisfaction-
The parson ain't a whale,
An' can't eat all the fixin's
In the butt'ry, I'll go bail;
An' when they've left the table
I reckon there will be
A fillin' up of "sonny."
When the parson comes to tea.

An' Sis an' I'll get even-
I'll tell her so tonight-
If she doesn't want the parson
To get a sudden fright,
An' skip her blooin' halter,
She'd better try to be
Most awful good to "sonny",
When the parson comes to tea.

DANCING WITH MY SISTER
by Linda Nemec Foster
Witness, 1995

A poet and member since 1980, Foster wrote Living In The Fire Nest (1996). Her poetry appears in The Georgia Review, Indiana Review, Quarterly West, Mid-American Review, River Styx, and others.

For Deborah

We're not talking those crazy Polish weddings
in Cleveland, where we both learned how to dance,
clutching each other's sweaty hands, galloping
to the Beer Barrel Polka, and trying not to bump
into Uncle Johnnie and his whirling Chicago Hop.

This is now, tonight, in a smoky bar in Detroit
where two women dancing together can scandalize
any pimp within range. Where the hot-shot
bartender can mix anything and has the wide eyes
to prove it: bloody mary, wallbanger, a zombie
with a spike of lime that will raise the dead.

Above the crowded dance floor, in the maze
of cat walks, the geek of a lighting man
(who reminds us of every boy in high school
who fast-danced with his hands behind his back)
shines the spotlight right on us. And we glow.

Girl, do we glow. Not for the memory of those
distant high school boys whose faces we can't
remember. Not for the fluid desire ebbing
around us on the floor and beyond where silent
men sit in the dark. We glow for the raw truth
of Aretha's voice spelling out RESPECT;
for the way our hair curls down past our shoulders;
for our legs that can out-dance any young thing;
for the miracle that we survived our childhoods —
mother's obsessive cleaning, father's factory shifts,
the Erwin Street mob of pre-juvenile delinquents.
We glow because we came from the same burnt-out dream
of second-generation immigrants and learned to smile
at the closed mouth of loss and dance, dance, dance.

THE OLD WAYS
by Kathleen Ripley Leo
The Old Ways, Sun Dog Press, 1991

Kathleen Ripley Leo, a member since 1978, is a poet with five books of poetry: The Circle Is Assembled (Sun Dog Press), Town One south (Northville Arts Press), and others.

iv.

My grandmother's hands could sculpt ponczki,
chisel mountains of dough and slap out
small circles for pierogis. She flattened
huge sheets for noodles and cooked great
pans of borscht and czarina on the kitchen stove,
wrung the necks of fat hens,
sliced noodles, tender nipples of dough.

She drew up her flour to tall cone,
funneled it with eggs and salty water,
gathered into the dough, and like an ocean wave, she kneaded it
back and forth, her arms and shape given up to it.
She taught me to roll up half dried sheets of dough
after they hung like crisp linens over front room chairs.
Each day she made it fresh, folded it up fat and long,
took her knife and sliced it into pieces for the soup.

vi.

Her kitchen was the place she skinned rabbits.
Meat simmered in the beet soup, gravy red and thick.
This was the place she dressed poultry,
plucked feathers as the skin winced,
pink wings shivered against the white sink.
She dragged entrails out of dark cavities,
bloody worms trailed off her fingers as she cupped
a yolk and showed it to me,
"See, Katje, this chicken was going to have babies."

The kitchen was the place Aunt Olga
ate corn out of the pot, sucking juice from the cobs.
How small the kernels and how large her breasts.
"There are no bones in breasts," she answered.
I touched the sides of them, there are no bones.

The kitchen was the place my grandmother sorted
white shirts, dark pants, white underwear,
rubbing out stains with a shudder.
"Katje, being with a man is one step in hell.
The best is, know everything, then forget it."

It was also the place grandfather drank,
his shot and a beer poured ready for him.
In the old country he sang tenor in operettas.
Now he sang to furnaces he repaired on a night-job,
through the welded pipes and angel-legged tables
he tooled at his day-job. Once he made her sit
in the middle of the room while he yelled
about something in their language. She cupped
her chin like the yolk, her other hand
picked at her skirt, but she did not wince.

WEENG

by Hulda Hollands

When Michigan Was New, A. Flannery Co., 1900

Hollands, a charter member, joined the Detroit Press Club (later Detroit Women Writers) in 1900. She wrote: When Michigan Was New, Moccassined, Maria (novel), and Borderland Sketches.

Weeng was the King of Sleepy Land, and ruler over the little fairies who guarded the Indian children while they slept. During the daytime these tiny creatures hid in all sorts of curious places around the lodges and wigwams. They crawled under the loose bark on the roof, cuddled down in the warm ashes of the camp fire, or behind the birch bark mokoks of maple sugar. Each one was armed with a tiny war club. When the darkness began to settle down over the forest they went around among the children and tapped them gently on their foreheads to make them sleep. If one blow was not enough it was repeated again until the eyelids grew heavy and began to droop, the heads began to nod, and one by one the children all floated away into Sleepy Land. The Weengs were especially fond of the little papooses. They hid in the long braids of hair that hung down the mother's back, or perched upon her ear until it was naptime for the little one. Then they would tap the round black head very gently, until it began to nod, when the mother would whisper softly to herself, "The Weengs have called the papoose," and she would wrap him in the warm soft furs and place him in the bark hammock that hung from the center pole of the wigwam.

But it was not the children alone who felt the gentle taps of the tiny war clubs. The Weengs sometimes hid in the tobacco pouch of the hunter, and when he sat down on a log to rest and smoke his pipe they would climb to his forehead and give him a few taps that would send him off to sleep. Then the game would pass him in safety, and he would be obliged to return to his lodge and go to bed hungry.

Once a great hunter whose name was Iagoo went out with his dogs to kill a deer. He soon struck a fresh trail and followed it through a long stretch of forest. For a time he heard the baying of his dogs and then they were silent. He searched the forest but could not find them. At last he drew near a lodge which was unlike any lodge he had ever seen. The sides were covered with vines, and clumps of small trees grew out of the roof. Here he found his dogs stretched out on the ground and every one of them fast asleep.

This lodge was the home of the giant Weeng, the King of Sleepy Land. He was the friend of the timid deer, the hare, and all the other forest creatures that the Indian hunters called game.

As soon as the dogs had drawn near the lodge the good King commanded his little warriors to use their clubs and put them to sleep, thus allowing the poor frightened deer to escape from the hunter.

Iagoo tried in vain to awaken them. In despair over his ill luck he cast his eyes upward, when he saw the giant King perched upon the branch of a tree overhead. He was in the form of an immense grasshopper, with many wings fastened along his back. These wings made a low murmuring sound like that of distant falling water.

As the great hunter listened to the soothing sounds he felt the gentle taps of the war clubs on his own forehead and he found himself nodding and his eyelids growing heavy. He made a desperate effort to awaken, and at last succeeded in escaping from the home of the Weengs. But, much to his regret, he was obliged to leave his sleeping dogs behind him.

FACE OF FEAR

by Geraldine Nagle

Published in Parabola, Fall, 1998, Vol. XXIII, No. 3

Nagle, a member since 1992, published two art books: The Responsive Arts, and The Arts: World Themes. Her published articles appear in the Ann Arbor Observer and Parabola.

Fear wears the face of a woman called Dzonokwa. To ancient Native Americans of the Pacific Northwest she was the spirit-woman who personified their worst fears. Her image, culled from the art of story tellers and shaped by the art of sculptors, became a composite of all they considered ugly and fearsome.

Carvings of Dzonokwa show a giant with sagging breasts, excessive hair, and sunken cheeks. Masks of her face are painted black and occasionally outlined, ghostlike, in white. Her mouth, open in a perpetual shriek, is painted blood-red. Some masks have closed or half-closed eyes, others only deep, empty sockets. Every Dzonokwa image is a variation on a theme. And the theme is always fear.

What did these Northwest Coast Native Americans fear? Not the natural world, for powerful ancestor figures — half-human, half-animal totems — taught them how to live and prosper in this rich but harsh region. Sudden storms, swift tides, rain-drenched winters, dense forests, and snowtopped mountains amounted to a way of life they accepted without fear. Fear was the unexpected, the unexplained, the unknown.

Fear was the sudden terror of a nightmare. Fear was a missing child. Fear was taking risks. Fear was the realm of Dzonokwa. The sudden fright in waking from a nightmare, like the dream itself, could be blamed on Dzonokwa who roamed through villages at night. Sometimes she was only a vague presence, a phantom shrouded in fog. Other times, she announced her presence with an ominous whistling shriek. How to explain her? How to explain a nightmare? How to understand why a dream of something imagined, something made real only in the mind, causes such physical terror?

Dzonokwa *was* the "Nightmare-bringer." A tale belonging to the Kwakiutl of British Columbia tells of a young girl who carelessly wanders the woods alone. Dzonokwa finds the girl, grabs her, and stuffs her into a bag. The giant carries her victim to her house in some mysterious part of the forest. There, Dzonokwa shakes the girl out of the bag and squints her bad eyes to look the victim over carefully. The girl is numb with terror, but when Dzonokwa tells her she is pretty and points to her eyebrows, the girl thinks of a way to outwit the giant.

She offers to pluck Dzonokwa's thick ugly brows if only they can return to the village for the proper knife. Dzonokwa agrees, and as soon as they enter the village, a warrior kills the giant. Afterward, the girl leads villagers to Dzonokwa's home, where they find among other riches a mask of an eagle perched above a human face. The mask, known as "Nightmare-bringer-nest-mask" became the property of the girl's family and brought great honor to her clan and their descendants.

This story, like so many tales, was both a lesson in courage and a warning. Children grew up learning to fear the "bogeyman." *Stop crying or Dzonokwa will hear you! Disobey and Dzonokwa will get you! Wander too far from the village and Dzonokwa will find you!*

And what of children who disappeared and were never found? Blame Dzonokwa, who was not only a giant but an ogre. Horrible and gruesome as this concept is, at the very least, it may have eased some of the guilt and lingering dread concerning missing children. A quick death at the hands of an ogre could be accepted more easily than a death from wolves or grizzlies. At the same time, Dzonokwa tales always held out that one, small nugget of hope that missing children didn't have to die: that somewhere, somehow they were safe and living better lives than before.

Hope is an essential element in missing children stories because so many describe children with physical imperfections or handicaps. These are the children abandoned by families. Some are loners, some are social outcasts, but most have serious skin diseases or physical disabilities. These are children born into a society where survival depends on physical health and prowess. These are the children who can't "keep up." Accordingly, Dzonokwa always finds them, but they always outwit her and discover among her treasures a magic water that not only cures them but makes them extraordinarily strong and handsome.

Along with physical health, Northwest Coast Native Americans prized physical beauty. Some stories give Dzonokwa an ugly, hair-covered child of her own. Others give her a child who makes no sound, and in these tales, the giant goes about promising vast riches to anyone who can make her child cry or speak.

Belief in Dzonokwa did not end with childhood. An interesting aspect of Northwest Coast society is that its men felt safer hunting at sea than on land. They knew that sea lions were ferocious prey and that sharks and the ocean itself presented other dangers; yet they feared the forests and hunted there only when necessary. Forests were Dzonokwa's domain.

One of the oldest myths is about brothers who leave their village to hunt mountain goats. Before they start out, their grandmother gives them four magic charms, and their father warns them to stay away from any part of the forest where they see colored smoke. Of course, they immediately see colored smoke rising from a distant mountain and go right to it. What they find is an entire family of Dzonokwas. After one brother cuts his leg, the cannibal giants smell his blood and a chase ensues. When the giants get close, the brothers drop their first charm, a stone. The stone turns into a mountain, slowing down the cannibal giants temporarily. The chase continues. The brothers throw their second charm, eulachon oil, and this creates a lake. Soon, the brothers have to toss the remaining charms: a comb that turns into a thicket and mountain goat wool that turns into fog. Finally, they reach their village with the cannibal giants in close pursuit. Now, the entire village is in danger, so their father the chief yells to the Dzonokwas, "Don't bother with my sons! Come back tomorrow and we will offer you a real feast." The cannibal giants — never overly bright — agree. That night, the father tells his sons to dig a deep pit near the house fire and cover the pit with planks. Then he tells them to pile rocks on the edge of the house fire. The next day, when the cannibal giants come inside to feast on bloody raw meat, they are seated on the planks. As the cannibals gorge themselves, the planks are pulled out, the cannibals spilled into the pit, and hot rocks and boiling water poured over them until they burn to death. Happily, the villagers begin celebrating — until a breeze stirs the ashes causing them to rise in the air, transformed forever into swarms of mosquitoes.

Countless variations of this myth exist. Among Alaskan Tlingit, the cannibal giant whose ashes turn into mosquitoes is called Gooteekhl. Tlingit groups also have their own versions of Dzonokwa, whom they know as the spirit-woman of the woods: a fierce woman who tests men's bravery and scratches them with her copper nails. Victorious hunters wear their bloody scars with honor when they return to their villages with food and furs. They are men who have taken a risk, faced their fear, and won.

Among the Kwakiutl, Dzonokwa was an important crest figure. During potlatches, their great feasts lasting many days, they honored her as a bestower of gifts. When boats carrying potlatch guests approached the shore, passengers might be greeted by an enormous free-standing sculpture of Dzonokwa, her arms outstretched in welcome and largess. During the potlatch, a host family might use ladles and spoons carved with the ogre's face. Or they might serve food in a ceremonial Dzonokwa dish: a wooden vessel shaped like a woman with an enormous hollow bowl of a belly, splayed legs, and an ugly open mouthed face.

The Kwakiutl included Dzonokwa in their most important ceremonies. In *The Way of the Masks,* Claude Levi-Strauss describes how a male Kwakiutl performer, wearing furs and a Dzonokwa mask, sat among dancers but never danced. Instead, he feigned sleep or else mimicked the giant's lumbering, shuffling walk and her poor eyesight. His performance made a mockery of the song, "Here comes the great Dzonokwa who carries off humans in her arms, who gives us nightmares, who makes us faint. Great bringer of nightmares! Great lady who makes us faint. Terrible Dzonokwa!"

For one night anyway, the audience could see that Dzonokwa was not so terrible. For one night, they could hold fear in abeyance.

SWEET GRASS

by Hope Morritt

Published in Canadian Author & Bookman, 1991

Morritt, a member since 1998, had two plays produced on CBC. She has written three novels, two history books, and a memoir published in England, Canada, and the USA. She won short story competitions in Detroit magazine and Winner's Circle.

Sweet Grass chief of Crees
hears buffalo herds pounding
like distant thunder
fox tail grasses sway golden
& people hug river
where drums beat rhythmic tattoos
thanking Manitou
for riches of earth

Sweet Grass rides cayuse
sees sky curving over
world's end...August breezes
toss eagle feathers caress soul
maize whispers of summer dreams
& harvest moon rides high

at dawn the sun dance
will baptize young men
entering circle of chosen braves
Sweet Grass will welcome
new chief to guide people
into promised land

he spurs cayuse galloping like wind
his heart singing of love
at seventy harvests bountiful nature
lends youth to tired bones

A WORK OF LOVE

by E. Cora DePuy

excerpted from Pebbles and Pearls, Review and Herald Publishing Co., 1891.

E. Cora DePuy joined in 1904. A journalist and novelist, she wrote The Little Girl Who Picked Up Coal, A Christmas Eve, A New Year's Dinner, Temperance Work Of The World, and Bud, The Newsboy.

There are few women in the world who have done more to lighten the burdens, to cheer the hearts, to alleviate the sufferings, and to upbuild the manhood of men in prison, than Mrs. Agnes L. d'Arcambal.

By nature a philanthropist, her noble deeds have not been the dictates of a studied intent, but the outpourings of a generous heart, overflowing with love and sympathy for the sufferings of unfortunate humanity. Endowed with rare mental gifts, favored by financial prosperity, and strengthened by the love and tender devotion of a husband, a son, and four beautiful daughters, who were ever ready to aid and encourage any philanthropic project she might devise, Mrs. d'Arcambal was singularly blessed in taking up a life-work in which love and sympathy must form the greater part. Her work has ever been a work of love. With the renunciation of self a ruling power, her charity has embraced all kinds and classes, and endeared her to the hearts of thousands of her fellow-beings over whose lives misery and woe had held undisputed mastery.

Although the spirit of love is manifest in all her acts, it is most deeply impressed upon the men in prison, who, by years of contact with vice and deceit and human depravity, have grown calloused to the appeals of the ordinary exhorter. In visiting these men, Mrs. d'Arcambal has approached them as a friend, pouring her soul into theirs, holding with them a sweet communion that for the time lifts them above their worldly cares and sorrows, and inspires them to higher thoughts. By acts of kindness and thoughtfulness she has won their affections; by visiting them often and mixing with them in their varied conditions, by administering to them when enfeebled, by exercising that union of tenderness and energy and benevolence that analyzes and assimilates character, she has acquired a knowledge of the moral as well as the physical ills that afflict their weak natures, while to the overflowing love and sympathy of her own generous heart may be ascribed the tender commiseration of these unfortunate beings, a work which has so powerfully characterized twenty years of her long and useful life, and which has become of her own existence the better part.

At the time of taking up this work, Mrs. d'Arcambal lived in Kalamazoo, Mich. From early childhood she had delighted in bestowing charity upon the poor and distressed, but her most heartfelt interests were ever centered upon the unfortunate men and boys whose frailties and temptations had thrust them behind prison bars. Often she would visit the jail in her own city, taking a little basket of fresh fruit, or a book, or perchance a white handkerchief, to soften the misfortunes of some erratic creature. Similar visits were frequently made to the State Prison also, but not until 1872 did the thought impress itself upon her mind to work for all the prisoners. In November of that year, while making a visit to the prison, she noticed that a library was sadly needed, and asked the chaplain if she might send the prisoners some books. He assured her that books would be very acceptable, as they only had a few. Returning home, Mrs. d'Arcambal resolved to secure enough books to make a library for the prison, and at once threw her whole soul into the enterprise.

Obtaining permission of the Superintendent to address the different rooms of the ward-schools throughout the city, she told the boys and girls about her project, and asked each scholar to do something — sweep out an office, carry in some wood, or pick up some coal — to earn a penny, and bring the penny to the teacher. In this way, when all the pennies had been contributed, the room would be enabled to buy a book.

The enthusiasm was infectious. Every poor boy and girl in the whole school was soon seeking "penny jobs," while never in the history of the city were the stores and offices and curbstones and sidewalks treated to such a sweeping at wholesale.

Thoroughly alive to the importance of the work she had undertaken, Mrs. d'Arcambal did not stop with the school children, but solicited books of leading citizens and ladies of social influence, ministers, teachers, any one and every one with whom she could secure an opportunity to speak of her project. When a number of pledges had been secured, she would take her little daughter's hand-sled, and collect the books. Thus by Christmas she had a collection of five hundred volumes.

JAGGED LIGHT
by Julia Grice
TOR Books, 1991

Grice, a member since 1969, has published over 20 books in several genres including glitz, non-fiction, and suspense. Her first historical romances, Lovefire and Emeraldfire (Avon) were on the New York Times paperback bestseller list for eight weeks. Her suspense novels include Tender Prey, Jagged Light., and Pretty Babies. (Tor)

PROLOGUE 1980

Mick Jagger blasted from the car radio, his voice raw, silky, tough, sounding like a man who would do anything, anytime, to anyone.

Jerry Quick waited in line at the gas pump of the Shell Station on Lakeview Ave., watching while the attendant pumped gas into a Mercury Bobcat. He tapped out the rhythm of "Jumping Jack Flash" with his knuckles on the Buick's steering wheel and imagined himself kneeling between some girl's legs, pumping it into her in the exact, frenzied tempo of the music. The Stones. They knew how, all right.

It was 4:45 in the afternoon, and the sun overhead was molten orange, beating down on the streets of St. Petersburg, Florida. Rush-hour people sweltered in their hot cars, whizzing back and forth on the road, making Jerry glad he had the day off today. He took another swig from the paper bag he'd stuffed under the seat, and the whiskey made everything look brighter, hotter, the air full of yellow light.

The Stones pumped on, and Jerry diddy-bopped to the music, idly admiring the wedge-shaped section of his face that was visible in the rearview mirror. His skin was suntanned a cordovan shade of brown from hours of sunning himself at St. Petersburg Beach. Thoughtfully he pursed his lips, pressed them together, opened them, trying to decide whether, if he grew a mustache, the hairs would come in thick. He decided they probably would. He was twenty, and he'd been driving around for three hours, looking for the right sort of action.

So far he hadn't found anything right, and Jerry's lips pouted as he mimed in time to the music, waiting for his turn. He might as well go home, he decided. It wasn't going to work today. Maybe he would take a nap, eat some supper and go out and try again after dark. He had his regular route: Madeira Beach, Treasure Island, St. Pete Beach, a couple of high schools, the campus at U.S.F. in Temple Terrace. He guessed he'd try some bars he knew up near the college tonight.

Then the big silver New Yorker squealed into the station. It pulled up to the left of the pumps by the middle bay of the garage, long, shiny, chromed, and so clean that the sun mirrored off its paint. There were two girls inside it, a blonde and a brunette.

Giggling.

Jerry sucked in his breath. The blonde, who'd been driving, looked barely seventeen. She had hair the color of light ale, tousled and streaked with sun gold. She was his idea of a *Penthouse* girl, with her red mouth, haughty cheekbones, and perfect, beach-toasted skin.

From where he sat all he could see was skin, bare shoulders visible through the car window no bra straps at all.

Yeah, it seemed as if she sat there in that silver car stark naked. And laughing about it.

Of course, Jerry knew she wasn't naked; she was probably wearing a strapless bikini top or something. He let his eyes slide to the other one, the passenger. She wasn't as pretty. She had a narrow face with a chin that jutted and a mop of black hair half falling in her eyes. She wore a blue tank top; he could see the straps when she leaned forward to say something to the blonde. A mess of towels and suntan oil bottles stuffed in the back window said they'd been to the beach.

Jerry pulled in his breath, thinking *what if.*

Jesus, he'd been ready to go home and here they were, right in front of him; he couldn't have picked better himself. He believed in coincidences and omens, and he decided this had to be meant.

He tilted the mirror so he could study them without their knowing. Waiting for an attendant to notice them, they were having a good time, laughing, carrying on. The blonde let her naked arm dangle out of the opened car window, a birthstone ring catching the sun. A green stone, maybe an emerald, and not a little one.

Jerry stared. He had always hunted girls like her. He loved the way their skin was dark gold except for the bikini lines, and, down there, the tuft of gold-brown fuzz. He didn't like dark girls nearly as much, because they reminded him of his mother. In fact, dark ones somehow made him angry.

Apparently deciding no attendant was going to come, the blond one pushed open the door of the New Yorker and got out. Jerry's pulse surged in his throat.

Man.

She started toward the station, and now he could see why she'd looked naked. She wore nothing but a yellow strapless top and a pair of cutoff jeans cropped so high on the thigh that white pockets dangled below the hem line. Little threads caressed the insides of her perfect, tanned thighs. And the cutoffs were so tight that he could actually see her cleft outlined, her female parts.

It decided him. He shifted in the front seat, feeling a tightening in his own crotch. The girl sauntered into the station, and the way she walked was another advertisement. Did she see him watching her? He couldn't tell. Girls like that flirted automatically, and knew all the time they weren't going to deliver.

The car ahead of him finished, and he pulled up to the pumps, taking his time because the girls hadn't even started to get their gas pumped yet. The 70-year-old gas jockey waddled over, four days' worth of white beard covering his standard-issue mahogany Florida suntan.

"Fill her up?"

"Five bucks worth."

"Right." The geezer's face revealed what he thought of guys who didn't fill up their tank.

While the gas was being pumped, Jerry watched the blonde who was now framed in the station door, talking to the kid inside. Pointing to her car, wanting something looked at. She had long, slim legs, baby legs, Jesus, so perfect he could crawl all the way up between them and eat her with a spoon.

When she walked back to her car and leaned in to say something to the other girl, the cutoffs tightened, pulling into the crease of her buttocks exactly like a picture in *Penthouse.*

Jerry couldn't believe it.

Did she *know* she looked like that? Hell, sure she did. She probably posed in front of a mirror when she was alone. Women loved to tease, holding it back like a guy didn't have a right.

His breathing tightened, and his erection pushed so hard against his jockey shorts that he had to squirm around, trying to relieve the pressure. They were two little rich bitches, he decided. Probably lived down on the Bay in a big house that overlooked blue water, with a big Chris Craft boat moored in a fancy boathouse. Even the boathouse cost more than Jerry made in the last two years as a parts clerk in an auto supply shop.

He paid for his gas with a five, then pulled around to the side to put air in his tires, timing it so that he finished just as the girls were paying, with a credit card the blonde fished out of a little pink leather purse. She was such sweet stuff. His heart hammered as he thought of the roll of duct tape, the knife, stuffed under the front seat along with the whiskey.

This was exactly what he'd been driving around looking for. It had ridden into the Shell station in a big Chrysler and he wasn't going to let it get away. When the girls pulled out, heading east on Lakeview Ave., he followed.

Hell, when a girl wore shorts like that, she knew exactly what she was doing. She had no right to hold back when she wore clothes like that.

She had to expect what she got.

Whatever she got.

ALIEN

by Helen Janet (Miller) Schuler (Mrs. Otto K. Schuler)

From Sonnet Sequences, Sept., 1931, Vol IV, No. 4, 40th issue

Schuler, a DWW member from 1930, was a poet, reporter, ballet dancer, model, secretary, in real estate and insurance, director of a sales corporation and then a plant nursery. She was listed along with Carl Sandburg and others in Muse Anthology. Poems from her book, Songs After the War , and other poems, appeared in the Detroit News, the New York Times, and the Chicago Tribune.

He does not know the ways of city streets
That hem him in their canyon depths of fear,
Or draw him down a peopled lane that beats
Its garbled sounds upon his alien ear.
They look upon him strangely, half amused
At his long silences, and wonder why
In all this frank enticement, his confused
Sad eyes should be upturned toward the sky.

But I have seen him by an ocean's brim
watching the lift and drop of tangled seas
That reached beyond the sky's gray-darkened rim,
Through flecks of moonlight in a shadow-snare,
The silver rippling on his copper hair.

THE SIMPLE EPICURE
by Della Thompson Lutes
excerpt from The Country Kitchen, 1936

Lutes, a 1936 member, wrote My Boy In Khaki, 1919;The Country Kitchen, 1936 (18 reprints): Millbrook, 1938: Gabriel's Search: Country Schoolmarm: Cousin William: and Homegrown, 1937. A prolific and well-respected writer of memoir, family recipes were often interspersed with Lutes charming recollections of growing up in southwestern Michigan. Her use of present tense in some chapters precedes, by many years, its fashionable use today.

When it came to doughnuts my father was quite content with my mother's product, but he liked these, too, hot from the kettle, and insisted on a fresh batch three times a week with no impairment to digestion.

My father called them "friedcakes." That was what *his* mother had called them and that was what they were. He said he didn't know what a doughnut was, and he didn't care. Friedcakes were what he wanted, and friedcakes were what he would have. Moreover, he had to have them fried in a certain iron kettle, huge, heavy, and unwieldy. Unknown to him my mother once bought a lightweight, clean-looking kettle of granite to take its place. When, however, he came in and saw the cakes sizzling about in this alien pot, he threw what is vulgarly known as a fit.

Who in tunket, he stormed, ever heard of such a thing as using anything but an iron kittle for friedcakes? He picked up one of the cakes, perfect in contour, light as a thistle, golden brown in color, bit into it with pursed lips, and threw it down with a contemptuous verdict.

Not fit to eat! What could she expect, coming out of that liver-colored contraption? *Where was the kittle?*

You fry cakes, Mother told him, in the *lard,* and it don't make any difference what the lard is in so long's it 's hot enough.

Father snorted and waved his arms. She needn't tell him, he shouted, that she could fry cakes in that thing. She had only to *look* at them to see. He demanded the *kittle.* He said he would get the kittle. He got the kittle and banged it down on the stove.

My mother sought to calm him. She urged him to try another of the cakes and expressed herself as willing to wager that he could not tell the difference.

Tell the difference! he roared. Of course he could tell the difference. They tasted of that stuff on that tarnation pot she was cooking them in.

She pointed out that this could not be so, as this was a granite surface and nothing could come off it.

Father insisted that there was a decided taste of tin or something, but followed the first sample with another and another, doubtless to verify his original opinion. He had never expected, he grumbled, in *his* time, to eat such friedcakes. They might as well be thrown to the hogs. My mother remarked tartly that it looked as if there wouldn't be many to throw, but she apparently did not consider the battle worth waging, for she went back to using the iron kettle and used it as long as I can remember — but not the same kettle.

A little while after this the iron kettle was knocked off the table and cracked. Mother said it was an accident and she was sorry, but it couldn't be helped, Anyway she had the granite kettle, which would do quite as well, but Father declared he would get another iron kettle before the sun had set. He dropped everything, hitched the bay mare to the buckboard, and took me with him. He stopped at all the near-by farmhouses and asked if they had an iron kettle to sell. Some of the women were willing to part with one (doubtless in the hope of acquiring one more modern), but none of them was what Father wanted. Some were too large, some were too small; one that otherwise might have done had a chip in the rim; another had a slightly cracked ear which endangered the safety of the bail. No slightest flaw escaped his eye.

We stopped at two secondhand stores (there were no antique shops then) and at the junk dealer's, but nothing would suit. The perfect kettle was not found.

On the way home somebody told Father about an auction that was to be held on the morrow where there would be a lot of household goods. So, as soon as an early breakfast was over, he hitched up the bay mare and we set forth. The auction was some eight miles away over a dirt road. (As if all roads were not of dirt, in that day!) The sand on this particular road, however, was unusually deep and the day was hot. We proceeded slowly while Father perspired and the horse lathered. Father took off his alpaca coat and vest and opened his shirt collar. When we came to a stream he drove through it on the shallow side of the bridge and let the mare stop to drink. He said it would soak up the fellies on the wheels as well. After we had driven through he told me to get out and pick some elderberry leaves and wet them in the stream. He put these inside his hat and I picked some more, wet them, and stuck them in the bridle to keep the flies away from the horse's head.

Eight miles was a goodly journey in those days over a dusty road, but we reached our destination shortly after the auction had begun. My father immediately began to prowl among the junk which was gathered on tables, benches, and on the grass. There were several kettles, but again none suited him. Vexed and disappointed, he turned away, and was making toward the buggy when a leather-faced, horny-handed stranger approached and said he 'd heard my father was looking for an iron kittle. Father said he was.

"I got one over to my house," said the stranger, "that's had more friedcakes cooked in it 'n you c'd put in a hayrack. House 's just down the road a step. Come down, I'll show you."

We followed him down the dusty road, his bare feet plopping in the dust, fringed overalls flapping about his thin, dirt-encrusted ankles.

"This-here kittle," he volunteered, "was my mother's and her mother's afore her, and just as good today as t'was then. Hain't no wear-out to it. My first womern set store by it, and fried a million cakes in it. But this here one — " A flip of the hand, significant expectoration of tobacco juice expertly aimed at a ragweed taller than its thousand mates along the road, and scornful lift of moustached lip (badly discolored) gave mute commentary on the housekeeping standards of this-here present "womern."

"C'min." He pushed open the dilapidated door of what was clearly the most desolate, rickety, junk-strewn excuse for a house that ever disgraced a township. "Womern 's up t' the auction," he explained. "I'll git the kittle."

Rattling and banging about amid the general debris in some outlying district he designated as the woodshed, he came back triumphantly bearing an exact replica of the late lamented article for which we were seeking a duplicate. "Thar she is!" He set the kettle down on a cluttered table and, giving it a hasty brush with his sleeve, stood off to observe the effect of this miraculous consummation of a desire.

My father clutched the kettle, struck it resoundingly with a knife which he picked up from the table, listened critically, and nodded his head. He inspected the rim for nicks, the ears for cracks, and the handle for balance. His investigation seemed to give him complete satisfaction.

He inquired, tersely, the price. The owner, shifting ballast to the other jaw, hitched his overalls a notch higher, squinted speculatively at his customer, and said with equal brevity, "Fo' dollars."

My father took a worn leather bag from his pocket, counted out four silver dollars, and handed them over. He took the kettle carefully in hand, bade the man good-day, and we started back to the scene of the auction, where our horse was tied.

As we were about to climb into our buggy a slatternly woman approached.

"Got that kittle from the ole man, didn't you." Which was a statement rather than an inquiry. "How much d'ja pay for it?"

"I paid four dollars," my father said shortly, his voice edged, and his eyes sharp with suspicion.

The woman gave a toothless chortle, flinging her sunbonneted head back upon a dirty throat.

"He sure stung you good, mister," she said with obvious amusement. "He snatched that-thar kittle out'n the pile of junk over thar"— gesturing toward the auction — "when he hearn you was lookin' for one. Paid fifty cents for it."

My father made no reply, but set the kettle carefully in the buggy and bade me, curtly, to climb in. So far as I know, he never related the terms of transaction to my mother, nor did I.

ADULT CHILDREN SURVIVORS FIND THE GLASS VERY FULL
by Vivian De Gain
Excerpt from The Rochester Clarion, January 19, 1994

DeGain joined DWW in 1994. A journalist and poet, her work has been anthologized in Variations On The Ordinary.

Memories of my childhood aren't like "Leave it to Beaver," or "Home Improvement."

I lost my Dad when I was 16. No, he didn't die, he just left. At the time, I was glad he did.

I feel oddly grateful for the day he walked out forever. Being deserted is an angry, fearful, and unexplainable loss, and though it was over 20 years ago, it still hurts, feels like a jigsaw puzzle missing a few crucial pieces.

My siblings and I were not abused physically. We were confused to find him "sleeping" on the bathroom floor, learned never to talk with him first thing in the morning and really didn't ever know what to answer when he screamed at us in drunk, irrational tyranny. He treated Mom a lot worse.

Mostly, Daddy just wasn't there for us.

We just didn't have enough growing up, not enough of anything, and I'm not talking about designer hightops. Yes, sporadically, he worked a little. Then he binged for days, months, ending up in the local "hospital" or jail. Eventually, he came home.

When Daddy was home, we often wished he wasn't.

We knew better than to believe his promises — but we kept wanting to believe. I was the little girl looking for him at my piano recitals, my graduation, my wedding. He just wasn't there. His not being there was better than him being there drunk, adding to our humiliation in front of our neighbors.

Dr. Claudia Black, psychologist and author who works in the area of Adult Children of Alcoholics, says that children in alcoholic families learn three rules: don't trust anybody, don't talk to anyone, and don't feel anything.

I didn't know I was learning those rules growing up, but I was. I couldn't vocalize them, I wasn't aware of them, but they limited my ability to love and be loved.

When I spoke them out loud for the first time, with the help of a wonderful therapist here in Rochester and read them in the books by Dr. Black and Melody Beattie, I knew those words held a healing power, a power I wanted.

That power helped me overcome the childhood handicaps of confusion and shame, helped me see that I had the courage to look into those holes in my stomach and remember ... and feel. That power helped me learn that I could peek into those growling black places, known to me before as empty, and I could be whole.

I still could become an alcoholic myself.

Odds are for it.

In her book, *It Will Never Happen To Me,* Dr. Black says that chances are 50 to 60 percent greater that I'll be prone to the addiction, if one parent was alcoholic. If both parents were drunks — chances are as high as 90 percent. I've battled other addictions, smoking, compulsive eating, worrying and working.

There is a brighter picture, I'm not an alcoholic.

I haven't smoked cigarettes for 12 years and most people think I look like a normal-sized woman today, despite the history of being "morbidly obese," more than 100 pounds overweight.

I've learned to nurture myself emotionally and learned how to love. I enjoy every minute with my husband and children. He's a devoted dad, the kind of father I wish I had. He's taught me how wonderful it is to laugh, to play, to just be myself. We have tended to bring out the best in each other, and, yes, we have done it with professional help.

My kids have asked me about my dad, and what it was like growing up with him, what he looks like, what he was like, if I don't miss him. What I say to my kids is these are tough questions. Very tough questions.

INSIGHT
by Mary Beth Smith
1992-93 Vol. of Rajah, Rackham Journal of the Arts and Humanities, University of Michigan

Smith, a member since 1987, publishes fiction in Arizona Quarterly, Rajah, and had an award winning story in The Pen Syndicated Fiction Project. Her TV documentaries air on national PBS. Trimark distributed her screen play "Running Free." Her non-fiction appeared in Heritage and Tee-Up Michigan.

My grandmother had been old. I don't miss her but I wish I could feel something, some kind of emotion, as I stare at this mishmash collection. There is no order or sense of direction to it — like a love of spoons or even brass bells.

Disturbed dust particles cloud the swath of sunshine that cuts through the room. A lighted pathway ends abruptly where shelves cover one wall of an alcove. Dust has been allowed to gather on trifles that line the shelves. Carefully I wrap each item in newspaper and place it in a cardboard box beside me. Little poofs of dust animate the bright stream every time I remove another treasure. My mother is in the other room doing the same thing. We are helping my grandmother move from off this earth. Everything smells old.

"Take what you want for your apartment," my mother says. But this is just an assortment of cheap odds and ends. I push my grandmother's rocker aside. The shove sets it in motion. Back and forth it rocks as though someone were in it. I've hardly been here to visit since Grandmother moved to Florida. I try to imagine her in this corner, rocking away, listening to the radio, reminiscing or reading her mail — she loved to get mail. I feel guilty for never writing. I'd thought about it, but somehow never did, except to thank her for some birthday present that I knew my mother had bought anyway. But by the same token, my mother signed my name to birthday and Christmas gifts for Grandmother, I wonder if any of those found their way into this alcove. Long ago I decided I hated "things" sitting around. I like a bare look. Clutter depresses me, firmly convinced that possessions possess one.

The chair continues to rock, somehow perpetuating its own motion, confined within the sun's brilliance. Grandmother's brother had made the rocking chair. It must be perfectly balanced. It reminds me of one of those wooden birds stuck on the side of a bowl that once set in motion pops its head up and down incessantly, pretending to drink water. These are the kinds of things I remove and wrap, dime store variety, a painted pottery milkmaid with an opening on top that at one time probably held some fresh flowers, the kind of vase florists send, and a little clay pinch pot filled with rubber bands. The only book is a dictionary. At one time Grandmother did crossword puzzles.

Why would anyone keep all this junk? I want to throw it all out, but my mother is adamant about packing everything. Like mother, like daughter. Well, thank God I'm different. Thank God my shelves are filled with books. Is this how we all end up? So what if people "had" given Grandmother all these tacky mementos. Am I, too, destined to sit amongst them in lieu of people?

A patch of sun creeps behind me as I work my way along the shelves, I sense its warmth gently moving me on. Mechanically I pack item after item, none of which means anything to me. The rocker has slowed to a stop, its creaking silenced, now out of the sun's reach. I reach over and with a light touch start it rocking again. I like hearing it squeak against the floor.

"There you go, Grandmother," I smile at my foolishness. By squinting I can see my grandmother sitting there in a cotton house dress and sensible shoes. I want to picture her wearing a printed house dress rather than one of those polyester pant suits.

Automatically I reach for the next item patiently waiting to be wrapped into oblivion. A plain brown pot on the top shelf looks vaguely familiar and stops me. The jar has a pebbly stone finish. A small chip mars the rim of its lid. On top sits a crude-looking honey bee, one wing broken off, the other chipped at its tip. Slowly I rotate the jar. "Honey" is etched on the opposite side, yellow paint still heightens some of the letters.

Suddenly a little girl emerged onto a sunny sidewalk, scurrying along toward a garage sale. It was early summer, light and airy. Card tables displaying a myriad of objects filled a driveway in front of a house at the end of the block. She spotted the honey jar at once. No matter that the bee's wings were broken. It was marked 25 cents, her whole allowance.

I try to recall giving it to her, but all I can remember is buying it. She kept it all those years — it must have meant a lot. I shudder at the effect of dismantling my grandmother's life, penetrating into some deep unknown layer kept private. An impulse urges me to put everything back in its place.

For a long moment I sit immobilized, holding the honey jar, watching the slackening pace of the rocking chair, Rhythmically I tap the rocker with my toe. I think about where I could put the honey jar.

I jump when my mother suddenly appears at my side.

"What a mess," she moans as she plops down in the rocking chair. "I suppose I'll end up keeping most of it." She leans back to rest her eyes and begins to rock.

"Did you find anything you wanted to save?" she asks wearily.

I stare at the rocker, frightened by its abrupt transformation into the next generation. I turn away from the dizzying effect.

"No. I don't think so."

THE GREATER GRIEF

by Myrtle Reynolds Adams

from 1936 chapbook: Morning On My Street, the Ryerson Press, Toronto, Canada, 1958. Burton Collection, Box 9

A poet and DWW member from 1923. Adams was chosen Poet Laureate of the Michigan Federation of Women's Clubs. She won the Lyric Phillida Prize Canadian A. and B. for the best poem of 1975. She wrote five books of poetry including Morning On My Street, Remember Together. Her work appeared in the Detroit Women Writers Club Poetry, 1949

THIS is the grief that stabs —
After the dust to dust
To sit alone in the room,
The once warm presences just
Beyond, still felt in chair
And open book, still part
of this living now. Yes,
This must break the heart.

And yet a greater grief
Will be, when after the years
On years, the bitterness
and the long dried tears
To the slow windy sound
of rainfall in the night,
In the starless dark, you try
To remember — and cannot quite.

CITY NIGHTS
by Naomi Long Madgett
from Exits and Entrances, 1978

The published poetry of Madgett spans 58 years and includes eight volumes, five still in print, the most recent Remembrances Of Spring: Collected Early Poems. Her work has appeared in many journals and more than 160 anthologies. A documentary film, A Poet's Voice, was based on her prize-winning book, Octavia.

(For Gertrude and Eddie)

My windows and doors are barred
against the intrusion of thieves.
The neighbors' dogs howl in pain
at the screech of sirens.
There is nothing you can tell me
about the city
I do not know.

On the front porch it is cool and quiet
after the high-pitched panic passes.
The windows across the street gleam
in the dark.
There is a faint suggestion of moon-shadow
above the golden street light.
The grandchildren are asleep upstairs
and we are happy for their presence.

The conversation comes around to Grampa Henry
thrown into the Detroit River by an Indian woman
seeking to save him from the sinking ship.
(Or was he the one who was the African prince
employed to oversee the chained slave-cargo,
preventing their rebellion, and for reward
set free?)
The family will never settle it; somebody lost
the history they had so carefully preserved.

Insurance rates are soaring.
It is not safe to walk the streets at night.
The news reports keep telling us the things
they need to say: The case
is hopeless.

But the front porch is cool and quiet.
The neighbors are dark and warm.
The grandchildren are upstairs dreaming
And we are happy in their presence.

BOY ON A BICYCLE
by Naomi Long Madgett
The Vision Of Words, 1989

Slim blue-jeaned legs pump laboriously
up a wet incline while a steady drizzle
films a dark young face with a satin mist.
Summer vacation has begun.

It is midmorning, the twenty-first of June.
The daylight will be longer than any other
day of an uncertain year, but it is doubtful
that anyone will see the sun. The streets
are slick and treacherous.

Where is he going, young black boy
in a city full of clouds and shadows,
pedaling two wheels up a hill in the rain?

YOUR WATERCOLOR LOVER

By Lyn Coffin

from Crystals of the Unforseen, PlainView Press, April 1998

Coffin, in DWW since 1996, writes fiction, non-fiction, and poetry. Her plays include: Ave Maria, Played Softly, and The Armoured Girl.

Do you have any idea how I feel? she wrote. How could you? To say I hardly know you is a boast. I met you at your watercolor lover's show, your lover's watercolor show. You probably didn't even register me as a presence, didn't notice me any more than the leaves which kept shifting in the door that rainy night, that fall outside my window now... How galling it is to think about my exposure to you. As though I were some kind of photo-sensitive plate and you the strong, ignorant light. To hell with metaphor. I had been in the back room of the gallery, drinking champagne punch because it seemed like the thing to do. I came out and there you were, with her. She was elegant and sophisticated, and you so casual it was almost an affront to her. You wore a pale blue shirt, open at the throat, and dark blue corduroy pants, and a pair of rain-splattered work shoes. You had a tangled lion's mane of hair then, and you looked like an old-time movie star, but more sexual. If I could describe the way you took possession of that gallery couch, of the room, of her, of me, the accuracy of my words would be a flaunting of my talent, a way of revenging myself for other inadequacies. But I can't describe it. The fact reverberates in me, an arrow half-buried in the heart of a tree. Then she got up, to greet a possible customer, I suppose, or just to recover herself, to marshal herself against you. To me, it was as if I had done it: I had wished her gone, wished her away from you, and ssscchuup! she vanished. I sat down beside you on the couch — fiercely, literally taking her place. And we talked. I asked what you did, then cursed myself for asking that, then cursed you for making me curse myself. You said you were a carpenter. The corner was shadowy but your eyes drew me. I looked in your eyes, I looked at your throat, where your pale blue shirt parted from itself, and I wanted to reach out, to touch you there — to touch you anywhere... I wanted you to touch me. I was a rough plank of wood, and you could smooth me down. When she came back, I was almost grateful — she was a kind of release, a breaking of a spell that might have split me asunder like a locked door under an iron axe. And I pitied her in some way, even then, even before you left and she came into the back room crying, tears running down her cheeks like rain and the only wonder of it for me was that she, her face, the hands with which she brushed at tears, blindly, didn't run together, like a water-color. The grief itself I understood. I knew you hadn't wanted to cause it, that you loved her, in your way, and it was agony for her. And I decided the fates had been kind to me. She was like a warning, your watercolor lover — a white face in the dormer window of a forbidding house — signaling to me, Go Back. And I wanted to buy one of her watercolors because it would be a reminder of the fate I had escaped. I didn't have enough money but she was so eager to get rid of me, that she let me take the painting I liked — the one I had seen you glance at, as you left. She gave me her card, told me to send a check. That's what I meant to do, but somehow I waited until last night, when it rained again. And the rain made me think of you and long to see you and be glad I couldn't. I decided I had to settle my debt. And I came to her house and ran up her path in the rain, and she opened the door, and I gave her the money. And she was in a bathrobe and it kept raining and I mentioned there was a leak in my roof which made me think of the carpenter I'd met at the gallery because a carpenter would know what to do. And she laughed and said to come in. And I came in, and the room was dark. And there was a bed. And you were lounging, fully dressed, on the bed. I hardly recognize you, I said. He got a hair cut, she said. And you looked at me, and said nothing. She stood behind me: I could forget she was there. It might have been you and me on that bed... We talked, you reclining, and you took my address and said you'd come and look at my roof tomorrow, which is now, today. And the woman said You'd better write down her name and I, suffering from real wet feet, said I had to prepare for a French exam and you said I could study conjunctions while you were exploring the roof and I said prepositions were what made me suffer and we were having this coded exchange whose meaning neither one of us fathomed but whose drift I recognized as down. And she said again, you'd better write down her name and you did, and it wasn't until I had gone out again, into the rain, that I realized you'd written my name down without my saying it, which meant you remembered. But the flare of hope this sponsored went out like a match because your watercolor lover had probably complained to you about this person who hadn't paid for the painting and she would have remembered the name because it was her only hold on me.

Now here I sit, waiting, she wrote. And when it was time, she rose to answer her future lover's determined knock.

PRIDE
by Margaret Hillert
The Lyric, Summer, 1971

Hillert, a children's book author, grade-school teacher, and poet joined DWW in 1962. Seventy-six of her picture books for children have been published broadly and reprinted. Her poetry has appeared in many periodicals.

I would not have you think me lonely
After your leaving.
                    Sooner would I
Pound fist to bark and head to stone
Than make a single bleating cry.
I would not have your pity, no,
Nor have you sorry.
I hold no brief
For the poor losers but still must own
I would lay back my ears in grief
And howl the heavens to splinters, only
I would not have you think me lonely.

HOMECOMING
by Margaret Hillert
The Lyric, Fall, 1990

I have been coming home to you
All the days of my life, and I did not know.
The path was uneven, the miles without end,
No marker to point the way I should go,
With hill after hill and the climb never over,
And all the fierce longings kept close in disguise
Then sudden the turning, and you there before me,
And I had come to the love in your eyes.

THE TEMPTRESS
by Vera Henry
from A Lucky Number, Lippencott, 1957

Henry, a member since 1951, wrote books (A Lucky Number), short stories and mysteries for the Alfred Hitchcock Magazine, She taught in the Writer' Digest correspondence school.

There's no getting away from the fact that my mother liked men. She frankly and completely believed they were the most magnificent, fascinating creatures on God's good earth. They could unstick drawers and open stubborn jars and balance bank accounts. Under the shining approval in her blue eyes every male stood a little taller than he really was. All this might have led to complications except for one obvious fact.

All men had their splendor, but it was most apparent Mother believed that Father was the king of them all.

In fact her trouble with the laundryman would never have begun in the first place if she had stuck to Yardley's English Lavender perfume.

For years that clean, cool smell was a part of the house. There were dried leaf sachets among the sheets and in the bureau drawers, and when she went out Mother always sprinkled a few drops of toilet water on her hanky and the front of her dress.

I remember one time my sister Bonnie fell in love with, of all people, Tom Grecy (Tom looked distinguished, but actually it was just a good, healthy head of hair). We girls couldn't understand it. Then one night Bonnie woke me up. She looked white and shaken.

"I've made such an awful mistake," she wailed. "It wasn't Tom I liked. It was that lavender shaving lotion he uses. He smells just like Mother!"

All of us girls were very relieved thinking we were rid of Tom Grecy but he kept right on coming to the house to see Mother. All of our ex-boyfriends did. It was downright embarrassing sometimes, to come home with a new date and find three or four of his predecessors out in the kitchen eating chess tarts and telling their troubles to Mother.

When it came to attracting men, Mother could have taught Cleopatra a thing or two. Mother, in a size 42 print dress and black oxfords, with no more make-up than a bit of talcum rubbed on with a chamois, could come into a room and every man there straightened his tie and made straight for her.

This never bothered Father in the slightest. It simply confirmed his own good judgment.

For years mother went comfortably through life getting seats on crowded buses or the finest steak from the butcher with a nice bit of suet thrown in, and then something happened.

My sister Bonnie gave Mother one of those perfume-testing sets for her birthday. It was a little crystal box filled with about a hundred tiny tubes of different kinds of perfume with wonderful names like My Sin and Breathless and Perhaps. (Actually, Bonnie had an ulterior motive in giving the set to Mother. She thought she would be able to borrow it back.) Mother, however, was as delighted as a child with a new toy.

"Why would anyone want to smell a hundred different ways?" she wondered.

"You don't," Bonnie explained. "You try to find the perfume that expresses your personality."

Mother was so pleased with the whole idea, she couldn't wait for one perfume to wear off before she started trying a new one.

"Angus, dear," she said to Father, "do you think my right or my left arm smells better?"

Father, who did most of his bookkeeping at home, looked up from his roll-top desk bewildered. "Is there a difference?"

"Of course, dear," said Mother. "My left arm is an Oriental Blend and the right is a Single Floral fragrance."

Father looked baffled. "How do you know?"

"Because it says so on the bottle. I had no idea that choosing a perfume was so complicated. I'm definitely not the Woodsy-Mossy type. I like the Spicy, but it doesn't like me — evaporates right off my skin. So far I seem to be the Fruity Blend. Would you have said I was the Fruity Blend?"

"I've never really given it the proper amount of thought," Father admitted.

"The Modern Blend might be better," she said. "But it seems so sophisticated. Smell again, dear."

He took a deep sniff. "They all smell the same to me."

"You've blunted your nose," Mother sighed. "If you smell too many kinds too close together you blunt your nose."

"Personally," said Father, "I like people to smell like people."

Even Father's lack of co-operation didn't stop Mother. She just went on trying out new types of perfume. The place took on a strange, hothouse smell. Pumpernickel, our dog, looked as if he were on the verge of a nervous breakdown. Father went around muttering that he felt as if he was living in sin with a different woman in his room every night.

Then something terrible happened.

Mr. Mendleson, the laundryman, tried to kiss Mother. Mr. Mendleson was a quiet little man with strong white teeth like oblongs of laundry soap. He had never acted like this before and Mother was very upset.

"I can't imagine for the life of me what came over him," she declared. "You know how pleasant and prompt he's always been about deliveries and replacing that old muslin sheet with a nice percale when it was lost."

"Calm down, dear," we said. "Now just what happened?"

Mother wrung her hands. "He put the laundry on the dining-room table, just the same as usual. I remember I said something about how easily he carried that heavy bundle. I opened my purse to pay him, and didn't have the right change, so I got it out of the teapot. Then I noticed he was breathing sort of funny and I asked if he was having trouble with his asthma again. Next thing I knew, he — he tried to put his arms around me. I was that surprised you could have knocked me over with a feather. I got away and ran outside — I can't imagine what the neighbors thought — me being chased around the petunia bed by the laundryman. I was never so mortified in my whole life."

Father reached grimly for his hat (the one Mother said made him look like a bank manager). "I," he said, "am going to have a little talk with Mr. Mendleson."

Mother tried to stop him, but Father was a stubborn man.

After he was gone, she was almost frantic. "Your father just doesn't realize his own strength," she kept saying. "Suppose he hurts that poor little fellow."

There was a dreadful silence while we pictured lurid headlines that said, "PROMINENT BUSINESSMAN SLAYS LAUNDRY DRIVER."

Bonnie began to cry. "Poor Daddy," she wept. "Poor Daddy. We must all stand by him."

"I wonder," said Senna, "If people really do bake saws in cakes."

Every time the phone rang we all rushed for it, but it was only boys trying to make dates.

About five-thirty Father came home. He gave Mother a kiss that skidded off the side of her cheek. "Sorry I'm late," he said. "What's for dinner?"

"How about Mr. Mendleson?" we all demanded. "Didn't you see him?"

"Mendleson?" said Father vaguely. "Oh, him — As a matter of fact, I did."

"What happened?" we asked. "What did he say?"

Father took a long time to light his pipe. "Flora," he said to Mother, "you're sure that maybe without meaning to — you didn't lead him on a little?"

"Lead him on! Lead him on!" Mother's blue eyes filled with outraged tears. "Angus, how can you say such a thing! You know perfectly well, all the years we've been married, I've never as much as looked at another man!"

Now this was quite true. It was the men who looked at Mother, though up until now, only with wistful respect.

"He was willing to come over to apologize but I thought it wasn't necessary," Father said. "As a matter of fact, I felt sorry for him."

"Sorry for him!" cried Mother. "Sorry!"

"He said he couldn't help himself," Father went on. "And in a way, I don't blame him. I know how it is. I, myself —"

He stopped at a warning cough from Mother.

We girls looked at her thoughtfully. She had brought us up to be polite, healthy and well behaved, but had she told us All?

"He said he looked at your blue eyes," Father told her, "and then he smelled perfume and he seemed to completely lose control of himself."

"The perfume!" we cried. "That was it! All it took was Mother plus perfume to push him over the border."

Mother sat down heavily. In her mind I think she was remembering those perfume ads with lovely scented ladies pursued by smoldering-eyed young men.

"But it wouldn't have the same result on an old lady like me," she protested.

We'd seen Mother in action without perfume.

"All I hope," said Senna, "is that when I'm Mother's age, some man will want to chase me around a petunia bed."

"What perfume were you using, Mother?" we demanded eagerly.

If it worked for Mother, by some lovely miracle it might work for her daughters too.

We never knew. Mother had simply opened a little bottle, used it and thrown it away. It might have been Passion or True Love or Forever Yours or any other of the hundred brands. The secret was lost forever. Mother was so provoked at Father for doubting her that she gave him the smallest piece of raisin pie for dessert.

Before he went to bed that night, Father fixed the pulley on the clothesline, the bathroom faucet that had been leaking for a month, and put up a new shelf in the broom closet.

Although it was a weekday, Mother made popovers next morning in the iron gem pans that our great-grandmother had brought over from Scotland.

As for Mr. Mendleson, he gave up his route and retired to a chicken farm where he did very well. We had a new laundryman who was quite prompt with deliveries and good about replacing things that got lost.

Just to be on the safe side, Mother went back to using Yardley's Lavender.

WHICH?

by Bernice Ireland Powells

found hand-written, in Box 16 of the Detroit Women Writers collection, part of the Burton Collection located at the main branch of the Detroit Public Library. Poem is dated 6/14/55.

Powells, a DWW member from 1925, was a dramatist and a poet. A 1934 newspaper article speaks of her leading a twice monthly drama group.

Sue moves in an orbit like the moon's
To gauge her closeness to me
From perigee to apogee gives me no palpitations

But Mitzi makes my heart chaotic —
Her moods are all tangential.
A quandary I must soon resolve:
Which treatment's preferential?

THE FABULOUS FLEMINGS OF KATHMANDU

by Grace Nies Fletcher

from The Fabulous Flemings of Kathmandu: The Story of Two Doctors In Nepal, E.P. Dutton & Co., Inc., New York, 1964

Fletcher, a DWW member from the 1920s-1930, was a prolific writer. In 1932, she collaborated with Frederic Bohn Fisher to write, That Strange Little Brown Man: Ghandi. She went on to write: In My Father's House, Preacher's Kids, No Marriage In Heaven, I was Born Tomorrow, and The Whole World's In His Hands.

This is the fantastic story of two space-age missionaries, Dr. Robert and Dr. Bethel Fleming, who trekked happily together over the high Himalayas and slid down a mountain of mud to bring modern medicine to the fabled Valley of Kathmandu. They found Nepal's nine million people fighting a losing battle with almost every known disease from cholera to worms. There were only a handful of qualified doctors and five trained nurses. In this Hindu-Buddhist country it is against the law to change another man's religion, so the Shanta Bhawan Hospital couldn't even be labeled "Christian." Yet last year these Silent Samaritans, who live their creed in deeds, not words, treated 100,000 patients.

Strangely "Dr. Bob," as he is affectionately known in Kathmandu isn't even a physician; he took his doctorate in education and is an ornithologist who knows more about the birds of the Himalayas than any other living scientist; he has collected some 700 species for the Chicago Natural History Museum.

Dr. Bethel has been a doctor of medicine for over thirty years, mostly practicing in India. Since 1956, when she started this now 200 bed hospital in Kathmandu, Shanta Bhawan has included among its clientele patients as diverse as the Queen Mother of the Royal Family of Nepal; the Russian ambassador; Nepalese farmers and street cleaners; Tibetan refugee weavers of yak wool with their holy Buddhist priests; lepers banished to the streets by their frightened families; American Peace Corps boys and girls as well as Embassy and USAID officials; mountain climbers from Europe, Asia, or the Americas who had frozen their feet or contracted pneumonia; harlots whose noses had to be sewn back on after being cut off as punishment for their crime of cohabiting with a man of other than their own caste. All nations, creeds, and castes are alike welcome, for Shanta Bhawan means its title of "Palace of Peace."

Dr. Bob, who climbed the Himalayas as a different kind of scientist, is a deceptively mild-looking little man with an impish twinkle that starts in his eyes and lights up his lined pleasant face; but be has a tough wiry body that can take off up a mountain at the chirp of a bird. His voice is the slow pleasant drawl of the school master; only the gleam in his bright blue eyes and the jaunty tilt of his flowered cotton Nepali cap over one ear clues you in that this is a man completely unafraid of any creature that crawls, walks, or flies. To get a good specimen of impeyan pheasant, he will cheerfully scale a precipice or swim a river in flood; he considers any mountain under 8,000 feet a hill and calls climbing it a picnic, because he takes along his lunch. Tigers roaring or wolves stalking around his tent at night are merely occupational hazards.

"We Christians waited two thousand years to get into Nepal," Dr. Bob is fond of saying. "Then when the Lord was ready, he sent a bird to show us the way." The miracle happened while Dr. Bob was teaching science in Woodstock High School in Mussooric, India. The Rana hierarchy, headed by the Maharajah, still controlled Nepal tightly, keeping its frontiers closed; even King Tribhuvan, shut up in his ice-cream-colored palace in Kathmandu, was allowed out only when the Ranas permitted. It didn't seem likely they'd welcome an American scientist wandering about their private mountains. But Dr. Bob had a restless, strangely compulsive urge to try anyway.

"I knew that Dr. Ripley of Yale had gotten permission to cross into this mysterious country where, in 1947, he had discovered the spiny babbler, a species that had not been seen alive for over a hundred years," Dr. Bob Fleming recalls. "I was on fire to go bird-hunting in Nepal. I didn't really think I had much chance of crossing the closed border but I wrote anyway to the United States Embassy in India to see if they could get me permission. To my amazement, almost at once I got permission to conduct an ornithological expedition in Nepal for six months! I had never heard of the Orient working this fast in all the twenty-five years I'd spent teaching in India.

"You can call it coincidence if you like; but as Dr. Bethel and I look back, the Lord's good Plan for us to work with sick bodies and eager minds in Nepal is plain. My request had 'just happened' to land on the desk of Roy Bisbee, the son of a Methodist Missionary, who had been a former student of mine in Woodstock School. He walked across the street to the Nepalese Embassy and 'just happened' to find a man in charge who was intensely interested in Himalayan birds, so he said 'Yes' to a fellow ornithologist. I had 'just happened' to have developed a good pair of mountaineering lungs by climbing about in India for years. So I was ready for the Nepalese Himalayas."

ERRANDS

by Judith Guest

Excerpt from Errands, Ballantine Books, 1997

Guest, a member of DWW since 1977, has published four novels, including Ordinary People, which became an award-winning film directed by Robert Redford. She now lives in Minneapolis, Minnesota, with three children and five grandchildren.

Harry unlocks the door, brushing snow away with his boot. Rex, behind him, sticks his hand through the square hole in the storm door.

"What happened?"

"Jimmy locked it on me."

This morning he'd gotten halfway to the bus stop before he realized he'd forgotten his backpack. By the time he got back home, the door was locked against him, with Jimmy laughing on the other side. He'd given it a vicious kick and, to their mutual horror, the glass had exploded into the room. Julie, sitting at the kitchen table, had shrieked as if she'd been stabbed. They'd cleaned it up, dumped the broken glass into the garbage can; all the time she was collapsed in a huddle on the floor, refusing to be comforted. Finally he had yelled at her: "It's just a stupid door!" and she'd sat up, wiped her eyes, turning it all off like a faucet. He'd like to kill her when she does stuff like that.

"Hey, Lucky. Wanna go for a walk?"

Rex leads the dog to the door and opens it, as Lucky jumps and whines in joyful frenzy, whereupon he closes it again.

Harry rummages in the refrigerator, finds the two Cokes hidden in the meatkeeper.

"Walk, Lucky?" Rex is saying. "Wanna walk? Huh?" He opens and closes the door again.

"Don't tease the dog," Harry says, handing him a Coke. Rex inclines his head toward the stairway, putting his fingers to his lips and miming a swift, deep intake of breath, as Julie comes down the stairs.

"Where'd you find that Coke?" she accuses them.

"What're you doin' home?" Harry counters. She flounces to the TV, turns it on.

"I had a dentist appointment. Mom dropped me off."

"So, she saw the door."

"Nope. She let me out in front." A small grin. "But I told her." Then, turning to Rex: "You have the weirdest haircut I ever saw on a human being."

"Little peahead tattler," Rex makes a grab for her. "Let's teach her a lesson!"

She avoids him, plops on her knees in front of the TV, pointing to the screen. "That woman is evil; we want her dead, she's a B-I-T-C-H." Her pink ballet slippers peek out from beneath her butt.

They take their Cokes and go upstairs to Harry's room. Harry pulls a pack of Camels from his desk drawer; they light up.

"Wanna go see Melanie?" Rex asks, as they puff smoke out the open window.

"Not really."

"Okay, then. Piccadilly Circus. Cousineau and Pappas are gonna be there."

Harry shakes his head. "I dropped six bucks there yesterday."

"What *do* you wanna do, then?

Rex prowls around the room, picking up stuff, putting it down. Jimmy's bookbag lies, open, on his bed. Baseball cards, comics, dirty socks, Pjs, homework, a wet towel — everything strewn everywhere. Why won't he keep his crap on his own side of the room?

"Where's your brother? I thought we were gonna ask him today."

"Not yet. We haven't even picked the store yet."

"Best Buy," Rex says. "That's where they got the most stuff and it's easiest to get to the door."

"I think we need to work on the plan first."

Rex shrugs. '"Work on it all you want. Sooner or later you gotta just do it. I've lifted bigger stuff than camcorders, anyways. We just need a lookout."

A knock at the door.

"Go away," says Harry.

"I need to talk to you," Julie says.

They hide their cigarette butts on the outside of the window ledge, and Harry strides across the room to open the door. Julie stands there, twisting a curl of her hair.

"Mrs. Bennett's missing. She's been gone since this morning."

"She's around. Just go watch TV. We're having a private conversation."

"She always waits for me on the back steps."

"It's just a cat," says Rex.

Julie stares at him coldly. "You're an infant. You don't have any brains." She turns away. "I know you guys are smoking up here."

Harry closes the door, and they finish their cigarettes in silence.

"Let's go to Melanie's," Rex says, but Harry shakes his head.

"I gotta hang around here."

"For what?"

"I just do."

He has no intention of taking Rex to Melanie's house. He barely has the nerve to go there himself. Her parents are both lawyers and they live in a mammoth place in Huntington Woods. He might be in love, but he's not stupid. He's not about to introduce her to any of the weird people he hangs out with — at least not yet!

After Rex leaves he goes downstairs, where Julie is standing beside the sliding door, her forehead pressed against the glass. It's raining. Her hand wipes across the glass. *Screep, screep.*

"I can't figure out where she'd be. Sometimes she goes down to Conroys'. I hope nobody decided to steal her."

"Nobody's gonna steal her, for cripes'sake!"

She leaves the room, then comes back, shrugging into her parka.

"Where you goin'?"

"Out to look for her."

"It's gettin' dark!"

"I know that."

"Okay, just a minute. I don't want Mom gettin' pissed at me over this." He grabs his coat from off the chair.

They walk quickly, looking left and right. The rain is a heavy mist. He knows this is pointless. She could be anywhere; she could be on the block they just finished searching. Julie calls out 'Mrs. Bennett! Beeee....!" into the gloom. Just the way old Mrs. Letofsky used to call her dead cat in the middle of the night. It gave him the creeps.

"Let's go up Brookview and circle around."

"Jule, it's too dark. She might even be back home by now."

"You think?"

But he isn't sure; her anxiety is contagious. Blackness yields up strange shadows, ominous shapes in the road. Near the corner a bluish mound settled into the darker blue of the street.

"That isn't her," Julie says firmly. "She's bigger than that."

He walks in front of her, keeping his eyes on the mound. It could be a squirrel. Or even a chunk of ice that has fallen off someone's car into the road. But he's known in his heart since he saw it. Damn it, he doesn't want to be right about this.

At last they reach it, and he bends to look. Gray, wet fur lying near the curb, tiny ears, tight to her head, pink nose.

"Is it her?" Julie whispers.

A car pulls up next to them. "Listen, this is what happens when you let animals run loose! You kids don't take care of your pets. If you're not going to look after them, why have them at all?"

Harry looks up at the man behind the wheel. It is no one he knows. Beside him, Julie's hands clutch at her coat. Tears are rolling down her cheeks.

"Where d'you kids live, anyway?"

Harry stands, glaring toward the car's dark interior. Angrily he waves the man off. Julie is moaning softly. He picks up the cat in his arms, and she is weightless, the body limp, sightless eyes staring at him. No blood, no sign of a wound.

"She's moving, isn't she?" Julie asks. "I see her paw moving. Maybe she's just asleep. Is she asleep, Harry?"

He doesn't answer, feeling a rush of guilt — for everything in this world he doesn't understand, for every way he's messed up.

They lay her body on a towel in the kitchen. Julie strokes it gently.

"She must've been hit by a car," Jimmy murmurs. "She was probably on her way home when it happened."

"We have to get her to the vet," Julie says. "I don't think anything's broken, and there's no blood..."

"Jule," Harry says. "She's gone."

A fresh flood of tears. Julie pushes at the cat's legs, as if willing them to move on their own.

"If we take her to the vet," Jimmy says, "they'll just keep her. We should bury her here."

They get shovels from the garage, and Harry pours boiling water on the frozen ground. The three of them take turns digging. Julie places the shoebox at the bottom of the hole with Mrs. Bennett, wrapped in the towel, inside it. Afterward they watch a rerun of *The Cosby Show.* Theo Huxtable airing out his bedroom so this parents won't find out he was smoking in it. Harry picks lint off the sweater Grandma Lewis gave him.

"What are we gonna do about the door?" Jimmy asks.

He doesn't answer.

"We should put a piece of plastic in there instead of glass. Then it'll never break." Julie is crying again. Her cheeks look red and raw. *Only a cat,* he thinks. *Like hot blue stars that have the shortest lives, highest internal temperatures. Like Vega, like the sun. Only a cat. Not like it's a person.*

"Anyway," Jimmy says, 'Now she's with Dad."

"Don't say stupid things like that!"

"Jimmy's right," Julie says. "Now they're in heaven together. You can have anything up there you want — pets, horses, anything."

"Fine. There's telephones, too. Call him up, why don't you?"

"What're you so mad about?" Jimmy asks quietly.

"Nothing! He's dead, that's all! He's in the ground! It's over, y'know?"

Jimmy looks at him. "You saying you don't believe in God?"

"I believe in him," Harry says wearily. "I just think He's a jerk."

FOR A VERY OLD CAT
by Margaret Hillert
The Lyric Fall, 1963

Living, I cannot think you dead,
And the soft purr stilled forever in your throat.
My fingers grip your bony head,
Trace hard against the pattern of your coat,
Grasp firm a fold of ageing flesh.
Your fur smells sweet and fresh.

You welcome my attentions, close
And open wide your paws in ancient rite.
The orange triangle of your nose
Touches me damply. Your old eyes light
With vestiges of former flame.
I gently say your name.

And there are those will wonder why
Such feeling should exist for a dumb beast.
But others, kin to earth and sky,
Who talk to trees, stargaze, and call the least
Small flower by name, find ample traces
That love has many faces.

WORD

by Mary Jo Firth Gillett
Harvard Review, Spring,, 1997

Mary Jo Firth Gillett (member since 1992) is a poet whose work has appeared in: CALYX, The Bridge, The MacGuffin, Sycamore Review, Third Coast, Michigan Quarterly Review, Harvard Review, Passages North, Plum Review, and others. Her chapbook, Not One, was published in 1998.

Not just a syllable, a ululation, click, roll, slur, trill. I want the whole damn thing, the roller-coaster ride of consonant, vowel, accent and innuendo. I want serendipity do-da, I want somnambulant rapture, and I want it mal, bad — malcontented, maladjusted, maloccluded. I want it alpha and penultimate — there is no end. I want the sound and everything it conjures up, the surprise — that wasp nest
still clinging to the eaves of memory, thin paper that seems empty but buzzes to life with a little warming — or should I say warning — a little onomatopoeic poltergeist in my head, a haunting, a mesh of sound and moment, a fit tight as tiles in a Moroccan mosaic, or the cowry shell wrapped about its softer insides, the subtle pianissimo of what it is — these sounds our companions, linking us one to another like some species specific duet — or should I say diet — the panda and its bamboo, the koala and its eucalyptus, how things are joined as, when I say a word — veranda, for example — or a name, Einstein — it never means strictly what I want it to because of the baggage, everything it ever was — including the madness — everything the seine net of memory can hold — squirming shiners, bits of vegetation, muck and grit and algae — the small, the smell of it, so that even now, dry and propped against the garage, this net teems, the wind catching at its webbing, the primal smell like bedsheets after sex — a skin, a skein of sound, whirl of x and y, both cargo and carriage — like any word — part cure, part tremor at the core.

AMONG THE BIRCHES
by Alice Bartlett (Birch Arnold)
from Birch Leaves, 1905. The dedication reads: These verses are for my dearest Mother, who was my severest critic and warmest admirer.

Oh "ladies of the forest"
  In gowns of silvery white,
Against the shadowed copses
  Agleam like bars of light,
Ye wear the crown of beauty
  The dryads wore of old,
And all the woodland vistas
  With witchery enfold!

Sweet "ladies of the forest,"
  With pastel shades of green
In the laces falling over
  Your gowns of silver sheen,
I follow where ye lead me,
  Bacchante to your spell,
Content in visual glory
  Forever more to dwell!

Section Two

* * * * * * * * * * *

Coming To Order

CONQUEST
by Naomi Long Madgett
From Exits and Entrances, 1988

If it comes on like a cave man
I'll write it.

If it kicks down the door
I'll let it overcome me.

No polite knocking, no pleading, no
waiting to see if I'll let it in. I won't

Unless it clubs me, subdues me,
drags me by my hair,

the poem
will never get written.

COMING TO ORDER:

DWW ORGANIZATION

A festive boat trip on the Detroit River and a fish supper at the popular resort of St. Clair Flats topped off the third annual congress of the Woman's International Press Union (WIPU) meeting in Detroit in 1900. Local women journalists and literary writers were excited. Hadn't they been praised as potential leaders and challenged for not taking that lead by one of the speakers?

One tenth of the 1,000 women journalists in the United States lived in Michigan, according to one speaker. The state already had the Michigan Woman's Press Association (1890) and the Michigan Woman's Press Club (1892) for women editors and publishers statewide. Mrs. Martha Louise Rayne, author and journalist, had founded a journalism school for women in Detroit in 1886, before she moved back to Illinois.

The Detroit women had been thinking about forming a press club, and they wasted no more time. They met that next week, June 5, 1900, and 13 of them founded the Detroit Press Club, the city's first press club. The founding members represented the city's leading daily and Sunday newspapers, where they edited sections or pages, wrote columns, contributed articles, essays, or poetry. Others were authors of books, poets, and non-fiction writers for major national publications. A few of them had already helped to found and had held office in national and state press associations of women.

The Detroit Press Club founding officers were:

Mrs. Lucy Leggett, honorary president, a book and manuscript revision specialist, the author of a book on United States history, *The First Century Under the Constitution.* She was vice-principal of the Sprague School of Journalism in Detroit, vice-president of the Woman's National Press Association, and its representative to the 1893 Chicago World's Fair. She had been president of the Michigan Woman's Press Association in 1888.

First president, Alice Elinor Bartlett, was the author (known as "Birch Arnold") of novels, poetry, and newspaper articles, and a department head at the *Detroit Journal.*

Pruella Janet Sherman, vice-president, was a special writer and editor of the woman's page of the *Detroit Sunday News-Tribune.* She wrote a series of "cypher stories" based on the cypher discovered in Shakespeare's and others' works.

Ida F. Wain, recording secretary, was the book reviewer for the *Detroit Evening News* and *Detroit Tribune* for seven years. She was known for her generous and unbiased criticism.

Mabel L. Ayers, corresponding secretary, grew up in her dad's newspaper office at the *Mendon Globe* and began setting type, reading proof and writing locals at age 13. She started a weekly, now called the *Trenton Times*, and was the Sunshine Department editor for the *Detroit Free Press* for several years.

Other founding members were: Josephine Voss, treasurer, author; Aristine Anderson, staff writer for the *Detroit Evening News;* Emma Stark Hampton, weekly magazine writer; Sarah J. LaTour, columnist; Hulda T. Hollands, poet and author; Hester Spinning, poet; Mrs. Franc Nicols, vice-principal of the Sprague Correspondence School of Journalism (1899-1908) and president of the Detroit Correspondence School for Writers (1909-1910); and Hattie C. Sleeper, manager of the Michigan Press Clipping bureau and former staff writer for the *Port Huron Weekly Tribune, Port Huron Daily Times,* and the Toledo *Blade.* In 1901 Sleeper walked the tunnel under the St. Clair river and wrote about it, the only woman allowed there before the tunnel opened.

Etta S. Wilson, an early member, was a founding member of the Grand Rapids Press Club and of the Michigan Woman's Press Association. She was the first woman reporter at the *Grand Rapids Herald* and later a staff member of the *Detroit Sunday News Tribune.*

E. Cora de Puy, another early member, covered all the news about Michigan journalism for *The Journalist,* a national professional journal in New York City.

Jennie 0. Starkey, an editor of several columns including the Letter Box and Society for the *Detroit Free Press,* was an early member.

The club met every other Tuesday night at the Buhl block in downtown Detroit where Hattie C. Sleeper ran her press clipping bureau. The new club welcomed "all women writers and authors living in Detroit." Prospective members had to submit a published copy of a story, article, or poem from an established publication, a local or national newspaper or magazine. This standard continues today. Dues were a dollar per year. Associate membership was available to writers living outside Detroit.

The Detroit women were part of a movement that started on the east coast. Male journalists formed the first American press club in New York City in 1872, and women were not allowed to join. Other male press clubs followed in the nation's cities, and typically women were excluded. By the late 1800's the women's club movement was in full swing nationwide, and it is not surprising that the growing number of professional women writers and journalists organized. The first was the New England Woman's Press Association formed in 1885, and soon followed by the Woman's Press Club of New York in 1889 and others.

In Detroit, however, the women organized first. When the male journalists founded a Detroit Press Club in 1904, the women's group became known as the Detroit Women's Press Club, and the name was officially adopted in 1908. Another name change in 1914, to Detroit Women Writers Club, signified that the group was open to semi-professional members who were published writers. The word "club" was dropped in 1966, further underscoring the serious professional credentials and aspirations of the group.

From the first the Detroit Women's Press Club promoted discussion of writing techniques and workshops or critique sessions on members' writing. They brought in guest editors and writers as speakers and held writing contests. Fifteen of the members in 1904 composed a "composite" mystery novel, which was not published.

Twice monthly meetings with guest speakers and workshop sessions led to an annual writing conference for the public in association with Oakland University beginning in 1961. Josephine Winn headed the planning for the first conference, collaborating with another member, Priscilla Jackson, who worked at the OU Conference Center. The conference now draws 400 to 500 aspiring and established writers each October and brings in top editors, agents, and authors.

In 1976 four members, Judith Goren, Eleanor Rose, Gay Rubin, and Elaine Watson edited one of the Detroit Women Writers' first books, a collection of poetry by members. *Echoes From the Moon* was successful, and proceeds were used to fund poetry contests for young people and prize scholarships to the writers conference.

Another successful book in 1987, *Voices on Writing Fiction,* featured 28 DWW member authors who discussed structuring, writing, and selling fiction. This book was a choice in the *Writer's Digest* book club, and proceeds were used for other writing projects and seminars Elizabeth Kane Buzzelli and Carolyn Vosburg Hall, came up with the idea and headed the editing committee of Pearl Kastran Ahnen, Bettie Cannon, Cynthia King, and Gladys Leithauser, with additional final editing by Lenore Bechtel and Edith Dunbar. This book received seed money from the Michigan Council for the Arts.

The organization grew steadily through the century from the original 13 to 29 in 1913 and 65 in 1928. Membership remained at that level until the 1980's when it doubled. By the end of 1998 there were 153 members, and over the century there have been 500 members. In early years some honorary memberships were named. Inactive membership is available to those no longer living in Detroit.

The 1914 constitution specified that the object of the group was "to foster a spirit of unity and good will among all the women in the city writing for publication." Membership was for women "regularly connected in a literary way with any reputable newspaper or magazine or professionally engaged in writing for publication."

The regular meetings focus on writing techniques, manuscript preparation, and marketing. Writing contests for students and professionals and recognition awards have been held in some years, and often subgroups are organized to focus on a specific genre, with the novel, poetry, and drama the most popular.

The current work of the organization requires active participation of twenty officers and chairs, and the budget runs around $10,000. Current dues are $30 per year for active members. Recent activities include collecting the organization's oral history, publication of a literary anthology, and holding seminars. Detroit Women Writers contributes to the Friends of the Detroit Public Library, where regular meetings are held. DWW archives are kept at the Burton Historical Collection of the Detroit Public Library. The group has never had its own club rooms, but has met at various local libraries and at the Detroit Women's City Club from 1937 to 1967.

Since 1924 a monthly newsletter has been edited by volunteers from the membership. In 1959 an annual list of achievements was published. It included books, articles, and poetry published during the year plus conferences, lectures, and workshops by members. A current directory of members who are available for lecturing, workshops, and editing has been published since 1995.

Although women's writing opportunities have increased over the century and professional women journalists have several organizations open to them, DWW's focus on promoting good writing and creativity continues to serve the primary needs of this group, while providing networking opportunities and creating friendships through shared work. Several new members are admitted each year on the basis of their published work. The club affirmed that membership was not restricted by race, creed, or color in 1966 and admitted its first black member. In 1994 the first of two male members was admitted.

With the increase in women's employment outside the home and the expansion of Detroit's business and commercial activities into the surrounding metropolitan area, noontime lunch meetings in the heart of the city began to attract fewer members. In the 1970's a typical noon meeting with a lecture and workshop would have 15 to 20 members, but in the 1990's only a handful regularly attend. Luncheons and special events still draw groups of 30 to 40, and the board meetings, committee work, and genre subgroups keep the DWW and its workshops alive and healthy.

Marion Tuttle Marzolf, co-editor

FOUR POEMS
by Alma Carmichael Reith
from Smiles Ahead, Acre Press, 1979

Reith, a poet and DWW member since 1973, has written light verse for 19 national magazines including The Saturday Evening Post, Good Housekeeping and McCalls.

CONCRETE SENTENCES

Writing's like walking on fresh laid cement.
You're stick with what's printed — no matter what's meant.

BE PREPARED

A writer of verse can be proud as a bell
When folks like her verse and will quote it.
But her skin must be tough as a black walnut shell
When they add, "But I don't know who wrote it!"

SILVER LINING

When editors return the verse I've mailed,
My optimism claims I haven't failed,
For on each envelope of each rejection,
There's postage for my son's used stamp collection.

TWO HOURS, PLEASE

Both you and I would surely thank
Inventors for a time-filled bank
Where busy folk could go to share
The time that others have to spare.

DECIDING WHAT'S WOMAN'S NEWS

by Marion Tuttle Marzolf

Abridged from Media Studies Journal, Winter/Spring, 1993

Marzolf, a member since 1980, is a University of Michigan professor emeritus who specializes in journalism history. She has published three books, several articles, and book reviews. She now weaves and writes features on fiber arts.

"News is what I say it is." Arrogant? Sure, but in its brash simplicity, perhaps it is just the right answer. In any case, it has been that way for generations of white male editors. Only in the 1990s, when women represent 39 percent of the newspaper newsrooms, are they, too, starting to have a say in defining what's news.

Will that make any difference?

It may. There are no rules, no formulas, no precise standards to meet in producing the daily news product. News is always what we choose to tell each other about our worlds; what gets told depends largely on who is doing the telling. Traditionally, that has been the world of politics and business, of winning and losing.

We tend to forget that what appears to us as the social norm is really based on a masculine, white, middle-class view of the world. That's always been the only view that counted, and it still retains most of the power. But recently the media professionals have started talking about "women's issues." Well, who defines that? If women don't, those in power surely will.

Women's issues and women's news have been around for a long time, mostly shunted to the side into a separate sphere, reflecting the status of women in our society. Women's pages in the newspapers, now a century old and only recently eclipsed by the 1970s lifestyle sections, are making a comeback in a few newspapers — to the delight of some and the consternation of others. We are caught in a familiar dilemma: women wanting to be fully equal as human beings yet realizing that there are gender differences that must be acknowledged. For women of color, the problems are compounded. Ironically, the fear is that acknowledging differences will push women back to the marginalized, powerless spheres, separate and unequal sections of past newspapers. But adapting and assimilating to the dominant culture poses still other problems — the denial or subordination of a vital part of herself. This is the dual reality of a woman's life in 1993: An outsider who is also an insider in different parts of her life.

Another option exists, but it is likely to be much more difficult. Women and men could share the power and modify the dominant values

— news would be defined to incorporate multiple and multicultural visions. "Mainstreaming" of women's news in all sections of the newspaper was supposed to be the fair way to cover the news. Despite a few newspapers' attempts to assure that some news about women and minorities regularly gets into the news pages, news about women and minorities still lags behind social reality. In most print and broadcast news products, the women's issues and women newsmakers are still rarities. Women readers are also deserting the daily newspapers faster than men; in 1991, 60 percent of women read newspapers, down from 77 percent in 1970. Lifestyle sections, adapted in the egalitarian, unisex 1970s and 1980s, have become mainly peeks into the lives of the rich, famous and sensational, who also happen to be selling their television shows, movies, music, books and food products.

Womanews, a new Sunday section introduced in May 1990 by the *Chicago Tribune,* proclaims its goal as an all-woman news section — news from a woman's point of view and for all colors, nationalities, ages and incomes. It does not want to bring back the fluff associated with past women's sections, nor to be patronizing or irrelevant. Its editors say they intend to write about women — where they are now in their worlds. Early reports are that advertisers and readers approve. At least 10 other newspapers have introduced similar new sections for women, and media consultants are warning publishers that women stop reading the newspapers when they no longer see themselves reflected in them. Women's reality is, more often than not, employment outside the home plus responsibility for families, the configuration of which has changed drastically. When women sit down to read, they want something that speaks to them and interests them — in-depth stories and explanation about the problems and possibilities of everyday life for women in their personal, work and family roles.

Mainstreaming, which applies to news of women and racial minorities, still holds out the promise of equity and acceptance of diversity in the news values and coverage, but it is still only a promise. Instead of serious, day-to-day treatment of these issues, mainstreaming tends to catapult a story briefly into the spotlight, then abandon it. Whether the answer is a return to special sections, or more attention to make sure this news stays in the main news stream, or both, news values are not going to change significantly unless today's women media professionals, including those of color, who are now insiders, take on the responsibility for making change. The male editors who do "get it" are important allies but are still too few. And why should they be the change agents?

It may be an unsettling idea for many who thought the battle was over once "we" got inside, but that was only the beginning. As mass communication scholar Gertrude J. Robinson points out, women in the newsroom are running into a power "threshold;" the final ascent to "social equality in the home and work worlds will be even more difficult to achieve than the legal equality gained in the past 20 years ... (because it) fundamentally rearranges established private and public power patterns."

Perhaps we will decide that we need both gender news reporters and editors and special sections, in order to provide both breaking news coverage of these issues and in-depth features and analysis that would be most salient. A revisited women's section need not be a retreat to the ghetto, but a modified lifestyle section designed to deal with the quality-of-life issues for people of all classes, races and persuasions.

However this gets sorted out, the point is that the diversity called for in the 1970s and partially attained today in terms of newsroom staffing will not automatically translate into changed news values. Today's editors do believe that having more women in the newsroom makes a difference. Women have introduced new subjects and "have allowed us all to do stories we never would have considered news before," as one editor put it. Editors also see women as having different approaches to news sources and improving newsroom work interactions. And women have successfully "pitched" stories in daily news conferences, where they now have a voice and are learning how to use it. Some of these stories were previously ignored: homeless women, single mothers and poverty, spousal, sexual and child abuse, abortion, AIDS and women, sexual harassment and breast implant dangers.

The twentieth century brought many significant changes in the lives of women in the United States, including far greater access to higher education and the professions, a wider range of job choices, better pay, fairer treatment by insurance, credit and pension companies, legalized family planning information and abortion rights. The percentage of women in the work force age 16 and above rose from 18.3 percent in 1900 to 44.8 percent in 1989. Working mothers are no longer a novelty, nor are households headed by women. The very definition of "family" had to change. But women still clustered in low-paying jobs and received 66 cents of every dollar paid to a man in comparable positions in 1988. Those who aspired to management often found a glass ceiling blocking them from powerful jobs.

Mainstreaming of the news about women's issues, including those especially pertinent to minority women, seems to have some drawbacks, because social-issue news generally has not had a high priority. It takes crisis, action or confrontation to get attention in America's news mainstream. Complicated social problems that expand traditional news boundaries and raise thorny economic and political issues take more time and care in the writing, editing and reading. Most women's issues are in this category, and so are routinely shortchanged. But there are vigorous editors and reporters who fight to make a place for these stories in the news, and some of these people have good academic training in the social sciences and race and gender issues. This expertise should be put to use in defining the daily news.

One way to define women's news is to frame it as information with the greatest impact on women as a category, regardless of race or class, linking all women across educational and financial divides by the physical, social and cultural characteristics they share. Women bear the children and provide most of the care giving in our society. They are still treated differently and compensated less well in the workplace. The Equal Rights Amendment failed for a second time in a century. Women are still vulnerable to sexual abuse, rape and harassment. Their legal right to abortion is eroded and still bitterly contested. Women are still being culturally stereotyped and objectified as sex objects to sell products.

New options and independent female role models for the contemporary woman do exist, but they are often ignored and even ridiculed by the mass media. Nevertheless, women's and men's roles and responsibilities are changing, and in some ways, even converging. There should be a new definition of the modern woman for the twenty first century. Maybe then the American public and the media will realize that women's issues are issues for society as a whole.

WHAT I THROW AWAY

by Karen Chorkey Renaud

from Everywhere is Somewhere Else, PlainVew Press, 1998

Renaud, a DWW member since 1998, has poems anthologized in Almost Touching and Everywhere Is Someplace Else (PlainView Press) and in literary magazines. She is a business owner, creative writing teacher, and zoning official.

On my way home, I see
something in the road ahead.
Rain and dark splotch my vision;
I think it's a deer, but it's my trashcan.
I watch it toss this way and that.
This isn't the first time
I've found my discards
tousled alongside the road.
I watch what I've thrown away dance:
first drafts I've given up on,
old love notes,
rejection letters — a whole trail of them.
The wind mini-cyclones, papers rise, rise,
swirl,
search out those words I've
never been able to reach.
Like the way I feel at that precise moment
my cries turn to laughter,
or the way my veins surge,
under the stars, when ice-covered
grasses tattle in the breeze.
Or how my grandbaby's hunger
echoes
inside my breast.
Finally, I am able to drive past
the remains, secure
in the knowledge that, one day,
the right words will come.

MYRA : The Life And Times Of Myra Wolfgang, Trade Union Leader
by Jean Maddern Pitrone
excerpted from "Myra: The Life and Times of Myra Wolfgang, Trade Union Leader," Calibre Press, 1980

A DWW member since 1960, Pitrone wrote short stories for Writers Digest for 17 years. Her tenth book, a biography of Martha Raye was published by the University of Kentucky Press. Her biographies have won several awards.

Synopsis: Myra Wolfgang came into the union movement in Detroit in the 1930s, the Great Depression era when the trade-union movement began to acquire muscle and clout via struggles and strikes. She became a leader not only of the Detroit Local 705 but also a vice-president of the Hotel and Restaurant Employees and Bartenders International Union as, for more than 40 years, she fought fiery battles to benefit the service workers whom she represented.

Myra Wolfgang's long-term minimum wage struggle was interspersed by the fierce battle she waged against the newly opened Detroit Playboy Club in late 1963 and early 1964. Even before the club opened, Myra began her campaign to discredit it by sending her 17-year-old daughter to apply for work when prospective Bunnies were interviewed. She also saw to it that reporters were fully informed of what took place during the interview, including providing a description of the clothing her daughter wore — black and white checked skirt that swirled around her slim legs, bright orange velvet top over which her long hair flowed, and a guitar under one arm.

The results of the interview were very much what Myra had expected. Keith Hefner, brother of Hugh, offered the under-aged girl a job and told her she could make $250 a week in tips. When the girl asked about salary, she was told there was no need for a guaranteed salary; tips were generous.

Myra went into a flurry of activity, inserting an advertisement in the Detroit union's *Review* that asked for volunteers to picket the Playboy Club. Then she set up headquarters for the pickets in a motel room near the club.

Her intent was that the picketing should provide a forum to make the public aware of what Myra referred to as "Playboy's archaic labor practices." She was sure that she had chosen the perfect issue and channel for flaunting her witticisms and for rallying support from other groups. Ministers and Catholic bishops roused their congregations to action as they wrote letters of protest to newspapers. Monsignor Clement Kern, the priest who had first been attracted to Myra's work when she called waiters and waitresses out on strike on behalf of the lower-paid "pearl divers" (dishwashers) now came to join the unionists in picketing the club each evening. Television cameramen and newscasters came to photograph and report on the proceedings.

A waitress who lived only three blocks from the Playboy Club prepared kettles of hot soup, sandwiches and coffee for the picketers as the hours for picketing were expanded. Myra spoke and wrote scathingly at every opportunity on "the matter of scanties" becoming a moral issue since "Playboy's no-wage policy makes the Bunny beholden to the customer for her livelihood." She scoffed at the Bunny costume as "more bare than hare" and insisted that the entire Playboy policy was "a gross perpetuation of the idea that women should be obscene and not heard." If Playboy were permitted to continue its policy, she envisioned the no-wage rule becoming contagious and spreading to other restaurants and clubs. Myra remained unimpressed by a Playboy spokesman's guarantee to pay each Bunny $90 a week if the employee did not collect at least that much in tips.

When the annual "Salute to Women Who Work" was held at Detroit's Cobo Hall that year, Myra and her friends reserved a table centered with a Maypole from which eight toy rabbits were suspended. A placard at the top of the pole was boldly lettered: "Attention, Playboy Club. 'Women Who Work' should receive wages." Waitresses, serving the dinner, placed a leaflet beside each of the plates. Each leaflet read, "We call upon you to join us in our fight against an employer who believes femininity is a commodity to be sold."

The evening became a public relations coup for Myra when reporters questioned the union leader about the leaflets. Her answer blasted Playboy's no-wage policy. "When you are saluting women who work, it is obvious they should be paid. These 62 Bunnies do not have pink ears and four legs. They are women working as waitresses without any salary at all. "

Before the end of March 1964, Myra was back in Washington where she was the keynote speaker at a Manpower and Retraining Conference. A few hours after her arrival at the conference, a telephone message from Detroit informed her that the Michigan legislature had finally passed the one-dollar-an-hour minimum-wage law for which she had fought so long and so hard.

Myra was in Governor Romney's office on the day the governor signed the minimum-wage bill. She had dressed carefully for the occasion in a dark V-necked dress set off by a butterfly pin and a pearl necklace. Her medium-length brown hair, drawn back over her ears, was fluffed out below a polka-dotted pillbox hat. She liked to wear a stylish hat because she had found it more difficult in recent years to control her fine, wispy hair, despite her regular dashes to beauty salons amid the rush of meetings and trip schedules.

Since the state's new minimum-wage law would become effective on January 1, 1965, Playboy Bunnies would automatically receive paychecks at that time although the club, like other employers, would be permitted to deduct specific percentages for the value of meals, lodgings, uniforms and tips — to a total of 40 percent if all four fringe benefits were applicable.

Before the January date, however, 7 1/2 months of Playboy picketing ended for Local 705 when the Detroit Playboy Club became the only unionized Playboy Club in the nation. On August 13, 1964, the "union shop" card was displayed in the luxurious Jefferson Avenue nightclub. When word of the agreement came, the pickets, in line for their lunch-time siege, burned their signs as television cameras focused on the ceremonial fires.

Myra recognized that the settlement had removed the media's compelling interest in Local 705's current labor disputes. But she was elated at the settlement because more than 2,000 members of Local 705 had been involved in the Playboy picketing for the longest period in the local's history. But there would be little rest for Myra as she prepared for tough negotiations for a new contract with the Detroit Hotel Association.

Branding the Hotel Association's offer for a new contract as "hopelessly inadequate," she told her unionists that the offer was "25 cents per hour under the $1.50 per hour needed to bring this group up to the barest level established by President Johnson in his fight against poverty. " In early January, crews walked out of the Whittier Hotel, the Statler-Hilton and others into a cold rain that poured down on pickets bundled into warm coats, scarves and hats, and shrouded with plastic rain gear. The Teamsters aided the strike by ordering the cessation of all deliveries of supplies to the hotel by their union. Elevator operators, maintenance employees, laundry workers and construction workers (who were involved in a remodeling project at one hotel) refused to cross picket lines. With all this backup reinforcement, the strike ended six days later as the settlement offer was made, and accepted, in Mayor Jerome Cavanagh's office. The manager of the Sheraton-Cadillac hotel characterized the settlement as "the best single packet ever negotiated for a group of hotel employees in the history of the industry. "

Standing at the microphone to speak to her unionists, Myra snatched off the glasses that she wore as rarely as possible and promised in her vibrant voice that "Next comes the Metropolitan Restaurant Owners Association, then the Club Managers Association, then the other contracts."

Her enthusiasm keyed up the union members to a delirious excitement. Now — more than at any time since the very early days when Myra spoke on soapboxes at street corners — she was, again, their beloved *"La Pasionaria."*

1944

by Mollie Michelson

included in the Detroit Women Writers publication DWWC Poetry, 1949

Michelson was a Detroit Women Writers Club member from 1936-1951

The moon is red
(And the battle-fields) —
The island ahead is Enchantment Land —
A lovely and dim and alluring land;
I dip — dip — dip the oars.
And sing a low song —
(But how long, 0 God, how long!)

MAN SINGS

by Rose Weinman

found in the Burton Collection, Box 20. Detroit Public Library

Weiman was a DWW member between 1936-1951

The world,
A giant cage
where man the bird sings songs,
Rapturous ones — broken ones,
But Songs.

AN AMERICAN FAMILY

by Mary Augusta Rodgers

Excerpts from An American Family, Redbook, November, 1964

A member of DWW since 1958, Rodgers (Schoen) published Country Roads Of Kentucky. Her articles and fiction appear in many magazines and newspapers: Woman's Day, Ladies Home Journal, Family Circle, Redbook, Gourmet, Washington Post, and the New York Times.

A friend said that she was downtown, shopping in a large department store, when the first announcement that President Kennedy had been shot in Dallas, Texas — exploded over radio and television. Browsing in the record department, near a display of television sets, she suddenly noticed clerks standing together and staring in the same direction. Their faces indicated that the view was frightening, and she thought, Oh God, somebody's having a heart attack back there, or some awful kind of fit.

She left, or fled.

Back at her car, she threw her packages in the back seat and started home. On the expressway she noticed that here, too, something was wrong. No cars were passing, or changing lanes or even driving faster than 30 miles an hour. "It was eerie," she said. "Just like a funeral procession." Then she turned on the car radio and heard the news.

When something like this happens, something so shocking and sudden, with such reverberating consequences, it helps to put the event in a frame of some kind; to make a personal connection. All the stories that begin, I'll never forget. "I was on my way to the post office when it started to rain, so I ducked into a drugstore and ..." serve the same purpose, whether the speaker is talking about the assassination of President Kennedy or Pearl Harbor. The familiar details lessen the unbearable feeling of helplessness: they put us in the picture...

Afternoon faded into evening, and the Presidential plane was somewhere in the sky between Dallas and Washington. Waiting, we felt like people in an airport; the same restlessness and uncertainty, the same determination not to miss the next announcement.

Finally, on the television screen, we saw the plane land. For one last moment, it was possible to believe that everything was as it had been that morning; that a crowd would murmur, "There he is!" and there he would be. But there was only the coffin. And then Mrs. Kennedy, the new widow, and the waiting ambulance. And the new President, Lyndon Johnson, facing a battery of microphones and speaking against the roar of airplane motors in the background.

The evening was an interlude. What seemed strange was that everything was exactly the same. In the kitchen, not even a cup had crashed to the floor. The goldfish swam in their tank; the roast was still in its pan, defrosted and ready for the oven. Dinner was late, and the television set stayed on...

Friday, Saturday, Sunday, Monday... the sequence of events is hard to recall, and it was confusing, even then. The weather, I think, was fine; the sun shining and the autumn air turning brisk. Thanksgiving was only a few days away and the Christmas decorations were up in the business district but all feeling of time and place was out of focus. Reality was the pictures on the television screen and that turned into a kaleidoscope of faces and scenes and voices.

We were taken to Washington, to Dallas, back to Washington again. There were news bulletins and reports, interviews and discussions, film clips and video tapes. We saw the face of Lee Oswald; an anonymous face, hard to remember, until it became, in a few hours, a face impossible to forget.

There was Oswald on film, airing his views on Cuba in a year-old interview from New Orleans; a rapid voice racing against the expected interruption, a guarded expression, the eyes bright and avid for attention. There was Oswald's mother, speaking in an immediately familiar voice and tone. (My son, he's a good boy, why should he get the blame every time something happens ?) There was Oswald's young wife, silent, bewildered, a baby in her arms. And Oswald's landlady, speaking in another familiar voice: "So I asked my husband to speak to him about the rent and frankly, he was real snotty about the whole thing ..."

There was the flag-draped coffin on the caisson leaving the White House, moving slowly toward the Capitol, being carried up the steps. And there was Jacqueline Kennedy, pale and controlled, moving like a figurehead on a ship, the admiration of the country rising in waves around her.

Churches were crowded that Sunday. At our church, a woman sitting near me broke down during the first hymn. "Eternal Father, strong to save, Whose arm doth quell the restless wave ..."

I cried too, but this was nothing new. I admire stoicism but that's as far as I'm able to go, being one of those unfortunate people who cry at weddings and commencements and sad movies and the sight of children in a school band, playing as they parade down a suburban street. During this weekend, I'd been tearful most of the time, humming hymns under my breath and dwelling on all the obvious poetry quotations; "0 Captain, My Captain", naturally, and "Goodnight,

Sweet Prince" and so on. But the woman near me looked as though she was struggling with a feeling of astonishment. "I never cry," she whispered apologetically, her eyes brimming.

After the service, we stood in the Sunday sunshine and talked about going to the special communion service on Monday. A friend shook her head.

"I can't take any more," she announced. "This assassination has killed me."

Then we went home, turned on the television set while we were having a late breakfast and — while passing a platter of bacon and eggs — we saw Jack Ruby shoot Lee Oswald in the stomach.

Disaster and sudden death have been well documented in our century, and the pictures form a fearful montage: the car of the Archduke and Duchess of Austria, assassinated at Sarajevo, and the open limousine in Dallas, with blood and roses on the floor; the Chinese baby alone and screaming after the bombing of Nanking; the children's shoes lying in the rubble of the black church in Birmingham, Alabama; planes, bombs, tanks; concentration camps and refugees; a body lying in the mud of a country road.

"History," people said as the shooting of Oswald was shown over and over in slow motion, like the movements in some monstrous ballet. "This is history."

So it was, and so is every day that is past. The winds of chance blow, a President is shot and dies and a door bangs open in every house. We shiver and, as soon as possible, we shut the door. For the present, everything at home remains the same. The pot of ivy sits on the window sill, the goldfish swim in their tank, the milkman arrives late, perhaps, on that weekend in November, but with the regular order.

In a way, it was a relief when the funeral began on Monday. The turmoil and dreamlike horror of the weekend was over. Now grief was given an ordered and eloquent expression, with prayers and military honors. Think of one moment and you'll remember them all: the slow march, the muffled drums, the riderless horse, the stab of amazement at the sight of General de Gaulle and Haile Selassie walking together down a Washington street. (It would have seemed no more fantastic if the announcer had mentioned the presence of Charlemagne and the Black Prince.) There was the son saluting his father's coffin, and his little-boy look of eager interest as the flags and horses and marching men went by; the final services at the grave, the lighting of the eternal flame, taps and the folded flag. "Eternal rest grant unto him, 0 Lord."

It was over. The limousines began arriving at the White House. The eulogies continued, but in a different tone; they had been prepared more carefully and some served other interests. "In this tragic hour..."

We are all left with our own memories. I remember our son Mark, then 15. He held his guitar as he watched the television screen and his fingers plucked out a melody; a folk song about pretty Polly-O.

The television program was a rerun of the 1960 Democratic convention in Los Angeles. *(0 Captain, my Captain, rise up and hear the bells! Rise up — for you the flag is flung — for you the bugle trills!)* Shouts, parading delegates, bobbing signs: *WIN WITH KENNEDY* and *WE WANT JACK*. It was the first political convention to command Mark's interest; he'd worn a campaign button, distributed leaflets, quarreled with his best friend, had a wonderful time.

A voice bawled. "And now, ladies and gentlemen, I give you ... the next President of the United States!" and Jack Kennedy smiled and waved to the roaring crowd.

"I can't believe he's dead," Mark said. The music stopped; his head sank down on the guitar. It's the moment I remember as the memorial service in our family. Only one out of millions, I know.

TO MY FATHER
by Hope Morritt
Libra Anthology, 1st prize, Trillium Books, 1988

I see no trenches
hear no guns
white headstones
march in silent file
where larks sing &
sunbeams flood
gold-green meadows

Block 295 — Grave 5
of this no-man's land
stir my marrow
you are not a number
of last posts — you are
gentle arms shielding
me from missiles
subtle humor & untiring love
etching horizons

Dear Warrior I see you
dancing — your sword sheathed
no battle cry upon your lips
only joyful shouts
that I have come
strong in limb & life
in the distant realm
to your last bunker

READING BETWEEN THE LINES: AN ENLIGHTENING ANALYSIS ALTERNATIVE

by Darlene House

excerpted from her Wayne State University PhD thesis

House joined DWW in 1989. She owns House of Communications — a writing, editing, and special events firm. Her degree project served as a reading assignment for subsequent college students.

The act of reading between the lines requires more than paying attention to literal meanings. It acknowledges the importance of figurative and implied meanings. It also provides an opportunity to explore the implications of related topics through detailed study.

Thus, readers are encouraged to look beyond what appears on the page to reach an enhanced level of understanding about the information. The act of reading between the lines helps one transcend from the obvious, initial levels of comprehension to the more advanced and profound.

Reading between the lines can assist us in the decoding process when studying communication created by Blacks. According to Molefi Kete Asante, indirection is an important component to code structuring that is observable in stylistic development. "Any Afrocentric analysis of Black communication must consider the importance of limited revelation, holding back on what one knows, restraint in speaking directly to strangers in the Mexican American culture."

Asante noted that Melville Herkovits, a pioneer in the study of indirection usage in Black language, believed it is a tradition that carries over from aboriginal culture for which Blacks came to America equipped with related techniques. The techniques of indirection are practiced in Black communication designed for a variety of publics and target audiences.

Essence magazine is ranked as distinctive among a large group of women's magazines seeking narrow groups. For many Black women, the 1970 inaugural issue was long overdue.

John Vivian claimed that magazines both reflect and impact their society. In his discussion of women's magazines, Vivian describes the evolution of a genre: The first U.S. magazine edited to interest only a portion of the mass audience, but otherwise to be of general interest, was *Godey's Lady's Book.* It was started by Sarah Josepha Hale in 1830 to uplift and glorify womanhood. Its advice on fashions, morals, taste, sewing, and cooking developed a following which peaked with circulation of 150,000.

Through the years, readers of women's magazines avidly turned the pages of "Seven Sisters" publications carrying on the *Godey's Lady's Book* tradition. These magazines are *Better Homes & Gardens, Family Circle, Good Housekeeping, Ladies' Home Journal, McCall's, Redbook,* and *Woman's Day. Cosmopolitan* is an eighth sister that focuses on a subcategory of young, unmarried, and working women. In addition, there are other newsstand alternatives that reflect more feminist perspectives. Black feminist scholar Bell Hooks said, "They got *MS* magazine; we got *Essence."*

Marion Marzolf concluded that the study of women's publications has been minimal in the past compared to other mediated artifacts. There is a need for more studies of this type. While studying Black Women's Thought, many other publications could be analyzed that are minority or mainstream.

Reading between the lines provides an alternative approach for looking at the diverse scholarly work of Black women who acknowledge the significance of Afrocentrism, Feminism, and Optimal Psychology. These women also contend those theories do not effectively address Black women's needs and issues. Black women scholars proposed Africana Womanism, Black Feminism, Afrocentric Feminism, Afrocentric Optimalism, and Womanism as alternative theories that are more inclusive of their race and gender. Instead of attempting a detailed study of all these theories, there was a comprehensive survey of Black Women's Thought.

The term Black Women's Thought was created by the author to provide a categorical means of reference for the diverse theories' discussion. Maggie Humm used the term Black Feminism to describe a "multilayered and multi-tissued approach to feminist thought that has changed feminism." Patricia Hill Collins describes Black Feminist Thought as being a comprehensive category. One thing Collins says about Black Feminist Thought is also true about Black Women's Thought. It can be presented as overly coherent or as a shifting mosaic of competing ideas . Nevertheless, excluding variations of the word "feminist" was deliberate because they are offensive for some Black women theorists.

Clenora Hudson-Weems's Africana Womanism theory vehemently opposes all feminist points of view. It speaks to the need for women of African descent to develop a heightened awareness of their heritage. Hudson-Weems argues that true Africana womanists must refuse to accept the basic tenets of feminism. This act of refusal enables them to focus on the 18 common Africana Womanism features that have also served as guidelines for literature analysis. They are self-namer, self-definer, family-centered, genuine in sisterhood, strong, in concert with male in struggle, whole, authentic, flexible role player, respected, recognized, spiritual, male compatible, respectful of elders, adaptable, ambitious, mothering and nurturing.

Along with Africana Womanism, Black Feminism is a major theory of Black Women's Thought. Black feminist scholars are prolific writers with work readily accessible through both academic and mass market publications. Bell Hooks has been described as "the most prolific, most anthologized Black feminist and cultural critic on the contemporary scene". As a result, the views of Black feminists are frequently presented as being representative of all scholarly thinking classified as Black Women's Thought making it a major area for study. In fact, there are diverse schools of thought within Black Feminism that provide different guidelines and models for analysis.

Black theories have been criticized for lacking scholarly technique and method. Asante reminds us that Black theorists went to the same schools as other scholars but developed different analyses. Negative critiques of Black theories encourage many critics to supplement their usage with those based on Eurocentric concepts.

The author found this technique to be effective when the synthesis of Black Women's Thought, genre and myth was used for analyzing a pop culture artifact. The decision was made because studying genre and myth enhances one's understanding of Black Women's Thought and how it is expressed. Thus, this study attempted to show how using theories not specifically focused for rhetorical analysis along with those that are can enhance the quality of tools used in scholarly work. Theoretical synthesis of this type somewhat responds to criticism of Black theories. This is deemed necessary because, although in many cases this criticism is not objectively presented, there are still significant issues raised for critics to address.

A case study involving *Essence* magazine issues served as the application for a theoretical synthesis. Throughout its first 25 years, the magazine evolved to become an interesting communication artifact. It simultaneously reflected Black Women's Thought, functioned within generic constraints, and attempted to dispel myths. The analysis focused on two magazine issues — the May 1995 25th anniversary issue and the one for May 1996. It reviewed a special issue of the publication and a regular issue with new features marking the start of a new era for *Essence.* By analyzing these texts, a study was conducted of how scholarly thought is expressed outside academic circles and its implications. Re-reading *Essence* on a more profound level revealed significant reasons for its communication success. They include planning based on women's magazine genre research, information presentations designed to promote positive images of Black women and responsive analytical techniques to creatively address feedback issues.

Black feminist scholar Marsha Houston Stanback explains why studies such as these are needed: At the very least, anyone who intends to study us should examine the fit between current theories and methods and Black women's communicative lives. At best, those who do research on us should employ theoretical perspectives and methods of inquiry that are developed for and thus uniquely suited to exploring the Black experience.

Studies of this type acknowledge the significance of theoretical perspectives and methods that focus on the Black female experience. Furthermore, they examine how Black theories can be synthesized with others. The studying of nontraditional artifacts provides a way to discuss scholarly thought that can be enlightening for a cross section of people.

Using texts that these individuals regularly encounter can increase their interest in learning more about related theories and other scholarly thought. Discussions based on nontraditional text studies provide more opportunities for people affected by information accessibility, literacy, or illiteracy problems to increase their awareness and knowledge levels.

As far as the many challenging opportunities that studying Black Women's Thought provide for the critic, let us say *vive la difference.* The conceptualization of Black Women's Thought as an alternative for theoretical analysis makes the study of frequently overlooked work essential. Their work eloquently addresses issues of gender, race, and class from a variety of perspectives. The study research process resulted in the discovery of very enlightening work by Collins and Guy-Sheftall. More efforts such as the survey of Black Women's Thought could enhance awareness of other unique contributions to our personal, professional, and scholarly quest for the truth.

By using customized lenses to study Black communication artifacts, the view changes and visions of new insights are possible. Thus, reading between the lines requires an intuitive initial reading or re-reading that can result in enlightening and rewarding experiences.

MAPLES

by Patricia Hooper

from Poetry, The Modern Poetry Association, 1995

Hooper won the Poetry Society of America's Norma Faber First Book Award for Other Lives. She wrote Flowering Trees (poetry) and two children's books, Bundle of Beasts and How the Sky's Housekeeper Wore Her Scarves. She appears regularly in many magazines.

When my neighbor cuts his trees down I don't want to see
the damage, so I don't look. I keep working in
my kitchen, but I notice how the light seems
brighter on the curtains and the bare floor. I don't want to
mourn anything not human, so I think about the few
deaths I've been given: one grandmother, two friends. Trees
can't match this, and I find myself going through old
griefs, weeping, though I thought that I'd stopped
grieving for many years. Now I remember how it was I
came back from those first loses, looking suddenly
upward at a sharp, quick song, some clattering in the thick
branches that shaded everything, my lawn and his. How clear
his house is now past the one scrawny magnolia and the back
fence: nothing between me and my grandmother's pale
face on the white pillow; nothing between me and the car skidding
over the steep, bright hillside, my friend's wild hair.

IN THE BACKYARD
by Patricia Hooper
At the Corner of the Eye, MSU Press, 1997

This morning a hawk plunges
straight for the squirrel at my feeder
and leaves only
its signature: blood on the snow.

All morning it circled the yard,
then dove, stunning itself
on the glass sky of my window,

and in minutes returned, braving
the thin, perilous channel
between hedgerow and house. I was watching
its path as it fell, its persistence,

and the squirrel, how it dashed
for the downspout, finding itself
motionless under the heat
of the hawk's body,

the claws in its rib cage, the sudden
tearing of wind as it rose
over the fence, the feeder,

the tops of maples and houses.
All morning it stays with me, not
the squirrel's terror, the hawk's
accuracy, but only

how it must feel to be lifted
out of your life, astonished

at the yard growing smaller, the earth
with its snow-covered fields tilting,
and what must be your shadow
flying across it, farther
and farther below.

AMONG COLLEGE STUDENTS
By Carol Chadwick, PhD
Prentice Hall, from Jump At Da Sun, 1999

Chadwick joined DWW in 1998 and has published essays in Public Voices, Private Lives (Univ. Of Texas Press), Jump At Da Sun (Prentice Hall), and Model For Adult And Lifelong Learning (Wayne University Press). She teaches at Wayne Community College.

For the last 25 years, toward the end of every semester I have been swamped with final essays, final exams, late papers, forms to fill out, requests for incompletes, students who go into labor just before the final exam, students who want to know how they can make up 14 weeks of absence in the next two days, desperate, cautious, worried students. Like clockwork, my mood darkens and I begin to feel that the whole endeavor of teaching in an urban inner-city community college is hopeless. I dream about winning the lottery and running away to the south of France. Then begin the plans for how I'm going to do it differently next time. Thank God, there will be a next time. Again and again, I, the groggy pugilist, go back to take one more swing at it. I don't care what they say in self-help books; it's failure that propels me, not success. The day I achieve what I've actually set out to do, I'll put it in a book on teaching methods and retire.

It's the challenge that keeps me going. Sure, I am influenced by the usual incentives, but I would have fled my job as an English instructor long ago were it not for the fact that after the end of every semester I have the opportunity to take another stab at it.

It begins during the last two or three weeks of school. First, I commiserate with friends and colleagues. We shake our heads and groan. We make sardonic jokes. This leads into "what if" and "why not" and before long I'm headed back to the drawing board, writing supplementary handouts and finding additional materials to clarify persistently muddled concepts. Before I know it, I'm engrossed in my newest attempt to achieve the impossible. Things, of course, rarely work out precisely as intended. Sometimes, one clarification leads to two new confusions. I write enlightening materials but overlook embarrassing typographical errors. There are delays and foul-ups in the duplicating room; I run short of materials; students are absent, the usual problems. Nevertheless I feel I am inching forward. I'm getting closer. I'm getting there.

Twenty-five years ago, when our college was groping through its infancy, my colleagues and I saw ourselves as trail-blazers. Adult urban education was a relatively unexplored territory and what lay before us was a whole frontier of educational opportunity and experimentation. We developed lessons, activities, and curricula, giving free range to our plans and dreams. Then we set them to spin. To our immense delight and excitement, many things worked well but, alas, not everything.

The harsh realities of the lives of our students sometimes wrecked our plans. Adult urban inner-city students have to cope with many things traditional learning theorists never need to consider. Non-traditional students sometimes have families to care for, often single-handedly, houses to keep up, part or full-time employment, unreliable transportation, health problems, money worries, and so on. Some of our best-planned lessons and activities are never completed because students are unable to find time at home to do the work or to come to school at all. Some have very far to go academically in order to compete with others with more traditional or privileged educational backgrounds. The needier the student, the harder the job for the teacher. Students can become very frustrated when they do not do as well as they hoped or when the tasks turn out to be more difficult and time-consuming than they anticipated. They may direct their anger and frustration at whoever is nearest at hand. That person, most often, is me. If voices could actually cut, I would be in ribbons. If looks could really kill I would have been dead long ago.

Not every student I teach is serious about education, yet there are enough good students to keep me coming back. In fact, all it really takes is one. When the brain becomes engaged, it can show on the surface. The student's eyes narrow and brighten and there is a tensing of the body; the student breathes differently, rapidly and less deeply. Then I know I'm getting through and that sets me off. Some days I fly.

Sometimes at social gatherings, we discuss what I do for a living. Some people wonder why I "waste" my time, the sub-text of which is "waste" their "tax dollars," teaching basic fundamentals of reading and English composition to adults who, in their estimates, should have learned what I teach in elementary school or, if truth be told, not at all. Here is when cynicism gives way and I hear myself asserting that in this democratic country everyone is entitled to a basic education. If, for whatever reason, people don't become educated when they're young, they should be allowed the chance to try again. By providing people with a second chance, we are making an investment which will eventually pay off for everyone. All of society benefits, because education makes people employable and, therefore, self-sufficient. Working people pay taxes which gives them a vested interest in their communities. People with jobs put money back into the economy by buying consumer goods and services. They have less need for public assistance and costly social services. They are less likely to be involved in crime, thereby decreasing the need for police, courts, jails and so forth. Having said all this, I either change the subject or someone does it for me.

At these events, I don't usually go into my personal reasons for supporting public education, but I will here. I was born in 1940 into a very poor dysfunctional family. From reading books, watching movies and observing the lives of others in the community, I reached the conclusion that education was the only way out of a life of hardship and misery. Thanks to the kindness and generosity of certain neighbors, teachers and, later, friends, I was offered social and educational experiences which enabled me to grow far beyond my initial potential. I owe an immense debt to them. Most of those individuals were dead and gone by the time I grew up, and I was not able to thank them in any conventional way. No single act or utterance would have been sufficient, anyway. At the community college where I teach, there are many promising but economically disadvantaged people who need the kind of mentoring I once received.

By helping people at the community college, I have the opportunity to begin to put back what I have been given. We read that certain percentages of students are failing the high school placement exams, that many Americans are at least functionally illiterate. Sometimes what I see in the classroom supports this. However, in our libraries and bookstores there are ever-increasing numbers of new and recovered publications by women and minorities. Thousands of people are finding their voices and they are doing so because of public education. Not everything they write about appeals to some of my colleagues and contemporaries nor does their style always meet with approval. There they are, nonetheless, to disgust, horrify, surprise, fascinate, and perhaps to enlighten. We can thank public education for that.

What I don't say to cocktail party challengers (because they would never understand anyway) is that I believe helping our fellow man is a moral, as well as social or personal, responsibility. I know that learning to read and write with even a moderate level of sophistication changes people's lives. For some people, especially disadvantaged men and women, there may be no family members, friends, or neighbors to serve as positive role models. The thoughts and actions of fictional characters, biographies and autobiographies may be all there is to guide them. Learning to read well (that is, accurately and critically) opens doors not only to inspiring people and events but also to the very acts of reflective, introspective, associative thinking that can begin to enable people to get a grip on their lives. Learning to express oneself clearly and understandably on paper gives one a voice that has power and breadth. It provides the ability to be recognized, and offers a way to manifest innate personal worth.

So, as the years pass, I try and I fail and I try again. I have lost track of whether I am the challenger or the challenged. Now it's too late to change, says she who never quite gets around to quitting.

TEA LEAVES
by Pearl Kastran Ahnen
from Heart Songs, Poetry Society Of Michigan

Ahnen, a member since 1981, writes articles, plays, fiction, and poetry. She was awarded the Michigan Livingston Art Council Award of Distinction in Literary Arts in 1992 and 1996. She teaches and directs conferences.

In my memory, Mother,
you sit at our kitchen table
and gaze into my tea cup.

You tip my cup — this way, that way.
Leaves fall and rise by the stroke
of a spoon, stirred by an
easy breeze on the tea cup pond.

You spy a tea leaf linked with nothing,
isolated at the bottom of the pond,
and with wonder and anticipation
your voice slices through the silence.

I see your dreams coming true
but I cannot wait.
You smile, caress my cheek.
I have an urgent engagement, you say.

Mother, you had no right to die
before your child did something to make you proud.

THE RELIGION BOOK
by Beth Aviv Greenbaum
the Jewish News, 1998

Greenbaum, in DWW since 1981, writes fiction and essays, and teaches.

When I first met Lori, I saw her as my Palestinian counterpart, I am Jewish and married to an Israeli. She is Christian born to Palestinian parents. We both have thick dark hair, and blue eyes. She teaches fourth grade. I teach high school English. We had both volunteered to work for the school district to revise the *Religion Book,* a book meant to tell the history, and beliefs of our community's religions and to increase levels of sensitivity and tolerance in students and staff.

In February, during Lent, Lori drove me in her aging BMW to her home for lunch, I admired her art, the fabrics on her sofa and chairs, and her Persian carpets. She served me delicious food — tomatoes on rice, Armenian string cheese, fresh olives, and warmed pita bread her mother had baked. We shared the same loaf, breaking off corners until we split the steaming middle,

The next day, I drove Lori in my aging Volvo to my house for lunch. She admired my art, my furniture, and my Persian carpets. I made her a meal she could eat for Lent and served it with fresh bread I'd baked. I was giddy and excited with our new, friendship — at the sense that one by one, we could prove history wrong. We could form the links necessary for peace.

I shared with her my fantasy of visiting her family with her in Ramalah and bringing her with me to meet my family in Tel Aviv.

At breakfast with my husband the morning of our last meeting, *The New York Times* spread beyond my coffee and toast on the kitchen table, I read him, as I always do, paragraphs from the paper. And then he has to listen to my diatribe.

The week before I had ranted about Har Homa, the housing project to be built by Jews for Jews in East Jerusalem. It triggered a suicide bombing in which four Jews died having lunch at Apropos, a trendy restaurant in Tel Aviv, just down the street from where my husband grew up. Netanyahu, the Prime Minister of Israel claims the land for the apartments is 75 percent Jewish owned. I intruded on husband's reading of the funnies in the *Detroit Free Press,* "Shouldn't 25 percent of the units be reserved for Palestinians if they own 25 percent of the land the apartments will be built on?" I asked.

And then my husband read from the *Free Press*, about Bernie Gleiberman who wants to put up integrated housing on a vacant stretch of Woodward.

"That's what they should do in Israel, put up integrated housing," I announced raising my cup of coffee into the air.

My husband surprised me "Wait. That's not so far- fetched," he said. "It would take private money. An American Palestinian and American Jew could do it."

"Integrated housing for Arabs and Jews? We could talk to Max Fisher or Al Troutman. We could talk to Lori. Maybe she knows a philanthropic Palestinian."

When I left for the meeting I left with optimism and hope. I was excited that perhaps two women in Detroit could instigate the building of integrated housing in Jerusalem. Yes, Lori knew a wealthy Palestinian. She would speak to him. As we chatted outside the meeting in the hall, I felt that maybe through our talk we could do something. Maybe we could do in Israel and the West Bank what has taken so long to happen in America. Maybe we could raise a roof under which we could all live — where our children might play. Then we went back to the meeting in the windowless conference room to review the chapters we had revised, and the old issues began to replay.

On the first page of the chapter on Christianity, Jews were described as responsible for Jesus' crucifixion. Not an auspicious way to begin. Then responding to my chapter on Judaism, Lori objected to my describing ancient Canaan in present-day Israel and Lebanon. It was also Palestinian land, she said. Everything began to have an emotional and political cast. And when Gail, Jewish parent on the committee, objected to my not mentioning the Holocaust and I said that it would be in the "Lessons section," the reverend said, "That's propaganda."

My head went into a spin. Ron, the Deputy Superintendent, levitated momentarily from his chair. Gail's face turned red and beaded with sweat. I turned to the reverend and said in the most rational voice I could summon, "What do you mean?"

"It's history," he answered. "It's not part of the religion."

I quoted Eli Wiesel, still trying to remain adult and reasonable, "Yes, but in the Holocaust only Jews died because of their religion. Not all victims were Jews, but all Jews were victims."

"A lot of people have suffered from genocides," Lori interjected. "'The Armenians. The Cambodians, the Bosnians."

Then Gail said she still lives with the fear that it could happen again, and she always keeps a suitcase packed, her passport in it. And

Lori told how her mother fled her village in 1948 in a bus in the middle of the night with only the clothes she was wearing, "Should my family have had to lose their homes?" she demanded.

And Gail, whose father survived Auschwitz, whose half-brother survived execution when his young mother pushed her five-year-old son into a pit of the already dead and dying just before she herself was shot, demanded, "Should my family have had no place to go?"

Lori responded, "Gail, do you think you are the only ones who suffered? Not only do I understand your suffering, but I've experienced it in the same magnitude. I want to understand you, and you to understand me. We can move forward, but how can we accomplish that without openness?"

We had ripped past our trendy clothes and civil facades. The beliefs we all hide in such civilized ways erupted. In that room of mustard yellow walls, fluorescent lights, and Formica tables, the power of history was alive and painful. Fifty years after the last Jews were freed from Auschwitz, almost 50 years after the last bus carrying young Palestinian girls left for Jordan, we remember. There is no propaganda in these stories. Only truth. And from this truth, I hoped, compassion.

The following week Gail and I told Ron, the Deputy Superintendent, that we thought the reverend had crossed a line. We wondered if a man who would call the Holocaust propaganda should serve on a committee charged with honoring diversity.

I called Lori at home. Lori pleaded that we all continue to work together. Gail and I should forgive the reverend. We could not.

After the reverend resigned, Lori too, resigned. Her uncle is the father-in-law of the man who cuts my hair, the father of a man my husband works with. Lori's sister cuts my husband's hair. How intertwined our lives are. And yet, despite the intimacy of her sister's fingers in my husband's hair, her cousin's fingers in mine, despite our wishes and modern ways, like our counterparts in the Middle East we felt governed by our beliefs and our blood.

But unlike our counterparts in the Middle East, we live in America. We live in similar homes and work at similar jobs. Several months later, Lori came back to our meetings. Ron, the deputy- superintendent, had called her and told her we still consider her an integral part of our planning. When we saw each other for the first time since our schism, we hugged — tenuously at first, and then she pulled me close to her, and I drew her to me, Then we released each other, and went to work.

SIGHTING THE EAGLE
by Loren Erickson
Ridgeway Press, 1992

Erickson, a DWW member since 1980, writes fiction, drama, and poetry. She taught at Washtenaw Community College,. She founded Northern Spies literary journal and is managing editor of The Bridge.

She said she saw it,
the bald eagle, I mean. In the city,
where it wasn't supposed to be.

She was driving, listening to news
of the probable
war in the Middle East.

We shot eagles out of Lansing,
Kalamazoo, Detroit,
even Ishpeming years ago.

So what was this woman doing
driving down 13 Mile
with her eyes on the trees?

I don't mean to ask
why wasn't she watching the road,
only — why was she looking for eagles?

Did she believe sighting
that fierce beak and eye,
head crowned in white feathers,

its flat wings stalled
over a Royal Oak strip mall,
off target and losing altitude,

would raise a lump in her throat,
hold her hostage to the flag
and the riderless horse

and Oh say can you see,
when it's only a bird winging
to Florida — or the nineteenth province?

I say, keep your eyes
on the road, woman;
pray for the sparrows.

BERTRAND RUSSELL'S INTELLECTUAL ODYSSEY

by Gladys Garner Leithauser

from her doctoral dissertation, Russell As A Man Of Letters, this segment published in Free Inquiry, 1995

Leithauser was a professor at University of Michigan-Dearborn where she taught writing and communication, and is editor of The World of Science: An Anthology for Writers.

Bertrand Russell is a major writer, prolific and venturesome. His 70 books and hundreds of essays for both general readers and specialists are sometimes ground-breaking and often controversial. The writings range from highly technical expositions through popularizing discussions of science to commentaries on social issues and ethical problems. Probably few readers have worked their way across the breadth of the canon, but many have become familiar and impressed enough with Russell's writings to make his ideas part of our culture.

What motivated such prodigious productivity? The answer seems to be the metaphor that underlay Russell's life: the great quest. Centuries old and part of the narrative of many societies, the quest theme is often religious. Surprisingly, it is almost that in Russell's case, despite his famed stance as an agnostic. Having lost his religious beliefs, he continued his search elsewhere for certainty and immutable truth. Readers who remember his encounter with geometry at age 11 — he called it "as dazzling as first love" — understand his transfer of the quest to mathematics, which he once termed "stern perfection." The search took Russell through a philosophical development that Ronald Jager, quoted above, considers an "odyssey." Though Russell never found his answer, he pressed on, and his writings record the innovations and advances the effort produced. In calling Russell "the great intellectual adventurer of the century," Jager gives both the man and his methods epic stature. The evaluation reminds us this year, the 25th anniversary of Russell's death, to focus more consciously on his journeys to the frontiers of modern thought.

As a young man studying Hegel's system, Russell devised an ambitious plan for his own work: two series of books, the first on the philosophy of the sciences, moving from the abstractions of mathematics to the concrete illustrations of biology; and the second on political and social matters, becoming progressively more abstract. The two series were to culminate in an encyclopedic volume, a Hegelian synthesis of theory and practice.

Although the series did not work just this way, Russell later remarked that to some extent he had accomplished his plan. Possibly, he meant that his books display a purposeful dichotomy. First is the series he considered "primary," works in which the subject-whether geometry, logic, or political analysis — is treated by completely intellectual, rational means. Second — yet vital — is the group from his complementary effort to base works on emotional perception, to admit feelings and values.

The dichotomy results from separation of the intellect and the emotions, as in Enlightenment thinking, based on Russell's conviction that only such disjunction allows a writer to trust the workings of the intellect. The presence of the second group testifies to Russell's growing interest in "knowledge" other than the rational. Again, his attitude reflects an 18th century view: reason and passion make the whole man.

Thus the Russell of the early years of the century emerges as a brilliant but dualistic and conflicted self. Characteristically, he approached materials in terms of rational "principles" or emotional "perplexities;" while holding reason to be the governing factor. When as an "apostle of rationality" he feared that he was becoming a "logic machine," he strove to balance his achievements in the realm of rationality (as evidenced, for example, by his innovations in symbolic logic) with a corresponding creativity in what he saw as the subjective realm of human values.

This complementary effort brought him out of the academic world and into the public forum. A first step was to enter politics. While such an interest was a family tradition — his grandfather, Lord John Russell, had been Prime Minister for Queen Victoria — Russell's bid for Parliament in 1907 was especially progressive in that he stood as the Women's Suffrage candidate. Undeterred by defeat, he went on to even more dramatic political activity, speaking and writing for pacifism and against conscription during World War I. The result was a six-month prison sentence. Soon his target shifted to the left; in 1920 he criticized the Russian communist regime in *The Practice and Theory of Bolshevism.* Standing again for Parliament in 1923 as a Labour candidate, he lost once more. But, as we know, these experiences did not destroy his activist propensities, which continued as opposition to the atomic bomb and, in his old age, culminated in leadership in nuclear disarmament.

One way by which Russell consciously developed what he called "the truth of vision," which he saw as opposed to the "truth of science," was by letter-writing. His habit of full and thoughtful message sending grew to include an astonishing number of correspondents. The most important was Lady Ottoline Morrel, with whom he fell fervently in love several years after the bleak discovery that he no longer loved his first wife, Alys. His correspondence with Lady Ottoline enabled him to explore aspects of his personality that he believed were not nourished by the austere worlds of mathematics and logic. The *affaire* with her became a central event in Russell's life and gave her influence for a time over the direction of his creative efforts.

Eventually, Russell's thematic quest for certainty covered a great range of experience. He moved from undergraduate days and the hope of finding certain knowledge in mathematics to his seasoned conclusion in old age, as stated in *Portraits from Memory:* "Cocksure certainly is the source of much that is worst in our present world." Between those statements lay the long, intense exploration of philosophy that resulted in numerous books, his award of the Order of Merit in 1949, and the Nobel Prize for Literature in 1950. For the Prize, Russell's particular citation was "in recognition of his varied and significant writing in which he champions humanitarian ideals and freedom of thought..."

To use Russell's own amusing word, the Nobel Prize conveyed a kind of "respectability" and placed his writings more securely in the tradition of British letters.

Reading the evaluation almost a half century later, we are aware of steady progress in Russell scholarship and ongoing commentary on his life and array of ideas. We are heartened to realize that Russell, struggling with the divided self, used his situation to conquer loneliness, despair, and the disappointment of the unrealized quest. He wrote: "To teach how to live without certainty, and yet without being paralyzed by hesitation, is perhaps the chief thing that philosophy, in our age, can still do for those who study it."

Russell readers have as exemplar a philosopher who, by treating uncertainty as a challenge, made an odyssey of intellectual adventure and gave freedom of thought enormous value by his unwavering dedication to it.

CELEBRATING FAMILY: Make 1997 A Giving Year
by Lisa Luckow-Healy
Observer & Eccentric Newspapers, 1996

Healy, a DWW member since 1997, writes the "Celebrating Family" column for the Observer & Eccentric, and freelances for six other newspapers, and Metro Parent magazine. She is president of Trendz Inc., a marketing and public relations firm.

On August 31, 1995, my life changed forever. It was the night I lost my 18-year-old brother, Mark, to an automobile accident. My family and I were devastated. Acquaintances passing the funeral home that week told us they thought a celebrity had died because so many people were going in to pay their respects. The funeral, itself, was reminiscent of a movie scene with the dozens of caring friends and family converging upon the burial site.

Since that horrible night, my family and I have had many long hours to reflect upon our past, present, and future. Losing a loved one has a profound impact on your life. It makes you realize that all the daily activities, rushing to school, planning your life around a client dinner party, worrying about a forthcoming business transaction or holding a grudge mean absolutely nothing without the love and support of family and friends.

As a family, we've repeatedly reminded each other not to dwell on the "should have, would have, could have" phrases, because nothing is going to change the past. But the memory of Mark that lives on within all his family and friends has been an inspiration to reach out and touch the lives of others in need of help and support — to make a difference in someone's life by putting that individual first.

With the New Year just a few days away, this is a good time to set New Year's resolutions, to help someone less fortunate. Ask yourself and your family how you can combine your love and support through volunteer efforts. There are hundreds of volunteer organizations throughout Michigan and the United States that depend on volunteers like you not only during the holidays but the whole year through.

One such organization is Lighthouse of Oakland County, a non-profit that assists low-income individuals with emergencies. Students, families, and church organizations are some of the volunteers who reach out to the Lighthouse. " One local corporation brings their entire staff to Lighthouse at Thanksgiving to help prepare meals for needy families," says Noreen Keating, president, Lighthouse of Oakland county. "If corporations can do it, more families can too by getting involved as part of their child's school community service project. A local man and his child work with the Comerica Bank and Trust office in Birmingham to gather the soft drink can returnables on a monthly basis, turn the cans in for their deposit, and submit that money to us to help others."

Sheila Clemons-Steger, Manager of Development Services, Make-A-Wish foundation of Michigan, asserts there are numerous ways families can help her organization grant wishes to children with life-threatening illnesses. "Our new program, called Kids for Wish Kids, is a Community service project many schools are tailoring to their needs, " says Clemons-Steger. "Basically, students in grades K- I 2 can participate by working together to raise money to grant a wish for a child in their area. The program teaches students how to focus on individuals other than themselves by demonstrating how they can pool their resources to make a difference in a seriously ill child's life."

Kids for Wish Kids is a program that promotes team-building between the students and their families. "Parents can foster the spirit of giving in their children while encouraging other members of the student body to participate and tackle the awesome responsibility of making another child's wish possible," says Clemons-Steger.

Paint the Town is an organization that selects a community in the city of Detroit and in its surrounding satellite cities to send volunteers to paint homes and perform general repairs. This widespread volunteer effort takes place in mid-August. "Students in Cub Scouts come out with their parents to lend a hand and receive merit badge credit for their participation," says James Jackson, Loan Administration, Standard Federal Bank in Troy, a corporate sponsor of Paint the Town. "The young people who volunteer with their families, many of whom are employees of companies who support the organization, are exposed to community service at an early age."

The Lighthouse of Oakland County, Make-A-Wish Foundation of Michigan and Paint the Town are just a few of the hundreds of local and national organizations looking for volunteers like you to help make 1997 a giving year.

SPINDRIFT
by *Mary Jo Firth Gillett*
Crab Orchard Review, Southern Illinois University, 1997

What hasn't already been said about the moon,
the stars? And though, love, we are
not heavenly bodies — no constellations —
in our eyes there still lingers the light — somehow —
of a collapsing star, light too dim to pierce
these onion days. But see how the very world
works for us, nothing wasted, nothing lost —
each tear that slips to the anonymity of collar
or floor, each molecule of rain that seeps
to alligator sewers — I've read — once coursed the points
of pyramids, knew the likes of Cleopatra,
and after a season of spindrift or snow will
melt again to hot sands, thirst that is
sudden artesian and slow Paleozoic,
tiger's teeth and trilobite's scuttle across salt seas,
both larger than the sky's red giant,
smaller than the radium atom emitting its lethal dose
to Madame Curie. In this time, both briefer
than the engineer's nanosecond and longer,
much longer than the 100 million years
it has taken us to get to this moment, stripped
of its coverlet weight, I marvel at our bodies —
each other's bookmark — keeping alive the passage
called passion, the red quickening pulse that,
like the ratchet sound of a child's wind-up toy,
like the edge of the evaporating puddle,
fades only reluctantly as each cell whispers,
I am here. You are here. It matters.

LACE AND FASHION

by Virgina Bailey Parker

from the International Old Lace Bulletin, 1992

Parker, a member since 1991, has written articles for newspapers, magazines, and journals. She owns Snowy Creek Press and Snowy Creek Video Productions. She lectures to children and adults on a wide variety of topics.

I had no idea when I began researching the clothing worn by the Puritans in 17th century Massachusetts that it would lead me down a path of lacemaking history. After all, are we not confident from the truths we learned in earliest grade school, that one had nothing to do with the other?

Picture, for a moment, the image ingrained so long ago of what a Puritan looked like. If it makes it easier, think of the Pilgrims, a splinter group of Puritans who founded the separate colony of Plymouth, as well as our time-honored feast of Thanksgiving. Our very traditions rest on the bedrock of knowledge that they were a people who dressed only in black clothes with plain white linen trim. (For the steadfast who resist change, read no further.)

Perhaps the misconceptions arose, at first, because the Puritans described their clothes as being of "sad" colors, but people in the 17th century understood this term to mean dark or deep tones. Popular colors in that era included russet, olive green, and most surprisingly, scarlet! The Plymouth Plantation in Plymouth, Massachusetts is an excellent place to view the styles circa 1627 of the Pilgrims. Here the interpreters begin to change our image of Thanksgiving's founders. In keeping with fashionable trends of that era, an interpreter may tuck a corner of her olive green skirt's hem into her waistband to reveal a scarlet underskirt. Apparently, Puritan men were no exception among 17th century males, who had an eye for full figures! Color is not the only surprise. We have considerable evidence that the Puritans also wore lace. We find the first concrete clues in their laws. The General Court enacted a series of sumptuary laws to curtail what the leaders perceived to be excesses in apparel, however, it is clear from studying these laws and the resulting court cases that clothing restrictions served, in part, to distinguish social classes.

The first of these statutes, passed in 1634, banned certain fashion details, including the making or buying of lace; however, we can presume that the Puritans continued to enjoy their lace because the Court saw fit to include a provision which allowed the colonists to wear out their current apparel, provided it was not too extreme, Two years later, the Court passed another statute specifically allowing a small edging — meaning narrow lace — to trim clothes.

The Massachusetts Bay Records addressed the issue of lace and social status head-on in 1651. In that year, the Court declared its "utter detestation that men and women of meane condition, education, and calling should take upon them the garbe of gentlemen by wearinge of gold or silver lace..." Another of the numerous, similarly minded laws, enacted by the Court in 1662, forbade "apparell exceeding the quality and condition of their persons or estate."

Court cases further bore out that the fine fashion was condoned and encouraged as a way of demonstrating social class. For example, two women who were brought to court for the infraction of wearing silk hoods were discharged because each proved her respective husband was worth two hundred pounds. Other cases followed in a similar vein.

Portraits provide additional information which disproves the popular myth of drab Puritans. Not only do gentlewomen appear with broad (wide) lace, but so do Puritan founders like Governor John Winthrop who donned a lace-edged ruff. Estate inventories, too, record the existence of lace.

I have found no portraits of the Pilgrims at the time of their settlement in 1620, but I suspected that, since they had emigrated from lace-rich Holland, the Pilgrims must also have worn lace. I contacted Pat Baker, Department Head of Wardrobe and Textiles at Plymouth Plantation, who kindly took the time out to discuss the matter with me. She confirmed that, indeed, the Pilgrims did wear lace, particularly bone lace, which was inexpensive enough to be affordable. They possessed no aversion to lace, per se; rather its use was determined by social station. They objected to anyone dressing above their station in life as that was contrary to God's will. Among some of the population, a dislike of starch and ruffs seems to have been a greater issue.

Alas, first scarlet and now lace: our image of the Pilgrims will never be the same! Nonetheless, these aforementioned sources, as well as a look at the distribution of lace among people of similar backgrounds in England leave no doubt. True to this knowledge, Plymouth Plantation interpreters who portray prominent citizens do wear lace on occasion.

The portraits painted decades later of the Pilgrims and their descendants clearly demonstrate a fondness for lace and fashion. One dated 1651 of Edward Winslow, a founder and governor, and another dating to 1670's of Elizabeth Paddy Wensley both display lace. Mrs. Wensley's collar, stomacher, and ruffles below the elbows are all of broad lace. Her hood is trimmed in little lace, and she donned a pearl necklace and earrings as well as ring for the occasion.

In studying these fashions, we learn something about what the Puritans thought and valued. Their esteem for certain things cuts across the lines of time. We lacemakers, in particular, share an appreciation of beautiful lace. And each time we create lace, we perpetuate our link to the past.

FOR JANE
by Ella Lull

Lull was a member of Detroit Women Writers from 1932 to 1951. Her poem "For Jane," was found in Box 16 of the DWW Collection in the Burton Collection at the Detroit Public Library, Main Branch. No citation of publication was given

I sit
and knit and knit
my love and happiness with you,
together with balls of heavenly-blue wool yarn
and make a "shoulder shawl" as light
as south wind's song, and soft as
petals of the blue forget-me-nots.

I hope it keeps you warm as camaraderie
which flows unceasingly between us two.
I sit and knit for you.

WHITE BIRD
by Judith Goren
The Bridge, 1994

It lived caged in the boy's room,
where window blinds cast bars
along the walls. Its song
woke him like a morning kiss.
He taught it to perch on his finger,
to hop when he whistled,
to give up fear.
Sometimes he opened the cage
and the room filled
with the music of laughter and wings.
The bird learned to land on the boy's head,
its feet buried in his hair
the way the boy walked barefoot in summer grass.

I

One November morning the boy,
wearing his bird like a crown,
watched an unexpected snowfall:
flakes large as feathers
filled the air, covered the ground.
As the world transformed itself
he felt his blood pound, his breath come fast.
Forgetful of his crown,
he dashed outside, face turned up,
and in that unreclaimable instant
saw a winged snowball rise
to be devoured by the sky.

A LIFE IS SAVED

by Virgina Law Burns

Enterprise Press, from William Beaumont, Frontier Doctor, 1978

Burns, a member since 1960, writes juvenile biographies published by her own Enterprise Press. Her latest book Gentle Hunter: Biography of Alice Evans, Bacteriologist, led to Evan's induction into the national Women's Hall of Fame. Burns is on the Children's Book Writers and Illustrators board of advisors.

That night, Dr. Beaumont returned to his house. It was late. He stepped carefully along the dark hallway and into the bedroom. A lantern glowed feebly, casting a pale glow on Deborah. She sat propped up in bed, reading the Bible. Her heavy, brown hair was tucked into a nightcap, and her face was calm as she lifted her head to welcome her husband.

"I am glad thee art back, William. My time cannot be far off, judging by the ache in my back!"

Dr. Beaumont smiled at his wife and bent over to kiss her.

"Life does go on, doesn't it?" he said quietly, stroking her hand and looking beyond the fluttering curtains that were pushed open to let in the cool, sweet night air. There was the smell of fresh water of the big lake as well as the minty odor of the island's wild fern.

"The youth I just treated, Alexis St. Martin, took the full discharge of powder, wad, and bird shot in his side and chest at no more than two or three feet distance from the gun's muzzle. Those present feel certain it was an accident, but we'll probably never know exactly how it happened."

"Oh, the poor lad! Is he from the island?"

"No," the doctor said. "He appears to be a trapper from Canada. What stuff he is made of! A normal man would have died instantly. The force of the blast carried away flesh larger than the palm of my hand; it broke the fifth rib and blew off and fractured what remained of the sixth rib. I found the left lung torn apart and the stomach was cut open by a bone that was blown through his coat."

He paused, then sat down at the foot of the bed and tugged at his boots.

"All around the broken ribs and cut muscles were the lead shot, and the wadding and fire had burned the clothing and flesh to a crisp. I found a piece of the lungs — as large as a turkey's egg showing through an outside wound, and below this, also showing, a portion of the stomach!

"At first I could not believe it possible, but when I looked closer, I saw it actually was the stomach, with a hole in it large enough to admit my forefinger!

Deborah shook her head sympathetically.

"What a strong heart he must have," she said.

"Indeed. His blood pressure was low, but it remained steady, even when I was working on him. Why, I was forced to clip off the sharp point of a rib with my penknife before I could put back the exposed piece of lung! Then I picked out rib fragments, old flannel, wad and lead pellets that had been driven together under the skin and into the muscles. I put on a dressing of flour, hot water, charcoal and yeast, and bathed the parts around the wound in a solution of muriate of Ammonia in Spirits and water.

"I shall change the dressings every eight or ten hours," he went on, "but the medicines I gave him by mouth escaped through the stomach wound."

Deborah's face became a picture of horror.

"Thee mean he was conscious all this time!"

"Yes, and no, Deborah. He was in shock and felt little pain. I daresay he will die before morning. I shall just rest a bit and go back down to him."

Twenty-four hours later, St. Martin still lived, but pneumonia, lung infection and a terrible cough began. Dr. Beaumont opened a vein and took about fourteen ounces of blood from the patient.

Doctors today know that a great loss of blood, especially for an ill person, is dangerous. Yet early medicine considered "bloodletting" or "bleeding a patient" generally acceptable and curative. The desperately wounded St. Martin, however, clung to life in spite of the blood losses. Dr. Beaumont spent much time with him, in addition to his regular post hospital duties.

During the first forty-eight hours after the accident, the exhausted, young assistant army surgeon plodded up and down the steep fort road, caring for the bleeding, semi-conscious boy at the bottom of the hill, and a beloved wife, having her first child at the top of the hill. Finally, on June 8, a healthy baby, Sarah, was born; and Dr. Beaumont was able to leave Deborah resting comfortably, blissfully, in their fourposter bed.

Bone-weary, William walked slowly into the living room and eased himself into the tall chair in front of the fireplace. His blue eyes were glazed. He closed them and sighed. The high cheekbones and the slightly aquiline nose were gray with fatigue. Still, the sensitive, full lips drew into a smile and his chin dropped. He had earned a rest.

Summer slipped into fall. Little Sarah grew and thrived. Her father's army duties fell into a steady routine, and Alexis St. Martin, having been transferred to the fort hospital, continued to recover from the extraordinary wound. Dr. Beaumont made an entry every day in his medical journal. He wrote:

"Four months after the injury, an abscess formed about two inches below the wound . . . . very painful and extremely sore: produced a violent . . . . fever." (Again, it looked like St. Martin could not live out the week.) "After applying . . . . poultices for a few days, the swelling pointed externally, and I punctured and laid it open for about two or three inches."

The result of this operation was that a piece of shot, and a small portion of wad was exited in about three days, and in another three days, more fragments of the ribs and cartilage came out. It continued, that during this four or five weeks, pieces of cartilage worked their way through this same opening. Alexis was in great pain at this time, and the healthy healing of the wound stopped. Both doctor and patient were relieved when there was no more discharge from the inflamed part, but it was a short reprieve. Directly, an inflammation appeared at the other side of the wound, this one as irritable and painful as the first one. Using a poultice and the same kind of operation, Beaumont opened it "an inch or two." In a couple of days, a piece of cartilage measuring about three inches came out. The next day, a smaller piece could be seen, and Beaumont drew it out. After this, the sore healed and there was no more action. Alexis was past danger.

THE CLUB WOMAN'S GLOSSARY

By Peggy Cameron King

a chapter from Ladies, Please Come To Order, Grossett & Dunlap, 1968

King, a DWW member since 1959, wrote fiction, taught creative writing, and mentored many aspiring writers.

If you've somehow managed to reach voting age without joining a club, your first exposure will confuse you more than an expressway cloverleaf. Nowadays, a club is an organization which a girl joins to develop her id. You're not familiar with that term? Call it what you like — psyche, mystique, libido, personality — that's *id.*

Don't be misled by Webster's varied definitions of the term "girl" as: 1. a female child; 2. a maidservant; 3. a sweetheart; 4. a roebuck less than two years old. Under these narrow interpretations, most members won't qualify, so in clubwork any reference to *the girls* is concerned only with sex, and includes females of any age, even those long past their prime (that is, over thirty-three). On formal occasions an acceptable synonym for "girls" is "ladies" even for the ones who tend to be vulgar.

"Will the meeting please *come* to *order?"* is the standard opening and you should not interpret it as either an insult or a threat, even though the presiding officer is armed with a mallet. Business will be conducted largely by *motions* which have no relationship to calisthenics. If the chairman asks, "Do I hear a motion?" it isn't because she's deaf; she's just making a desperate plea. Although *seconds* play a vital role, just as in a duel, the chief physical activity is of the tongues, since a verbal hassle results whenever anyone makes a suggestion. The preliminary rounds involve not only motions but *amendments,* and sometimes amendments of the amendments. You don't have to be a gracious hostess to *entertain* a motion. Finally, one of the girls will make a motion which is either *carried,* or is *tabled* (without using the furniture). In extreme cases it may be *killed* (without violence).

The fine points of protocol are dictated by the *constitution.* Some clubs never get around to drawing one up although no artistic talent is needed. Just as you need an annual physical, a club's constitution should have periodic overhauling.

Even though the president knows everyone personally, she will sometimes announce that she wishes to *recognize* a member. If she's in a generous mood, she may even *give her the floor.* It is customary for the president to *leave the chair* if she wishes to make a motion or voice an opinion; but lots of presidents voice an opinion without leaving the chair if they're mad enough.

There's very little physical exercise in a regular meeting although some of the terms imply it. You can *spearhead* a *drive* without either a weapon or a car. No one who is *running* for office actually does any sprinting. Some clubs encourage their members to *go through the chairs,* but they don't want the furniture demolished. It is permissible to make a suggestion *from the floor* without lying on it, and *standing* committees are allowed to function sitting down, just as *outside speakers* are allowed to come indoors. Even when it is announced that the treasurer's report *stands approved,* nobody rises.

When you are told to *listen to the minutes,* don't hold your watch up to your ear, and if asked "What is your pleasure?" you're not expected to launch into a recital of your hobbies. The presiding officer's request for a *"show of hands"* doesn't mean that you're in for a motherly inspection. Be assured that the fact that the group has seven vice-presidents is no reflection on its morals. Also, a *chairman* has other responsibilities than looking after the seating arrangements, just as a *toastmistress* performs at banquets not breakfasts. If you are told that everyone is *going Dutch,* you don't wear wooden clogs. Any talk of *operating expenses* has nothing to do with surgery.

At the annual meeting, the nominating committee will *present a slate,* but only theoretically, because slates went out with hatpin holders. After you've been associated with the organization long enough to give its interests top priority, but not long enough to be completely fed up, you'll be asked to *accept an office.* By now you'll know that this doesn't mean rent-free occupancy, and that with other officers of the executive you will assemble periodically for *board* meetings, some as dull as they sound. And of course, when you *retire* from office, you don't go to bed.

But I have an idea you'll need to when you get home from your first club meeting. Is there any second for the motion?

Section Three

* * * * * * * * * *

The Middle Years

FIVE POEMS
by Elinor K. Rose
from Echoes From The Moon, DWW, 1976

Rose, a member since 1957, wrote humorous verse for the Detroit News and was syndicated in 350 newspapers across the country. She cc-edited the DWW poetry anthology, Echoes From The Moon, and arranged scholarships to their annual conference by holding a poetry contest.

GETTING THE WORD
Our puppy chews chairs, a deplorable caper;
We slap his behind with a roll of newspaper.
This training is having amazing success.
For even a dog knows the power of the press.

LIBRARY FINES
I check out a dozen, forget to renew;
No notice is sent till they're weeks overdue.
My money's aghast at the way I can fritter it;
I'd doubtless be solvent if I were illiterate.

EBBING ALPHABET
My Christmas cards from A to G
Have long and chatty notes from me.
My lines get briefer, by and by;
All T to Z receive is "Hi'."

LIMBO LOST
My mind is like a parking lot;
Each memory has a separate slot.
I don't forget a name or face;
I just can't find its parking place.

OPEN MINDED
He keeps old keys in jumbled scores
To cars now gone, forgotten doors,
To ghosts of locks of long ago
And sagely nods, "You never know. .."

THE MIDDLE YEARS

MEETINGS AND MEMBERS

Thirty years after the 20th century arrived, Detroit horses still pulled milk wagons, delivered bread, coal, and ice. Outer Drive had replaced Grand Boulevard as an unofficial city limit. By the third decade a car became as necessary as indoor plumbing, although streetcars rumbled along all the main corridors.

Phenomenal changes in lifestyle and outlook are not always for the better. The optimism of 1900 and the roaring 20's dimmed with bank closings, rampant unemployment, and dust bowl realities. In 1900 a house could be ordered from the Sears Roebuck Catalog; in the 30's buying a new house melted into a day dream.

In the Great Depression dime-clutching survival techniques made the kitchen-table craft of writing more appealing than ever. Small sales could be a godsend. An extremely humble DWW treasurer's report of March, 1932, lists total disbursements as Yearbook and other postage, $2.20. Every aspect of life was peeled back to minimum cost, yet Detroit Women Writers continued to gain members. The writing successes of other women spurred everyone on.

Meeting for criticism was essential, yet it is hard to imagine how any real workshopping on writing got done. Here, for example, are the minutes of a meeting in 1933:

> "The first (season's) meeting called to order by Mrs. C.R. Dudley at 3:00 PM. The question arose as to whether the Club should support the Detroit Symphony Orchestra by purchasing a book of ten tickets.
> Discussion: Federation of Women's Clubs requested that the DWWC vote two members to serve at table for the month. Passed. Interviews with caterers found one who would serve tea at $.50 each. Two delightful piano selections by Mrs. Spaulding, to whom our thanks are extended.
> Women's City Club donated a room free of charge for the prose group. Speaker: Dr. Pickett; subject —Modern Trends in Philosophy. Meeting adjourned at 4:32."

Note the mention of a "prose group." There seemed to be a pecking order in which prose was given priority and extra privileges. The wide variety of speakers shows that members were interested in civic and political affairs; in keeping up with the newest findings in health science, social welfare, world trends, and more. Inquiring minds wanted to know far more than the latest gossip. Programs aimed to provide food for thought and inspiration from unexpected sources. There was a doughty sense of civic duty, with no loss of genteel propriety.

Presidents' reports were written formally in the third person, first names seldom appeared, and married titles were insisted upon. In three or four small ledgers, such minutes as survive are in carefully tilted handwriting suitable for personal invitations or calling cards. Telephone numbers were still in four digits. Priorities tell a lot. Eight persons ran the program committee while the hospitality group had seven members. The women met in homes or in a local library until moving to the Women's City Club in 1937.

Program planners handled difficulties with the delicacy of Miss Manners. One of the few handbooks left on the library shelves says, "A slight change has been found necessary in preparing our yearly program. The names of those who have charge of the evening's entertainment are given, but topics are omitted. We have learned that it is not wise to give anyone a subject months in advance... (the) topic ... may not coincide with one's mood at the time chosen, for everyone knows writers are the most 'moody' of individuals."

The back of the book listed ten names of those who had passed on, with these words; "One by one they cross the bar, and we shall follow when we receive the call."

In 1933 the Detroit Women Writers Club had $47.32 in the bank; untouchable because all bank assets were frozen as of March 14, 1933. Cash on hand amounted to $5.50. It was suggested that an effort be made to raise the balance to $10. Miss Marie Racy, parental advisor for the Board of Education, spoke at a meeting. "The new psychology," said Miss Racy, "has halted the old way of writing about people who were born great (royalty), whose faults were submerged. Modern bios are about personalities and are read for profit."

Still clinging to some of their grandmothers' basic dictums, women guest speakers tried bravely to address new trends, as long as the approach was noble and uplifting. One guest is quoted as saying, "A book may not be called a book unless it makes us more courageous in the face of any fate, or gladder in the face of any joy."

Social affairs in those shaky days certainly helped people to forget deepening economic drabness and disturbing news from Europe. The writers put on Mother and Daughter dinners and President's Day teas. They formed committees to report on social legislation, child welfare, home economics, public health, Americanization, and civics. Even conservation was on their list of concerns.

The pursuit of journalistic excellence had new outlets *in* the form of writing contests and recitations at programs. Serious writing gained steady ground, even as the rumblings abroad grew louder. In 1939, Hitler invaded Poland, and World War II was at the nation's doorstep.

With all its madness and valor, World War II was another watershed era for women. The manpower shortage opened windows of opportunity as women filled jobs they never would have been trusted with in earlier times. They ran banks and tested airplanes. Rosie learned to rivet and kept assembly lines moving. Women moved into the press room, took their places behind police desks, and ferried finished ordnance to military bases.

DWW's Sheila Holden, a concert contralto and poet, became the Red Cross director of the army induction center at Fort Wayne in charge of Italian prisoners of war. She helped them stage operas, and started to write about America's Happiest Prisoners.

For social scientists, the winds of change were blowing in all directions. The Women's City Club, for example, was home to one of the best restaurants in Detroit, but no liquor was served. To the joy of ladies who lunched, the City Club opened a chic cocktail lounge one floor above the restaurant. Women now had their own respectable and private place to go for a little nip of sherry. A few members fought against this radical advance, but it was an immediate hit.

The 40's gave women wider venues, yet when peace finally came it brought unexpected set-backs, usually seen through rose-colored glasses. The good news involved a high priority dream of ex-servicemen and their wives to own their own houses in the suburbs on a large lot and have three or four children. The government put the dream in tangible reach with the GI Bill of Rights, the most generous education and home loan subsidies ever offered.

The stern dictum that working women were taking jobs from men was a popular logic. Men needed all factory and bank jobs. Putting hubby through grad school by pitching in with a job was seen as a necessary evil, while the parallel message was not to seek employment unless the family was really strapped. The good life a la *Better Homes & Gardens* became a fixed high-hurdle goal. Mom in a starched apron making cookies with her little elves, fathers knowing best, and the family that "plays together stays together "were among the rain of catch images and phrases that put a guilt-trip on women with outside personal ambitions.

The baby boom was hardly an accident.

Much as in the Depression, women of literary bent who stayed home filling expectations, found the DWW group to be an intellectual lifeline and writing a mutual cottage industry. Most work was done peck by peck on manual typewriters, although swift electrical machines had arrived. Television was a seven-inch screen novelty in the early 1950s, but the possibility of future markets in the new medium was discussed at many a meeting.

Only published writers could join DWW. It was a measure of the times that membership went up in the post-war era then doubled in the fifties. Dues inflated to a new high of $3.00.

Jeanne Duran became a member in 1952 with sterling credits as a *Detroit Free Press* columnist, as a radio personality, and fiction writer as well. As a member with the longest stretch of service to the Detroit Women Writers, Jeanne has been a resource person magna cum laude, remembering the lean W.W. II years and living out the then-unfamiliar role of working mother.

Vera Henry, whose life included supporting an invalid spouse and two sons, joined as a noted writer of short stories and mysteries, and later did some writing for *Alfred Hitchcock Magazine,* taught for *Writers Digest*. Vera is warmly remembered as an outstanding mentor and teacher.

By putting a daily verse in 350 newspapers, including the *Detroit News*, Elinor K. Rose inspired dozens of women writers (and more than a few men) to hone their doggerel for print in general newsstand outlets.

Josephine Winn, a novelist, also joined the new 40's group, along with Priscilla Jackson, Aileen Fitzpatrick, and Kay Smith. Skilled writers in all genres applied for membership, some driving in from Ann Arbor, Brighton, and points north, to swell the DWW annual achievement lists.

In 1961 credit belongs to a number of people, but Jo Winn and Priscilla Jackson are given major credit for initiating the Writers Conference. Events at the time also caused DWW to play a major role in Detroit's change of attitude when the club unanimously voted to leave the Women's City Club due to its policy of racial discrimination. Not written into its by-laws, but a definite rule for the City Club was that no women of color were allowed above the first floor. In a seven-story building where most of the facilities were upstairs, this limited vision and narrow prejudice was impossible to justify.

Kay Smith, president of the DWW at the time, issued statements saying that "the Detroit Women Writers (now 96 members) had many inquiries about the admission of Negroes as guests and had been told by a City Club spokesman that Negros would not be allowed." Mrs. George Romney, wife of Michigan's governor, heard about the racial policy and immediately sent in her resignation, giving the

Women's City Club some very adverse publicity."

The Detroit Women Writers moved their meetings to the Conference Center at Wayne State University and later to the Detroit Public Library's Main branch.

Meetings in the decades that followed were held at the Library, in evening or afternoon sessions, in homes and in area libraries; Farmington Hills, Birmingham, or the Ford Library in Dearborn. Meeting schedules included an annual book and author luncheon toasting those who had published books in the previous year. Best-known, Joyce Carol Oates and Judith Guest were the biggest names on the list of an astonishing number of nationally successful publications.

Recently membership has remained at a steady level of around 120 to 150 persons. After a long debate on the subject of admitting men, two now appear on the roster. The general influence of this group generated by its own successes and by the teaching skills it has generously shared marks a proud record. Moving toward the new technical eras of communication, the basic wordsmith skills remain. The Detroit Women Writers will be there to write the book, edit the words, or compose for the Internet.

Doris Scharfenberg, co-editor

SIMPLE PLEASURES IN THE REGION OF RED GOLD

by Doris Scharfenberg
from Country Roads of Michigan, Country Roads Press, 1994

Scharfenberg, in DWW since 1967, won many travel writing awards including three-time Mark Twain Award. She has written five books, her first, The Long Blue Edge Of Summer, and the latest 88 Great Lakes Vacations. Her work appeared in the Detroit News, Detroit Free Press, Michigan Living, Better Homes And Gardens, Chicago Sun Times, chapters in Rand McNally Guides, and others.

Six years before the 49ers' dash for the gold and 50 years before silver fever hit Colorado, a stampede for copper was on in upper Michigan. Prime target, that finger of land poking into western Lake Superior, the Keweenaw Peninsula where chunks of the purest copper ever found on earth waited just beneath the surface.

Michigan's copper rush had all the frenzy of a wild west legend. Deep snow, ice, black flies, a babble of languages and boom towns. Include a lot of hell-raising and going broke... until wives arrived and things pretended to get civil. Unlike the gold and silver glory days in the west, however, Michigan's tales didn't make it into the national folklore. No "copper" movie has ever been made, yet the profits were richer.

In haunted beautiful Keweenaw the history of copper mining is woven through in ghost towns, great fishing, coastal-Maine scenery, ethnic pot-potpourri, and laid back fun. The gray beach noticeable as US 41 curves northward along Portage Lake is stamp sand from old foundry dumpings. In Houghton the road zips past Northern Michigan Technological University, founded as a college for mine trainees. The Seaman Mineralogical Museum in the school's Electrical Resources Center is a jewel mounted with 30,000 minerals and precious stones. NMTU, home to the Keweenaw Symphony, puts on a major Ice-Sculpture Contest and Carnival in January. On Houghton's waterfront the Ranger III waits for summer trips to Isle Royale.

Copper history is there when you cross the big hydraulic lift bridge over the Portage Ship Canal (a.k.a. the Keweenaw Waterway), a way for earlier ore vessels to avoid lethal rocks and storms around the Upper Peninsula's upper peninsula.

In Hancock there are street signs in Finnish, one of the major ethnic groups lured by copper. Suomi College is the only U.S. school to offer Finnish as a major; their converted-church Cultural Center reflects Finnish gifts for design. US 41 winds steeply uphill to a great overlook of the scene, and then passes the tall angular housing of

Quincy Shaft No. 2. This historic hillcrest relic marks a mine shaft deeper than six stacked Sears Towers; 1.5 miles down. A giant steam hoist built to haul men and ore such distances stands next door, open for inspection. (No, you don't go down).

Visit the restored opera house in Calumet, where Jenny Lind and Caruso sang, and Sarah Bernhardt emoted grandly. Calumet, now under 1000 population, came within an ace of being named state capitol in its 47,000-citizen glory days. Along with Laurium and the Quincy Shaft, Calumet is part of a new National Historic Park. Stroll through town and through the Coppertown Museum. In Laurium, home of the "Gipper" of Notre Dame football fame, a grand old mine-owner's mansion, Laurium Manor, lives again as a fantastic B & B.

US 41 curls to an end just past Copper Harbor and Fort Wilkins State Park. The Fort was built to guard miners from Indians, who were no trouble at all, but miners often needed protection from each other. Self-guided tours with costumed personnel.

In the village a nice choice of motels, eateries, shops, et al., plus transport on the Isle Royale Queen III to the National Park. Ask about trips to the harbor lighthouse, now a small museum. A drive to the top of Brockway Mountain (pause at first turnout for a view of Copper Harbor), ends 600 feet above Lake Superior. The whole peninsular topography spreads before you: forests, lakes, the Eagle River harbor, and on a clear day a shimmering hint of Isle Royale.

Keweenaw Mountain Lodge on US 41 was built by miners out of local logs and stone during the big 30's depression. Operated by the county: wonderful, dining room and lounge, nine-hole golf, single and duplex cabins with fireplaces.

Explore the coastal villages of Eagle Harbor, Eagle River, the singing sands and underwater preserve of Bete Grise, the remains of Central or Mandan. The Delaware Mine has an excellent, informative tour. US 41. Rustic outdoor furniture available in Mohawk, thimbleberry jam at a bakery shop run by monks on M 26, free blueberries in season atop Blueberry Hill near Eagle Harbor. Ask where the trail is. Old mine dumps sometimes yield pieces of copper (NEVER enter an old shaft). In this surprising territory, the top producer of basketball and dance floors in the world operates in Dollar Bay, and unofficial top ice cream parlor is Lindell's Chocolate Shop in Lake Linden. The Houghton County Historical Museum on M-26 here has its own treasures for history buffs to mine.

Woods and waterfalls, downhill skiing... Michigan's copper glimmers with gold.

BETWEEN THE BLUFFS IN MINNESOTA
by Carol Spicer
from Country Living, Travel Midwest, 1995

Spicer, a member since 1965, wrote (under the name of Barbara Brooks) a series of Detroit Free Press articles: Happily Ever After, We Are Three, and War Wife. Her articles appear in Parents, House Beautiful, Better Homes And Gardens, Saturday Evening Post, Vogue, Washington Post, Los Angles Times, Boston Globe, and more.

Look at a map of Minnesota and you will see in its southeastern comer a fat and undulating blue ribbon hemming the state's border with Wisconsin. The wavy blue line represents one of the most beautiful stretches of the Mississippi River, whose bluffs rise on either side and where, in certain areas in the spring, the pink and white blossoms of the valley's apple orchards transform the slopes and perfume the air.

From the river town of Red Wing, through Wabasha and Winona to the river town of La Crescent, Highway 61 winds through this wide valley of the northern Mississippi for 68 miles via rural lands and Victorian villages.

In Red Wing, grain elevators, reminders of the days when Red Wing was considered the Wheat Capital of the World, and a limestone bluff that looks like a long gray barn loom against the sky. The prosperous wheat days of the 1870s have left their mark on this town in other ways, too, as in the opulent Shelden Theatre, built with money bequeathed by Theodore Shelden, a wealthy grain merchant. With its plush, royal-red seats and its murals of gaudy goddesses and cherubs, the newly restored and redecorated landmark is a gem of late 19th-century architecture.

The prosperity brought to Red Wing by the wheat trade is reflected, too, in the imposing Italianate homes constructed during those years and in the St. James Hotel, built on the Mississippi for the convenience of riverboat passengers. One of the hotel's entrances that faces the river tells the tale of the days when guests came by way of the river. Walk through this door and you are in the hotel's original lobby, where travel-weary guests once checked in with bulging portmanteaus. Although the structure is grander now, its original marble columns, mosaic floor, and solid walnut check-in desk still greet travelers, and the gilt-framed portraits of the businessmen who, in 1870, pooled $60,000 to build the town's new hostelry still climb the main stairway wall.

The hotel's 60 guest rooms, all named after riverboats, today have private bathrooms and are much more elegant in a "modern-antique" way. Room #312, for instance, named "Columbia," boasts a 14-

foot-high ceiling, a handmade quilt on its four-poster, beneath which there is a trundle bed, lovely yellow wallpaper, wooden interior shutters, and a chaise longue. Each guest room is decorated differently.

Local attractions include the Red Wing Stoneware Co., a longtime pottery tradition in the town, where visitors can observe the pottery-production process through windows without disturbing the artisans. The company is located four miles west of downtown Red Wing on Highway 61.

The Mt. Frontenac Ski Area and Golf Course, located nine miles south of Red Wing on Highway 61, has the highest vertical drop to the river in southeastern Minnesota. The 18-hole golf course at the top of the bluff offers panoramic views of the Mississippi.

Meander 20 miles downriver to the old town of Wabasha and you'll find more grain elevators and another oldtime hotel, the Anderson House, which bills itself as Minnesota's oldest operating country inn. Built in 1856, the inn is best known for one eccentric, yet endearing, feature: its feline bed warmers. If you make arrangements when booking, you can claim temporary custody of one of the hotel's 15 cats during your stay.

Your furry friend will be hand delivered (along with litter box and food)to your door.

The Anderson House deserves recognition for its many other homey touches as well. A hot brick wrapped in a quilted envelope will warm your cold feet, if you don't cotton to cats; an always-filled cookie jar is in the lobby; flowers fresh from the hotel's gardens grace every room in summertime; a May basket awaits on guest room doorknobs on April 30; and your shoes will be meticulously shined and returned to you every morning, just outside your bedroom door. In the hotel kitchen, you're even allowed to cook fish you've caught in nearby streams. And the river side of the hotel affords expansive and stunning views of the Mississippi.

Wabasha is a scheduled stop for both the *Delta Queen and Mississippi Queen* riverboats. If you're there on a day they dock, join the crowd and watch the paddle wheelers pull in and the passengers disembark. To find out when they churn into view in 1995, phone (800) 543-1949.

Wabasha is also a favorite stop for the bald eagles that use the Mississippi as their North-South highway. At sundown, watch from the river's viewing platform as the great birds wing down into the trees; they are a sight to remember.

Out of town a way, on the now-familiar Highway 61, you'll come to the hamlet of Kellogg and its toy factory, L.A.R.K., where such life-size creatures as a giraffe and a rhinoceros are being hand carved for a carousel. Here, you can watch the making of wooden toys.

In Winona, located 23 miles downriver from Wabasha as the river bends, artisans' workshops have earned this town the title Stained-Glass Capital of the U.S.A. Sightseers can tour the largest of these operations, the Conway Universal Studios, and watch the artists at work. It's an absorbing, fine-tuned process that includes sketching the design, choosing colors, cutting glass into the design's intricate shapes, staining and firing each color separately, leading, and finally mudding to make it waterproof and airtight. Everything is accomplished — with the exception of firing, which is done in electric kilns — exactly as it was done 200 years ago. Informative tours are given between 9 A.M. and 2 P.M.

The heart of Winona, however, is always the river. The grand paddle wheelers put in here, as they do in Wabasha, but here, for less than $10, the casual traveler can board Winona's own *Jollie Ollie* and enjoy a two-hour paddleboat cruise on the Mississippi between the steep bluffs. A Sunday-brunch cruise is about $18; a three-hour weekend-dinner cruise featuring prime rib, champagne, and all the fixings is $5 more.

Chances are Samuel Clemens, a.k.a. Mark Twain, who wrote about his travels in these parts in *Life on the Mississippi,* would enjoy the Julius C. Wilkie Museum. It's a replica of a real operating steamboat replete with smokestacks, paddle wheel, and steam engine. Visitors entering from its berth at Levee Park are greeted by a magnificent staircase, gleaming brass chandeliers, and a stained-glass window depicting the original Julius C. Wilkie under full steam. Beyond the staircase is a treasury of river lore, including a rare collection of letters and documents written by steamboat designer Robert Fulton.

On the second deck is the Grand Salon, which is grand, indeed, with rich red-brocade chairs and drapes to match, crystal-prismed chandeliers, and stained-glass doorways. Another staircase leads to the top deck and the pilothouse. On the pilothouse roof is a huge, brass whistle that once alerted nearby boats and town that the steamboat was a-comin'.

Finally we reach La Crescent, where good soil and the sheltered location made by the bluffs combine to create conditions conducive for growing apples. In the spring, the town's thousand acres of apple trees are foamy visions of pink and white. The landscape is enchanting and reason enough to make a drive between the bluffs.

A SUMMER MOMENT WITH HEMINGWAY'S MOTHER

by Lucille S. DeView
from Up North, Indian Village Press, 1977

A member since 1981 DeView says "This essay inspired my play, 'A Summer With Hemingway's Twin' which received the 1997 National Play Award from the National Repertory Theatre Foundation."

The summer of 1939, at Walloon Lake in search of Ernest Hemingway (who never came), was my last summer of sad-sweet girlhood days filled with soul-searching and romantic longings.

I was a snobbish intellectual then, trying to live a bohemian student life at Wayne State University in Detroit, which in those days meant drinking tea, reading e. e. cummings, and staying up all night to argue about pacifism.

Money was scarce and so were summer jobs. The only one I could find was as a mother's helper at a cottage, a job I didn't want until I learned the cottage owner was Marcelline Hemingway Sanford, one of Ernest Hemingway's sisters.

I had a tremendous crush on Hemingway. I read "A Farewell to Arms" until my copy was threadbare. And the Nick Adams stories had their roots, I knew, in the very northern Michigan countryside where Mrs. Sanford had her cottage.

Maybe (just maybe) the great one himself (Ernest) might come to visit his sister and I could meet him and — .

My daydreams knew no bounds. We sang in the car going north. The cottage was modest and inviting, furnished with a hodgepodge of brightly painted, old furniture so it didn't hurt to sit around in wet bathing suits.

Always, whether we were swimming or I was serving dinner, I had my ears open for tales of the Hemingway family or of Ernest himself.

But the tales didn't tell me as much as the woods and the water.

At night, in my room, I could hear the sweep, sweep, sweep of waves on the shore. The rising, falling rustle of leaves stirred by the wind sounded like the faint shivers of distant tambourines.

He (Hemingway) must have heard the same sounds, I thought. Did they give him the tempo for his writing? This stand of birch, that point of land, in describing them did he learn how to make words pointed or how to let them float free?

I wanted to see and touch and hear all of what had fed and nourished this writer I so adored. I wanted to explore the very makings of his mind.

And though I quickly learned from the family that he never (ever) returned to the northern Michigan haunts of his early years, I continued to dream that he just might and that I just might meet him if he did.

And if so, I would show him the scribbles of poems and stories that were piling up secretly in my top dresser drawer and I would ask him: Why is this wrong? Why does this fail? Why here, in this phrase, do I think I succeeded?

It was an audacious daydream but then, I was in Hemingway territory which was pretty heady stuff and I was vulnerable.

On one of our canoe outings, the family pointed out a small, white frame cottage Ernest owned on another part of the lake. From then on, whenever I had an afternoon off, I would take the canoe and venture out of the sheltered waters of our bay and paddle to the shore in front of that white frame cottage.

No lesser goal could have tempted me to handle a canoe alone on the choppy, wind-swept, open lake, but my struggles were always rewarded when at last I reached HIS beach and sat on HIS stretch of sand and looked for signs of life in HIS cottage.

Toward the end of summer, Hemingway's mother (Grace Hall Hemingway) came to visit. Although she was getting on in years, it was part of her pride that she drove her own car everywhere. She had driven to Walloon Lake alone from Mexico.

When she pulled into the yard, it was like royalty arriving. Indeed, she was queenly. A big, large-boned woman, she wore full-length, flowered chiffon gowns which had long gone out of fashion but seemed perfectly suited to her artistic interests.

Mrs. Hemingway had been an opera singer in her younger years. She had composed many songs in her lifetime and could still, on occasion, be prevailed upon to sing in small private gatherings.

She had recently learned to paint in oils and had several showings in the West.

She spoke eloquently, often in metaphysical terms. She was deeply religious. She didn't smoke or drink. She used no makeup. She radiated such zest and enthusiasm that it was as if some exotic bird of paradise had flown into the midst of a flock of sparrows.

One day she asked me to drive with her to the family cottage where she and Dr. Clarence Edmonds Hemingway had first come from the Chicago suburbs to northern Michigan and where Ernest had spent so many summers with the family in his growing-up years.

She wanted me to come along to give the cottage a sweeping and she wanted to check over the property. I was excited.

We drove off in her big, white automobile and she told me how she had learned to drive by necessity. Once, one of her married children coming north had had a car accident. Mrs. Hemingway was alone at the cottage with one of the younger children when she received word of the tragedy.

Although she had never driven alone, she felt compelled to get into the driver's seat of the car and, putting the younger child at the window to tell her if she went off the road, she went in pursuit of her injured family. She had, she said, driven ever since.
She didn't, however, always remember to shift gears. Nor did she always make her turns in time. It was a wild ride and when the road ended she took off across the fields in the car and we bounced and bumped and careened to the foot of a small hill where the family cottage stood.

Mrs. Hemingway turned off the motor and sat there for a long time. Her enthusiasm was suddenly gone. It was as if, for a moment, she could not go on. That she could not get out of the car. That she could not go up the hill. That she could not unlock the cottage door (unlock the past).

I felt suddenly tender toward her, sitting there, this large lump of a woman whose husband, I knew, had committed suicide, and whose famous son had written books she felt she could not entirely approve.

I saw tears sliding down her wide cheeks.

"This was paradise," she said.

And later: "We were all so happy here."

I followed her to the cottage door. She unlocked it and went inside. It was empty of furniture. Our footsteps and voices echoed.

I felt I was in a shrine — a shabby shrine, all dusty, not restored as public shrines are restored, no velvet ropes to keep me out of rooms — and I thought of how Hemingway had always written of this place with tension, nerves tight, everything always ready to snap.

Conflict and tragedy were always on his shores.
And yet his mother had called it paradise. And said they were happy here. Could both be true? Could he have felt the conflict and the tragedy and still have been happy here?

I would have to reread him. I would have to rethink him. The artist. The person. How were they mixed?

Mrs. Hemingway asked me if I would please leave her alone for a while. I walked down the hill (on holy ground). There were some boys in a nearby apple orchard. They were picking hard green apples and throwing them at crows which perched on the posts of a sagging wire fence.

I tried to picture Hemingway as a boy, throwing hard green apples in that same place. I tried to picture him on a hot summer day walking down to the shore with his fishing gear, feeling the sun hot at his back, thinking ahead to where the bass would be feeding in a lily pond or a pike would take a certain bait presented in a certain way.

At the shore, I shoved aside the soft birch branches to get to the water and sand and imagined Hemingway, the boy, shoving aside the same branches.

And splashing in the shallow water to climb into his boat and shoving off but carrying in his head the day, the sky, the sun, the boat — and the tensions, the people, and what they made of the day and each other.

And putting it all into his stories.

I went back to the cottage and swept it, and Mrs. Hemingway locked the door and we drove away.

Hemingway, himself, of course, never came.

When I returned to college for the fall semester, I had thought to brag to my intellectual friends that I had spent the summer in the near-company of one of our literary heroes. But when they asked me what I had done — I merely said I worked for some people at a cottage at Walloon Lake.

I kept what really happened to me that summer private for a long time. Because if I told my friends I had gone in search of a great writer, they would have seen me as the silly goose of a girl I was.

But they could not have seen that in some strange way, I had found him.

TORO! TORO! TORO!

By Elaine Watson

from the Detroit Free Press Magazine, 1987

Watson, a DWW member since 1969, has published two historical novels, Anna's Rocking Chair and To Dwell In The Land, as well as verse, and articles on education, learning disabilities, travel, historical events, and personalities. She has instilled correct grammar in many students' heads at Ford Community College.

"They could just as well be going to a Tigers game," I thought, watching a small girl with a halo of shining hair disappear among a clutch of eager customers who pushed their way through ticket lines.

"One thing I won't do in Spain," I'd told friends at home, "is see a bullfight." But here I was, on my first Sunday afternoon in Madrid, mingling with crowds on their way into the Plaza de Las Ventas.

Balloons floated above hawkers selling ice cream and souvenirs, and bright posters were spread out on the pavement in the 4 p.m. sunshine. My desire to get the "feel" of Spain was paying off. Inside the stadium I saw the girl again, running down a corridor ahead of me. "Surely a bullfight can't be all that brutal if Spanish parents bring such an angel-faced-child here," I told myself.

After I found my seat, a narrow granite ledge, I saw families with small children everywhere — and, just in front of me sat — and bounced — my little *afectionada,* on a brown pillow. Directly behind me was the band.

While the band played a traditional tune, three matadors in bright embroidered silks and their entourage of picadors, banderillos, peons, and monosabics (who drag the bulls' bodies away) circled the ring, accepting the cheers of the crowd. Then, after they had all marched off, a trumpet announced the first bull, and he rushed into the arena. There would be five more.

I tried to make myself comfortable on my granite ledge. It was the last time I would be conscious of that hard seat for the rest of the afternoon.

Suddenly the picadors came dashing out on their horses — horses with blindfolded eyes and padded bodies. But when one of the picadors jabbed him, the great black bull jabbed back, beneath the horse's padding. While the bull's horns drove deeper into the horse's belly, where he lay struggling on the red earth, I heard my own voice yelling, "Shoot the poor horse!"

But then my little neighbor shrieked, *"Toro! Toro! Toro!* " The rest of the crowd cheered the fallen horse, but *she* had cheers only for the bull.

Finally, the bull's head was brought low by the banderillos, small harpoons thrust into his neck by the banderillos, and the matador accomplished a clumsy kill.

As the afternoon went on, chanting and response from the people on their granite seats rose and fell in a rhythm that convinced me that this bullfight was much more like a religious service than a baseball game at home.

At last came bull No. 6, a confused, slow-moving thing that appeared to be easy fodder for the arena. But suddenly the beast came to life, and in horror I watched the bull repeat the earlier scene ; except this time the matador was pierced by the bull's horns. He tossed the matador all around and finally dropped the limp body into the dust as other men swirling capes drew his attention.

I was sick.

My little neighbor's hands were folded tightly together, and her eyes shone. *"Toro,"* she whispered. *"Toro. "*

THE STATION
by Lyn Coffin
from Crystals of the Unforseen, PlainView Press, 1998

You know where you're headed after you arrive-
an empty station where a wind like
the desert sighing drifts in one door and
out the other, and the remains of windows
are glass daggers stuck like teeth in wooden gums...
My fingers fumble their way along cracks in
what were walls...   The roof lifted off — a big hawk —

and bricks, as if dazzled by sudden sunlight,
tumbled onto the bed like staggered children.
What lovers were left left long ago, in
the days counted — glass beads hung around necks
so slender no words came close, so hands made do,
covering that small warm throb with laced fingers,
days when the interlocked rings left on tables
by two wine glasses could be seen as a sign...
I cannot remember what I thought death was —
small birds' erratic wheelings darkening
the sky at dusk? Horses with slick sides
galloping riderless toward the ocean?
No. Someone shouts numbers penciled on old
phone books — A stubbled man in a tom jacket
clamps a fiddle under his chin, and pulls
a thin bow across four thin strings — whereupon
ghosts push back their chairs and square off for a dance,
a naked light bulb does an electric
dosey-do, hanging down from a ceiling where
a thousand holes drilled in rows more regular
than corn aren't enough to sponge up the silence
which swells like dark water under the music's
shivering glissandos. In the yard, ghosts in
kneepants swing on tires that dangle from the trees
in nooses of knotted clothesline, the black
receivers of abandoned conversations...
and all around the pinprick house, the ceaseless
prairie darkens — an untroubled ocean
of canvas grass stretches in all directions,
farther than the human eye can see,
a sea of parted grass through which they come as one-
pale horse, pale rider — at an easy lope...
Nothing to stop them and nowhere to turn.

LAST OF THE BIG BREAKFAST EATERS

By Jeanne Duran
Detroit Free Press, 1962

Duran, a DWW member since 1952, wrote magazine fiction, was a journalist for the Detroit Free Press, wrote a daily column, had a daily program on WJR Radio. She won two Catherine O'Brien national awards and the Family Circle Magazine Community Service Award. She still teaches, critiques manuscripts, and advises a writers group.

Cleveland Amory, social chronicler par excellence and last of the Big Breakfast Eaters, was in town Friday, to address the Dearborn Town Hall.

With reluctant gusto (reluctant because while he believes women may be dotted inconspicuously about a hotel dining room at breakfast they should never be at the same table with men!) — he shared his seven-spoon breakfast with me.

His lament on the lost art of breakfasting was preceded by a request that the temperature of the Sheraton Cadillac's Town Room be lowered by 10 degrees.

"Room temperature is as important as food temperature," he explained.

Amory separated a waitress from a small covey with a silk-sheathed blade. "Could you take our order — if it wouldn't be too much trouble?"

The pretty little pink-clad waitress went from a smile through confusion, amazement, and finally grim resignation, as she filled three pages of her book with his detailed order for probably the largest breakfast ever served in the Town Room.

Amory commented steadily on the right atmosphere and accessories, as well as the ideal foods for breakfast, as we ate and drank our way through orange juice and half a grapefruit (both, you understand); a large bowl of oatmeal laced with cream and sugar; two boiled eggs (he requested six-minute so they would come out four-minute — "if you order four-minute, they come out two and a half"); four pieces of toast, marmalade, three strips of bacon, four medium-sized pancakes, coffee, and more coffee.

The newspaper is important while breakfasting, Amory explained. Not the news — this you should have read earlier. But he likes a look at the stock market — it is cheering to see that a stock you didn't buy has dropped a bit, or one you bought against "expert" advice has risen.

It also adds a bright note to check obituaries and find someone much younger than yourself listed there, especially if the man has been a romantic rival, perhaps, or the kind who never tired on the tennis court, and stayed lean and hard through counting calories.

"Diet is a lot of nonsense," Amory declared. "A good breakfast alone should contain 2,000 calories — it's the only way you could possibly face some of those horrible reducing diets the doctors are always putting you on."

In an article in the December *Esquire*, Amory goes into reverse-rapture over the sorry state of breakfast, all across the country. He complains bitterly of "unintegrated canned orange juice, globby, sad-eyed greasily fried eggs, hairy bristle-brush buttered toast."

He admits, however, that coffee — while the American woman's mainstay and sometimes only interest in the morning, is the one item which is consistently better commercially than when made at home.

"But never in a paper cup," he warned.

On the Three M's in Society — Money, Manners, Morals, he said, "The first generation is usually all right, rough and ready but nice. Be careful about the second generation. They've been given everything the first one didn't have, so they're likely to be impossible. But the third generation gets ashamed of the second, so they get back to being nice people again."

Speaking about appearances, he feels a man can invite a woman, no matter who, to a luncheon, if it is large enough; dinner gets a little conspicuous; breakfast never! Tea is the one occasion which can be shared without any worry about lifted eyebrows.

We had used only six spoons.

He apologized. He explained that a really civilized breakfast called for a taste of honey, along with the marmalade.

I wouldn't know. I usually just have coffee in the morning.

TRIPLE TRAIL TREATS
by Mary Kincaid
Midwest Trails and Streams, premier issue, 1996

Kincaid, a DWW member since 1977, is a freelance writer living in Ann Arbor, Michigan. Her articles appear widely in magazines and major dailies. Visiting museums, attending concerts, walking, cross country skiing, and eating are her chief interests.

"I walk four miles a day here," says a svelte blue-eyed Ann Arbor widow. "I've done it for years. I like the asphalt paths on this side of the water better than the park's other paths," she adds, "I make better time on the pavement."

Other Ann Arborites and first-time visitors to Gallup Park along the Huron River soon find a favorite among the variety of trails, each with color-keyed marker posts at 1/4 mile intervals. The park stretches some two miles along each side of the Huron River. Willow trees and flowering shrubs, quacking ducks and honking geese provide foreground interest while gliding canoes and paddle boats enhance sight and sound experience. Here and there a Frisbee floats through the air near the play structures at each end of the park.

An aroma of roasting meat wafting from one of the outdoor grills whetted my appetite yesterday so I entered the snack house for a hot dog and coffee. Only one other person was there, a student doing homework at one of the four tables, so I quizzed the counterman, Jason Solomon.

"What usually keeps you busy here?" I asked.

"Lots of people order pizza and pop, and people that come to fish buy leafworms, crawlers, and waxworms from me," he answered.

"What about bikes? Do you rent many?"

"Definitely not many bikes," Jason said. "Canoes and especially paddle boats are what people want."

Not everyone needs equipment though. Small ones love to cross the four Japanese-style wooden footbridges arching from island to island. Tossing twigs into the water, then running to the other side to watch them float out from beneath the bridge is high drama for them.

At the opposite end of the park I saw a small boy grab his father's hand to show him a heron he spied from the new overlook built to view the five-acre wet prairie community to the north of that trail. The plant life is what early pioneers found in the region.

Although most people come here to follow trails, fish, or boat, the park's utterly flat surface attracts novice cross country skiers, too. Blue shadows falling across the snow and stretches of ice on the river provide a scenic treat as beguiling as the easy skiing surface.

The western edge of Gallup Park touches the border of the famous Nichols Arboretum of the University of Michigan. This 123-acre area is well known to most students.

Romances bloom there season after season, as well as flowers and shrubs. "Kick a bush in the Arb and it will kick you back," goes the local cliché.

Our enjoyment of the Arb didn't stop with student days, though. We lived close enough to bring our toddlers there dozens of times, escaping our cramped apartment to enjoy the Arb's hills and seductive meadows. What a thrill the children found in running down the grassy slopes to be caught in our outstretched arms! Noticing their first blue jays and crocus blooms excited them as much as more exotic wildlife would as they grew.

Self-guided tour maps can lead hikers through the 123 acres of steep ravines, rolling hills, and prairie to notice some of the 500 trees. These include 64 species, labeled with scientific and common names, as are the plants.

My most vivid memory is of the pine grove by the Arb's Washington Street entrance. On one sunny May morning I took our two pre-schoolers to that grove with their little wagon to collect pine cones. Suddenly, I clutched a tree trunk as labor began. We made it home, wagon, tykes, and pine cones, and within the hour their sister was born.

In early June those in the know flock to the peony gardens just beyond that pine grove. Seven hundred peonies grow there, numbered and identified in an invaluable $5 guide available from the University of Michigan School of Natural Resources, 3012D Dana Building, Ann Arbor, MI. 48109. With it, you can learn the names of the vivid reds and dozens of shades of pinks and whites as you inhale their perfume. Many of the older plants bear historical names: Victory Chateau Thierry, Pasteur, Mrs. F.D. Roosevelt, for example.

Matthei Botanical Gardens, slightly over a mile north of Gallup Park, boasts seven miles of trails along Fleming Creek, bringing further bird-watching and plant finding opportunities. Wildlife, including the occasional Massassauga Rattlesnake, can add thrills to wildflower hunting (not picking).

You're not out of luck to be caught in a rainstorm here. The Conservatory offers shelter and for a $2 admission, you may go beyond the lobby and gift shop to enter the greenhouse with its 2,000 different plants. The tropical area, with its orchid display and chocolate tree, fascinates most visitors.

If you require further stimulation while you are in town with family, try the Hands-On Museum, always a hit with children, the Natural Science Museum, University of Michigan Museum of Art, or the Kelsey Museum of Archeology.

Rain or shine, indoors or out, find your own best trail to follow in Ann Arbor.

ON CORCOVADO MOUNTAIN

by Naomi Long Madgett

Octavia and other Poems, 1988

High above the sands
of Rio, cloud and veil
the impassive face

of the Redeemer.
Momentarily
pale sunlight steals through

seeking refuge in
the folds of the stiffly
fluted skirt. Below

in the deeper shadows,
crevices of precarious hills

crouch faceless squalid
children whom those out
stretched arms will never
hold, never redeem.

WHY SNOWBIRDS FLY

by Priscilla Jackson
Slab City Messenger, Chittenden, Vermont, January, 1997

Jackson, a member since 1953, has written numerous articles. She was a prime mover in organizing various events such as the first DWW/Oakland University Writers Conference in 1961.

Starting September 1st, our local friends' greeting is, "When do you leave?"

Not for a couple of months — or more."

"Oh, good, not for a month, " they answer, but I feel the faint exclusion. We are only transients now. They suffer together through the snow and mud and pull each other out of ditches, but we steal away. They often end the conversation, "I hope we have a warm fall like last year." Fervently, I agree relieved to share that "we." Though part-timers, we are not ignored.

However, serious decision-making awaits: When will we leave? Nothing really draws us away, although everyone assumes it's the climate there. Actually I am repelled by the dreary prospect of closing up, of draining pipes, eating perishables, moving the valuables. I'm comfortable here — we've spent years arranging it.

And I have too much to do to pull up stakes, see local friends who've been busy with summer excursions and visiting family. The broken door's not fixed; dahlia bulbs aren't dug up. Why hurry away? A silk undershirt under wool makes bearable our semi-insulated remodeled barn; the wood stove and electric heaters take off the autumnal chill. Outdoors, a hooded jacket and boots protect me from the sharpening, north wind which clears the skies of clouds and the mountains of haze. It is so beautiful here.

"We'll stay until the fall colors fade, certainly," I answer my friends. I watch the sunset make the pink mountains across the steep valley. "Or maybe until snow flies."

One day, I hear noisy honking, and wonder who has been married. Why hadn't I heard about it? Then I remember to look up. in autumn's bright blue sky I find the V-shaped line — Canada geese — flying south. My neighbor phones. "Look east. The geese. And when are you leaving!"

"Oh, not for a while," I protest.

But is that high-flying V a sign? The warblers left; the Monarch butterflies took off for Mexico. Also the hummingbirds, I've been told. Migrating may be natural but not for nest-builders like me.

It's not natural to tear up your roots semi-annually, to organize two places. It's disconcerting to close off projects, to pack and unpack. Life should flow with time, like a river. The phone rings. "I want to see you before you leave," says a friend. "When are you going?"

"Not yet," I say. " I do apologize for running off and leaving you the ice and snow and freezing rain and mud."

"That's OK." she says. "I haven't been to Florida, but I don't have the yen to leave."

I know what she means. To the old colonial states of the East-Coast, Florida and California aren't serious. They're full of silly people gamboling on beaches, wearing loud clothes and sun glasses. But the Sun states have other facets. Elderly Ida nodded when I told her that. Her father had scorned Florida, too, she said. His children urged him to go, though in those days few did. His rheumatism, coughing, and temper were spoiling everyone's house-bound winter.

"What self-respecting person would doll up like that?" he'd growl. What worker would throw time away? But, for his 70th birthday, his children bought him a plane ticket. Grumpily he flew off, too thrifty to waste it. Three months later, on his return, townspeople crowded up: "How was Florida?"

"Should'a gone 50 years ago," he growled.

One night comes the killing frost. I wake to see my flowers stiff and shocked. A knife-edge wind cuts around each charming casement window. I run down the freezing hall between the heated bedroom and heated bathroom. My husband splits wood, lugs more armfuls in. Expensive electric heaters run day and night. Our eyes meet and we agree. "Let's leave."

Why do snowbirds fly south? Not for the lure of sunny climes, but to run away. The blustery face of this North-Temperate Zone is harder to face than any admission of shame. Plainly put, Old Man Winter drives us softies out. Us and the Canada geese.

THE TRIP THAT ALMOST STARTED ON TIME
by Marilyn Lyman
Ford Times, September, 1985

Lyman joined DWW in 1958. She has published two novels (Scholastic) which became course textbooks, and articles that appeared in the Observer & Eccentric Newspapers. Her articles also appeared in the Ford Times, the Toledo Blade, and the Dearborn Press.

I'd pay cash money not to attend a certain play put on annually at our house. It's titled "Leaving for Our Trip." The destination is changed but action and dialogue stay the same — a curdled sitcom.

Early on launch morning George packs softside luggage into narrowside car. There is the house lock-up and the no-breakfast bad temper. I duck in and out of the front seat stashing the must-haves until my hair looks like I rented it. George says, " The front seat is a junkyard."

I tell him, "Neat. You're too neat to live. Real life is not neat."

The last worst part comes when we are a block from home. He asks me, "Are you SURE you unplugged the appliances?"

"Absolutely," I say. And I was, too — until he said that. Now I wonder. Have I left the house to either burn all the way down or blow all the way up?

"Pretty sure anyhow," I finally say.

"Didn't you check it?"

"I thought you did."

"Dammit! Should we go back?" he hollers.

"Well."

This year I made a list on June 1st. " We'll be so organized by the 15th that we can get up and leave in one hour," I told him. "For once we'll start out in a good humor. Okay?"

"It sounds good anyway. " He looked unimpressed.

The next week all action aimed at smooth departure for San Diego to visit two cousins. The house was clean; the paper and mail stopped; I even hurried out for four new sets of underwear for George. Something about wearing spiffy new underwear makes a man feel confident, more cheerful. I could even picture George laughing as we left home.

But on the 15th, the bedroom clock read only 4 A.M. when George sat up alert, listening.

"Don't get up," I whispered. "Too early."

"Something's on the roof," he muttered. A flurry of hefty footsteps sounded above us.

"So, it's some cat."

"And he wears snowboots? No. It's raccoons. Bill Morgan was three months getting them out of his attic. The house got fleas."

"You worry too much. Get some sleep," I murmured.

"I'd better check," he sighed, pulling on his jeans. He took up his red lantern.

"Crazy," I said, snuggled down again.

But who could sleep with that brouhaha out on the front lawn? From the window, I watched George standing on the dewy grass, looking toward the roof. He stopped making loud hand claps and yelling, "Shoo! Go on!" Now he aimed his lantern upward, making a series of threatening hisses (cat) and threatening barks (dog).

I called out past the screen, "I've heard of dumb animals, but he'd be an idiot to think you're a cat AND a dog."

"Okay! Okay!" he answered. " Do you want raccoons coming from the fireplace flue, tearing up the furniture ?"

Shoving my slippers on, my blue nylon gown flapping, I ran out to the front yard.

"Go away!" I called toward the large lump sitting in the beam of George's lantern. The animal moved around slowly as though the light kept nudging him.

Then the raccoon, looking bored and superior, turned his back and sat down.

"Hell." George tossed me the lantern and sprinted toward the garage. He returned with our tallest ladder and a broom.

"Listen, they bite," I warned. " Don't climb up there."

"You want to raise raccoons in the house ? Now keep that light on him ALL the time. See if he runs away."

I did recall the police loaning the Morgans two animal traps; the destruction and noise in their attic; the danger of chewed electrical wires Would this intruder invade our house and keep us home ? I was getting mad too.

George rested the ladder against the house, climbing up and along the roof in his rubber-soled slippers. He advanced on the raccoon, swinging the broom and commanding, "Get out ! Go on!"

And he did. The raccoon waddled over where George couldn't walk. Then he climbed down into the fireplace chimney.

"Hey! He went inside!" I yelled.

George rushed back down the ladder, tossing me the broom before running into the house. " Don't move! See if he comes back out."

Our house lit up. I remembered it was almost time for the early paperboy and the milkman to come by and I'm standing around the yard in four ounces of nylon, holding a broom and a lantern.

I watched the chimney. Pale smoke rose against the dawn sky. Next rose the raccoon. Working his fat sides out of the flue, he disappeared smoothly over the roof peak.

Just then an old sports car came around our corner. Its lights swept past as I yelled out " He's gone !" I yelled again loud enough for George to hear, "He's gone !"

"Lady, you ain't gonna get the guy back with no broom," a man's beery voice called from the car.

Shivering, I went back inside while George doused the burning newspapers in the fireplace. He tied a rope from the flue damper to the iron log basket to anchor it tight. We checked the furnace flue pipe, too. We stood in the basement wide awake and smeared with soot. Only five o'clock.

"I guess we won't get back to sleep," I sighed.

"Right. Let's shower and get out of here."

Sounds of sudsy water running, slamming dresser drawers, zipping suitcases. I moved toward the sunroom, but heard George call out," I want to thank you for this underwear."

It was his "come here" voice. I was sorry I went back, though. He was a vision in white. The stuff hung on him like a formal.

"Who WERE you shopping for ? " he scowled into the long mirror, muttering, "Am I getting shorter?"

Rats. So much for fast shopping. No man could laugh in THIS underwear. More slamming of dresser drawers. The sun was coming up and the car truck was ready, finally. An old-time chime alarm clock he had saved for his cousin as a surprise went in last.

Puffing a little and starved by now, we drove down our street. I thought to myself, "Look at this. We're out an hour ahead of schedule and everything's fine. Planning counts."

So George says to me, "Are you SURE you tightened that loose shower head? It could leak a river in two weeks."

"I thought YOU checked it."

"Maybe I did. Are you saying we have to go back?"

"Before you start that stuff, tell me how come you started a trip in your bedroom slippers ?"

"Damn!"

ONE THING OR ANOTHER
by Ruth Cain
The Detroit News, 1977

Cain, a DWW member since 1994, was a Sunday Magazine Special Writer for the Detroit News. She is active in community affairs in the Metro Book & Authors and Cranbrook Writers Guild.

Most of life's little ironies are bitter, a few even tragic. The ones that are humorous are so rare we ought to appreciate them all the more.

Take my mother's efforts, which extended over my entire childhood, to fatten me up.

As a child I was — I sob when I think about it — skinny. And that's not surprising since I was completely disinterested in food. It was no reflection on my mother's cooking ability, which was quite good. Maybe it was a personality thing. In any event I found eating had a low priority on my list of interesting things to do.

My mother was convinced that my slight frame had to mean I also had a low resistance to disease. To avoid my early demise she resorted to all sorts of things — some quite bizarre —to make me want to clean my plate and put some meat on my bones.

You should know that my mother had a truly democratic approach to the practice of medicine. She would accept medical advice from a woman she had just met at the grocery store as enthusiastically as she accepted it from the family physician. I think she realized that the gratis advice might not always be as reliable as the professional sort, but since she hadn't paid for it she figured she really couldn't complain.

I don't know which of her acquaintances put her on to halibut oil, but he or she was responsible for a low point in my life.

There are many, many people in this world who think that cod liver oil is a truly revolting taste experience, perhaps one of the worst, but that is only because they haven't tasted halibut oil. My mother would add it to orange juice, firmly believing that if only I would quaff the concoction quickly all I would taste was orange juice. Try to convince her that oil and water do not mix.

Naturally, the slimy stuff floated to the top, coated my lips, tongue and teeth in a way that led me to gag before I managed with heroic effort to swallow the unholy mess.

This went on for several months. I don't know if it was my nightly retching that got to her or the fact that the witch's brew simply wasn't increasing my appetite, but after the second bottle was finished we stopped.

Another winter, once a week, my mother and I walked a mile and a half to the doctor's office. I don't remember if that was because he wasn't on a bus line, or we weren't on a bus line. I rather think neither of us was on the bus line.

The purpose this Arctic trek was to give me a sunlamp treatment, guaranteed to make me hale and hearty and hungry. It didn't. It just made me miserable.

I still remember the long walk in the darkness and the cold, with me shivering all the way. Once there I was stripped to the waist, my eyes covered with colored goggles while I was exposed to the sun lamp. The lamp made a humming noise, gave off a strange distinct odor and an eerie light, but strangely enough not much heat. As I recall, the doctor's office wasn't all that warm. Then we had to walk the long way back home.

At the time I was only concerned with my own misery. But my mother must have been equally uncomfortable. The strange thing is that my mother was an eminently sensible woman in most respects. But her fanaticism about my health clearly led her to park her common sense while we made our three-mile pilgrimage.

My mother's final effort occurred during my teens, when she sent me to camp. The theory was that the experience would result in my becoming the out-doorsy type who naturally ate well. Nothing could have been further from what actually happened.

When I returned from my stay at camp — which had been pleasant — the only difference in my appearance was that I had an outstanding crop of freckles. My mother looked at them nervously and declared that they were cute. I knew better.

How amusing years later to hear myself making that same statement — that freckles are cute — to my daughters and being treated with the same disgust and disdain.

That was Mother's last-ditch endeavor to get me to eat. I suppose she finally realized that over all those years I have survived, and in pretty good health despite my lean state.

Where is the irony in all this? Today it is only with the greatest self-discipline that I do not polish my plate and ask for seconds. And it has been some years since anyone described my bones as skinny.

There is one consolation. If mother can see me now, she must be rubbing her hands in maternal glee, declaring that it had all been worthwhile.

WHERE DID ALL THE APRONS GO?
by Anne-Marie Nilsen
Ford Times, July, 1977

Nilsen joined DWW in 1976. As a travel writer her work has appeared in over 150 magazines and newspapers including the New York Times, Los Angeles Times, Christian Science Monitor, World Traveler, and the Sarasota Herald Tribune.

I admire my granddaughter even while admitting she has this one small fault: she never uses an apron. She doesn't own an apron. She and her contemporaries run efficient homes, cook gourmet meals, sew fashionable wardrobes, and serve willingly on school and church committees. They not only don't use aprons, they give the impression they've never even seen one outside of *Godey's Lady's Book.* Flinching as I watched my granddaughter flick her fingers down a towel looped in her blue jeans belt, I asked her if she'd wear an apron if I made one for her. She stopped in mid-flight to peer into my face to see if I was joking.

"Heavens no, Gran. Who uses them?"

"I do."

She gave my shoulder an affectionate pat. "I know you do, but you're unique."

I had that dreadful feeling her tongue barely skated past the word "weird." I could have told her that that very morning my own apron had become an emergency dust cloth as I swished it across two table tops on my way to answering the door bell. I also could have added that there's nothing to beat an apron for toting. I bring apples up from the basement, eggs in from the hen house, wood in from the wood shed, and more than once have carried orphaned kittens in from the barn.

Those New England merchants who operated businesses that ringed the square in the town in which I was reared had no compunctions about donning an apron. The blacksmith wore a huge leather apron that covered him from chin to heel; the cobbler wore one of blue and white ticking; the ice man one of rubber; the butcher, the baker and the draper
. . . all wore aprons of style and materials suitable to their trades. Today a man wears one when he wants to be cute while barbecuing ribs at a picnic.

I used to be able to get my year's supply at a church bazaar, but those tables have become display areas for eye-catching gadgets that are not always useful. I suppose not all things must serve a purpose, but when gilded egg cartons or plastic bleach bottles are nudged into the "art" category because of a coat of paint, I begin to wonder why aprons were jettisoned in their favor.

My own mother was a practical woman who made her own aprons, as did most housewives of her day. There was a set ritual about her day that started at six in the morning when she donned a bibbed gingham affair that was kept on a hook behind the pantry door. As the morning progressed the pockets bulged as she went from room to room. A bit of thread here, a tatting shuttle there, or embroidery scissors, an "egg" for darning our long, black-ribbed stockings, a crochet hook or one of my father's misplaced collar buttons. The apron pocket dispensed as well as collected: It often held such surprises as a piece of fresh coconut, a chunk of rock candy, or even a new taffeta hair ribbon.

But, come noon, that sensible gingham apron was whisked off, to be replaced by a frilly organdy that barely hid her flowered dress but still was protection enough while she dished up the standard New England fare of creamed codfish over boiled potatoes. On Sundays she wore a black taffeta with two rows of ruffles and a pocket no bigger than a thimble. Her supply was endless, the selection kaleidoscopic.

New England ladies referred to them as "apuns." I wonder if they still do. Our grade school teacher's mood could be accurately predicted by the color of her apron: if grey or black, watch your Ps and Qs, but if white or lilac it was going to be good day. They were plain aprons , no ruffles, no embroidery, but they often did have a narrow insertion of crocheted lace at the hem. That little bit of lace made even those hugely enveloping aprons seem less austere than those worn by the Quaker ladies who lived north of town.

And today? Well, if one sees a woman wearing an apron it would make heads turn for a second look. I realize I'm an oddity in preferring to protect myself against splashes and dribbles, but aprons are as old as the beginning of the world.

When God's wrath was aroused at Adam and Eve, they made themselves aprons of fig leaves. The word "apron" is mentioned many times in the Bible. The Romans, the Egyptians, and the Greeks all wore aprons in one form or another. Many of those early aprons were made of fine linens and precious metal threads but I am not sure even those were as elegant or splendid as some worn by the proudly attired ladies at the church quilting parties.

Flaunting new aprons was, however, secondary to pride in the cakes (with inch-thick icings) and rich salads held together with honest-to-goodness whipped cream. While the ladies gossiped, I ate myself all out of shape with resultant stomach aches that were eased only by burying my head in my mother's aproned lap.

No matter how fine, or common, the apron, there is no better place to sob out one's physical hurts or bashed ego. Somehow, regardless of time of day or night, that haven always was available. Was it because it was a refuge from slings and arrows? Or was it an urge to stay close to the mother warmth? Whatever the reason, the apron was the cure for every passion.

The union of the old-fashioned apron with the jet age is, I think, singularly mine. When my grandson buzzes the farm, I run out to flap my apron, signaling I've received his message. By the time he's parked his company airplane, a bare two flight-minutes away, and boiled up the driveway, the steaks will be medium rare. As I set the table he ties on one of my aprons to toss the salad. Now why can't I get his wife to do the same? Maybe the right moment hasn't come yet, but I'll keep trying.

ISOSCELES CAT

Gwen-Kirsten Johnson

Arts Council Magazine, Traverse City, MI, 1981

Johnson, a DWW members since 1994, has had 35 poems published and has won or placed in 15 competitions. Her Raisin River Manuscripts was produced by a drama group as reader's theater.

Think of that perfect form
triangle
fleshed and poking through common trash
behind time's-up tenements
Think of triangle taking action
against a sea of troubles. Think
of Isosceles Cat with a haunch of mouse
A lucky spine of God
in it's perfect mouth
behaving perfectly. Form in transit
between hungers a philosopher
functioning
in the latter day as was promised us.

Plato waves from a passing Buick.
In his fondle is Isosceles Cat.

UP YONDER, A STORY ABOUT GRANDMA MOSES
By Lois Fromm Breitmeyer
staged at the Birmingham Unitarian Church, 1981

Breitmeyer, a member since 1964, has collaborated on several children's books with Gladys Leithauser. She has written scripts for a television series on Channel 20. Her play Janie's Mother won a Loyola University competition.

Scene: Back yard of farmhouse. Mr. Parker strides across the back yard to the porch steps. He extends his hand as he walks toward Grandma. Grandma stands and shakes his hand. Dorothy comes from the kitchen.

DOROTHY: It was real nice of you to come, Mr. Parker. I honestly don't know why Grandma insisted on taking up your time.

GRANDMA: Why, Dorothy, you most certainly do. I want a professional opinion about my pictures.

PARKER: You flatter me.

GRANDMA: You're a teacher at the University — so that makes your word valuable.

PARKER: I'll do my best....

GRANDMA: Gracious, I never had any teachers handsome as you. Course, all my teachers were women — and I never went to college either.

PARKER tries to laugh.

DOROTHY(quickly): Mr. Parker, would you like a piece of cake? I just took it out of the oven.

PARKER: Thank you -- perhaps in a few minutes. But first I'd like to see your work, Mrs. Moses.

GRANDMA: You walked right by it. And you may as well call me Grandma — everyone else does.

CUT TO: Backyard of farmhouse ten minutes later. Parker is studying the paintings on the table. Grandma stands near while Dorothy hovers in the background.

DOROTHY: Don't you think it's remarkable, Mr. Parker? Why, Grandma's almost eighty.

GRANDMA: I 'm barely seventy-seven.

PARKER: Hmmm, interesting... (PARKER holds "Maple Sugar Days" at arm's length) This is nice — for an amateur. But, Mrs. Moses — I mean Grandma — (PARKER puts the painting back on the table.) For one thing, it lacks perspective. All your paintings do, really.

DOROTHY: Do you think so? I mean, I don't know a lot about painting, but it seems to me that some of the people look farther away than hers.

PARKER: Yes, but... Oh, the paintings are nice, don't misunderstand me, but they're so simple. You know, art today is complex, obtuse, symbolic, varied, intense....

DOROTHY: Not many people take up painting at Grandma's age, do they, Mr. Parker? Isn't it just wonderful?

PARKER: (to Grandma) It must bring you a great deal of pleasure.

DOROTHY: Oh, it does. Glory, yes.

PARKER (with a sweep of his hand, indicates all the paintings on the table). Everything is sharp, too defined. Now, perhaps if you were to try to blend the objects, make he outlines less obvious — more impressionistic....

DOROTHY (softly)Your skies and trees are beautiful, Grandma.

PARKER: Then there's your use of colors. You don't have enough shadings, mix. Your colors are bright and clear — again too obvious. (He stops and looks at Grandma, she doesn't speak.) And your figures — they're rather dumpy — shapeless, in fact. On the other hand, the animals aren't bad. You must be interested in horses and cows, dogs too....

DOROTHY: Oh, she is. Aren't you, Grandma?

PARKER: Have you ever thought of taking a class — learning some technique?

DOROTHY (horrified):At her age?

PARKER: Oh, my dear, we all know, don't we, that the learning process goes on all of one's life.

GRANDMA: I'll answer that, Dorothy. No, Mr. Parker, I've never given a thought to a class.

PARKER: They must offer one at the high school in Hoosick Falls. Or perhaps there's a local artist who'd be willing to give you a hand?

GRANDMA: I'm the only local artist I know about. But thank you, Mr. Parker, for coming here today, for giving me your opinion. I'm very encouraged.

PARKER (puzzled): You are? Well, I'm certainly glad....

GRANDMA: Yes, you told me my pictures are simple, the objects are easy to figure out, and the colors are lively and cheerful. At least, that's what you appear to be saying in a backwards sort of way.

PARKER: I did? Well, I suppose...

GRANDMA: You see, I'm trying to paint pictures of my childhood — the way I saw things then, clear and simple. Guess I'm succeeding.

STITCHES IN TIME
by Debra B. Darvick
Metro Parent, 1997

Darvick, joined DWW in 1993. Her essays and feature stories appear in several Jewish presses: Forward, Jewish Parent Connection, Reform Judaism, Jewish & Family Life! webzine, as well as the Detroit Free Press and Detroit News.

The phrase "Mom's office" still sounds awkward on my tongue. After working in the basement for years, wading through Legos and Playskool villages to get to my computer, I've taken over the spare bedroom. I now have a room of my own in which to write. I have seven feet of desk surface, a window that overlooks our quiet street, and bookshelves, bookshelves, bookshelves. Feathering this nest within a nest came with no compromises to the family's needs or desires. It's my retreat, shared willingly, but there's no mistaking the room's purpose.

For 12 years, however, the space we now haltingly call Mom's office was referred to as the sewing room. Even though I long ago traded Singer and pinking shears for mouse and Mac, the name stuck, harkening to the days when creativity sprang from paper envelopes stamped Butterick and Vogue. Claiming this room for writing, winnowing a closet of sewing supplies into two 12 inch drawers, I realize with needle-sharp pain that I may never teach my daughter to sew.

My mother once made costumes for a theater in Atlanta. Each fall my grandmother sent us boxes filled with clothes sewn for my sisters and me. By the time I was 12, I was making my own clothes and embroidering samplers and pillowcases, if not with pioneer dedication, then with an affinity that puzzled my friends. Sewing was something I did from before puberty until after I weaned my last child. But, somewhere along the line, the need to write overtook the desire to sew.

The last thing anchored beneath my pressure foot was a dress for my daughter, Emma, now ten. As a toddler smitten with *The Wizard of Oz*, she pleaded for a "Dorothy dress." I complied with delight: blue gingham check topped by a slate blue corduroy pinafore. On the pinafore I hand stitched a contrasting gingham pocket for the plush dog she carried everywhere. Now older than I was when my mother first let me sit at her machine and turn the fly wheel by hand, my daughter doesn't even know what a fly wheel is. Each evening I cover her with a quilt I made while she slept in my womb. Some nights when I tuck her in, I remind her that I put a kiss and hug in each stitch. Will she be able to bind her children to her thus?

Emma has a sewing box, a gift from my mother. It holds a barely begun embroidery sampler and bundles of floss that are snipped to make Beanie Baby leashes. I never remember the sampler during her "there's-nothing-to-do" spells.

When am I supposed to teach her to use an embroidery hoop? In between tennis and piano lessons? After meeting car pools and newspaper deadlines? I no longer have patience for sewing. Today I stitch words into paragraphs, paragraphs into copy. The stories I once spun in my head while basting sleeve to bodice now come to life at the keyboard. But I can't shake the feeling that I'm cheating my daughter by not passing on the craft that once brought me yards of satisfaction and fabulous dresses at half the store-bought price.

A long time ago my mother said, "You want to sew? First learn how to rip." Her adage is a metaphor for any endeavor worthy of effort. You want to write? First learn to rewrite. Withstand the pinpricks of rejection.

In Mom's office we play Scrabble and word games. It pleases me no end to hear my daughter use the word "infinitesimal." For last week's English assignment she wrote, "The panther's teeth were as sharp as a bee sting" and "The town was so friendly you could invite yourself to dinner and no one would mind." In Mom's office she learns that anything done well takes effort. She hears of occasional strangers who call, grateful for essays that mirror their own lives' triumphs and struggles. She learns that words have magic and that it's the greatest thrill in the world to cast a spell with language.

I've traded velvet for vellum. But the thread that runs from my grandmother and my mother to me is the same one I wind around my daughter: Create something that fills you with joy. Do it and do it and do it until it fits just right.

DETROIT'S BEST CONEY ISLAND
by Pearl Kastran Ahnen
Balancing Act, Legna Press, 1997

George watched the girl sitting at the counter. He'd been doing that for the last ten minutes. Mustn't stare, he thought. That's no way to treat a customer. He turned away from her, leaned on the counter and looked out the window at Michigan Avenue. Cars cruised by. How many times had he counted cars on a slow night at the diner? How many times had he dreamed about owning one? Maybe a Cadillac. Might as well dream big. This was Detroit wasn't it, the motor city?

That girl interested him. How could he be expected to take care of the diner when he was concentrating on her? Not that she was good looking, because she wasn't. It was something else about her. Thin, with washed out blonde hair, plain, you might say. It must be her eyes, blue, but more than blue, misty, sad. She wore a simple print dress, pink and green. Why did she look scared?

It was a warm evening and she was the only customer in the diner. So George watched her shake salt onto the fries, squirt mustard on the hot dogs. She ordered three of them, jumbo fries and a large Coke. She ate like a truck driver, already two of the hot dogs had disappeared and most of the fries. But why did she look so scared? A leather brief case lay on her lap.

He might as well talk to her, thought George. They were alone in the diner. "Good, eh?" he asked, in his thick Greek accent. "My Theo Gus, excuse, I mean Uncle Gus, he make best coney island in Detroit."

The girl's huge blue eyes opened wide, "Yes," she said. "The hot dogs are good."

But why did she sound so scared? They were alone in the diner, but he wouldn't harm her. Maybe he could reassure her, take her mind off her fears. She must be afraid of something, George thought.

He said, "We also got best view in Detroit. Michigan Avenue — all the big cars drive by."

And lighting the street was the bright harvest moon. The diner had a southern exposure. All through the summer, George had sat at the cash register, taking in the sun, refusing to think about the obsession that surrounded his Theo Gus. Now he glanced around the diner he knew so well — six stools at the counter, three tables with bentwood chairs pushed against the dingy gray wall. George breathed in the mixed smells — onions, chili and stale smoke.

The store, a narrow, high ceiling structure, was squeezed in between two office buildings. Above the register was an old sign —

"Detroit's Best Coney Island."

George moved from the cash register to the counter and wiped it with a rag. Tall and athletic looking, George came to Detroit three years before from his Greek village. When he was seventeen, George's mother died. His only living relative, Theo Gus, sent money for him to come to Detroit.

He worked side-by-side with Theo Gus at the diner every day and went to school at night. It left him little time for anything else. Occasionally Theo Gus would take George to a dance in the basement hall of the Greek church down the block. The dance was free. Theo Gus avoided activities that cost money.

"Save your money, George," his uncle would say. "Money is king."

Then George would reply. "Money not everything. People important."

George frowned thinking back to the conversations and how they would always end. Theo Gus would spit on the floor.

"Phtew-w, that for people!"

Then the diner door slamming shut pulled George back from his reverie. He turned as Theo Gus barged in.

"Oh, hi, Theo Gus," George said.

The short, stocky man ignored the greeting and instead bombarded George with a volley of questions.

"George, you lock back door? Did dishwasher leave? Coffee urn clean?"

"Yes, yes."

"Good." Theo Gus glanced at his watch "Time to close up. " He turned his gaze to the girl. "George, you give lady check?"

She looked up. "I'm ...... but, I can't pay. I don't have any money."

"What you say?" Theo Gus snatched the check from the counter. "You owe $8.32 lady. You eat my hot dogs, now you pay or I call police."

"But...but," she began.

"No buts, lady, pay, now."

"Let her talk, Theo Gus."

Now the girl was crying. George offered her his handkerchief. The girl crying, the hiss and whining of the old refrigerator, all came together for George. He swallowed, there was a bitter taste in his mouth. Wasn't this America? Wasn't this where good things happened? He had suffered through a childhood filled with hardship in Greece, to face an even worse adolescence here in America, America where good things happened.

The girl had stopped crying. She folded his handkerchief and gave it back to him. "Thank you. Someone stole my purse, and my wallet."

"What?" George asked.

Now he listened while the girl told her story. She had come into Detroit by bus from northern Michigan. She hadn't eaten all day. She was hungry, tired from the long ride. Before she looked for a restaurant, she put her suitcase into one of those lockers at the bus station. A young man came up from behind her and grabbed the suitcase before she could shut the locker door. Another one snatched her purse. It happened so fast, for a moment she thought it was all a dream. Then she screamed, cried for help. Although there were people in the bus station, no one came to her aid. Now hysterical, she ran to the ticket clerk. He called the police.

"The police told me out-of-towners were easy targets for purse snatchers. They wrote everything down. I was so angry, so frightened..."

"And then what? "George asked.

"I just stood there. All my money, my suitcase gone." Her lips trembled. "I'm an artist. All I have left is my paint case." She showed George her case.

"I can pay for the food, I mean — " She did not look at Gus. "Sort of a trade."

Gus gasped. "What you take me for? I call police, for sure — you — you street woman!"

At that instant an outrageous image formed in George's mind: himself decades from now, an old man, like his Theo Gus.

"Theo Gus, no, listen to her."

"Listen to a street tramp, no!" He pushed the cash register shut and picked up the phone, rapidly dialed.

"Please, I didn't mean that," she began. "I came to Detroit because I have a new job here. I'm an artist, and I can paint you a new sign — for my meal. That's the trade I mean." She pointed to the old sign over the cash register.

"No, I call police."

"Theo Gus, give her a break."

"Who give me break?"

"People."

"You make me crazy all the time with people. Shut up." He slammed the phone down onto the counter.

"Yes, Theo," George said. He glanced at his uncle and the girl.

Outside it was dark now, and the street deserted.

"YES!" George could not control the anger coming up in him. "No, Theo!" He slammed his fist on the counter.

"No!" Three years! Three years. Always — yes, Theo. Three years." George's anger would not let him finish. He reached in his pocket and pulled out a ten dollar bill and threw it at his uncle. "Enough money to pay her bill?"

The old man did not move. "For all I do for you, George, you treat me — like this? Shame."

They stared at each other.

"And here," said George, turning to the girl while she wiped her red-rimmed eyes with the back of her hand.

"Here's 40 dollars, you paint new sign, eh?"

"Don't give whore — money," Theo Gus said.

"I can't take your money," the girl said.

"Yes, please take, get room tonight. Good hotel. No rough place. And Miss Artist, make us big sign, say..."Detroit's Best Coney Island."

Section Four

* * * * * * * * * * *

Expanding Our Scope

HOLD TO WHAT IS DIFFICULT

by Tina Michelle Datsko
Soujourners, January, 1982

Datsko, a DWW member since 1982, has worked for Sundance Institute and Columbia Pictures. and written and produced films and videos shown at festivals in Chicago, Toronto, and Havana and shown on Turner Network TV. She has taught at the University of Michigan and California State University.

In Memory of Rilke

Only the tiniest paintbrush
flowers grapple in the lichen-bearing boulders.
Rocks smooth as breadloaves,
gray and huge as whales' backs.
And onto such an ominous
stone a blowing seed dares.
A crevice catches it.
Roots unfold. Fine hairs
cleave to the rock.
They cleave bits and
grind them. So patient. Patient
like women's fingers weaving
washing, shelling peas.
Fingers crawl into depths to
eke out the slightest nest.
The paintbrush flower must
grapple its space,
must grapple its beauty
In such a hard place.
only the tiniest paintbrush.

EXPANDING OUR SCOPE:

CONFERENCES, CLASSES, COMMUNITY

The atmosphere is so redolent with energy and expectations at the annual October Detroit Women Writers/ Oakland University Writers Conferences that it could be bottled as elixir. For nearly 40 years attendees came from all over Michigan, eager to meet other writers, learn writing skills, and beguile editors into publication.

This event began in 1961, when DWW president Josephine Winn called a meeting of eight members including Priscilla Jackson and Marilyn Lyman, to design a conference to be held at the new Oakland University campus in Rochester, Michigan. This seemed a good idea for two reasons. Aspiring writers who needed publishing credentials to join the DWW often asked members for writing help. The members themselves wanted wider contacts in the publishing world. We can't all go to New York City, the group reasoned, so let's bring New York to us. DWW invited a few "New Yorkers"— an editor, an agent, and a renowned keynoter— along with DWW members as speakers for most of the varied sessions. Three hundred people attended!

By 1976 conference chair Julia Grice noted that 450 people gathered in the Oakland University crockery to hear the keynote speaker. She recalls one frizzy-haired smoker in the audience wildly waving matches who eventually set her hair on fire. Later, Mrs. Hair-on-Fire sat placidly in the front row of Grice's class... casually lighting up again. Exchanging such stories, out-of-town speakers and committee members staying overnight in Meadowbrook Hall laughed and carried on like college students, Grice says. The next day she sat near keynote speaker Peter Mayer, Avon Books editor, resulting in the sale of her first historical romance story.

In the first years, the conference selected mainly local speakers, but soon greater emphasis was placed on bringing in New York editors and agents. In addition, former attendees were now publishing on their own, joining DWW, and becoming conference speakers themselves.

Many "big name" conference keynote speakers lived and wrote here in Michigan. Elmore "Dutch" Leonard told witty tales of writing for years before fame, fortune, and the movies became his lot. DWW member Judith Guest described striking gold with her novel *Ordinary People* which became a Robert Redford movie. Michigan provides fertile ground for writers.

By the 20th year, and drawing 500 participants, the conference demanded enormous work to produce. At the same time Oakland

University restructured the continuing education department and reduced staff. Two DWW members, Bettie Cannon and Iris Jones, were paid to coordinate the conference but wearied of the hassle and resigned to write. So Helen Balmer, a public relations professional, was hired. Tasks were divided three ways: OU oversaw on-campus registration, class rooms, board and meals, and security. DWW recommended and selected speakers, assigned topics, arranged the schedule of sessions, presented sessions, and hosted speakers. Balmer contacted speakers, arranged transportation and pay, and prepared copy for the brochure.

Few conferences in the country then and now offer such a broad selection of speakers at such reasonable cost. The 25 to 30 sessions feature editors, agents, fiction and non fiction writers, poets, children's writers, playwrights, business and travel writers, essayists, columnists — whomever has useful information or inspiration to give. Talks range from technique on plotting, characterization or description to marketing, creativity, research, making contacts — whatever a writer might need to have. Private manuscript critiques, small writing workshops, social gatherings and an extensive bookshop add to the literary feast.

The year enrollment hit 550, guards were needed at the door of popular sessions, the lunchroom was bedlam, and the book store was jammed. Every year modifications and changes are made in hopes of perfection. Even so the hassle is worth the effort. Everybody benefits; both beginning and established writers as well as the speakers. Wunsch, young adult writer, tells of learning to give speeches at conferences. After a talk preceding Joyce Carol Oates as featured speaker (not then the literary lion she was to become) Wunsch stressed the importance of up-beat books for teens. "I like happy endings" she said. Joyce Carol Oates stood up, said "I write my nightmares," and sat down.

Conferences are a good way to keep in touch with literary and market trends, to meet agents, editors, and professional writers and to know aspiring writers from all over the state, but not the only way. In 1981 Cynthia (Toni) King and Julie Grice put together a two-day seminar on Writing Book Proposals at the Detroit Public Library. "The seminar was a huge success, both professionally and financially," King said. Paul Sculpholm, Executive Director of the Friends of the Detroit Public Library, suggested doing one each year on various topics. (As an aside, King mentions that when it was suggested that the "ladies" supply the food, she replied that we were writers, not cooks in this affair. Meals were catered.)

The next year, King and Susan Brown organized a Children's Book seminar. A seminar on proposal writing scored another success. What at first seemed to DWW members vital time taken from writing when King recruited members to help, came to be seen as a gift of experience and knowledge.

In 1985, a major effort, again under King, came to fruition. The Short Story Symposium, involving major fund and grant raising, brought in famous editors William Abrahams, Ted Solotaroff, and Gordon Lish. Local authors of repute included Charles Baxter, Gloria Whelen, Paulett White, Alan Cheuse, Max Apple, Beaufort Cranford, Ruth Coughlin, and more. The Detroit Public Library main auditorium was filled to capacity.

In answer to writer's requests, DWW and OU planned in-depth seminars in the spring. Elizabeth Kane Buzzelli and Carolyn Vosburg Hall chaired a Mystery Writers Seminar inviting three local mystery writers — DWW member Sarah Wolf, Loren Estleman, and Lowell Cauffiel— joined by a New York editor, a detective, and a psychiatrist to help "get the facts straight." Corinne Abatt and Beth Aviv ran a seminar called "To Market, To Market" on getting published featuring, among others, Ruth Langan on romance writing.

Some events were limited to DWW members, for example — Virginia Parker's seminars "For the Potentially Rich and Famous" on marketing oneself held at Schoolcraft College, and another on self-publishing held in Canton.

Often members planned less formal writing retreats, one in Kentucky, another in Canada, two big ones at the Emrich Center, Brighton, Michigan (the 1989 and '90 events pictured on the cover). Smaller retreats occurred at members' vacation homes. Members car-pooled, brought food, planned the program then wrote all day or walked and talked about writing and met to commune in the evenings.

Over the years the DWW members not only toiled at their own writing goals but continually emphasized professional standards in their community involvements. The DWW yearly achievement list tells the many ways the group interacts with the community. Members travel the state on arts grants for teaching creative writing in the schools, teach classes from children's to college levels, give talks to groups and on TV and radio, with the aim of assisting aspiring writers.

Some members over the years have inaugurated their own presses to assist poets and literary writers in achieving publication. Naomi Long Madgett's Lotus Press promotes black writers, Gay Rubin's Hot Apples Press published poetry and fiction. Virginia Burns publishes her biographies on famous Michigan people such as *William*

Beaumont, Frontier Doctor. Margo LaGatutta's PlainView Press gives many writers a chance for exposure.

The Detroit Women Writers has self published several group books; one called *Detroit Women Writers Club Poerty* in 1949, *Echos From The Moon* — a poetry book in 1976, *Voices on Writing Fiction*— 28 members give advice on all aspects of fiction in 1987 (co-published with Writers Digest Books), and in 1999, *Century of Voices* .

As a group and individually, the group finds many ways to reach the community. And often good things happen in return. In June 1999 a kick-off for the group's anniversary a special readings night "Authors On Stage" is planned, co-sponsored by the Cranbrook Writers Guild and The Village Players. Proceeds from this fund raiser pay for the Guild's annual university student conference and the Players' theater building fund.

"Authors On Stage" features selections from this book presented by actors to honor the Detroit Women Writers' first 100 years. Director Bob Carington and Corinne Abatt prepared the script which includes book chapters, poems, essays, and more, a lively olio of works.

As DWW moves into the next century, many plans are afoot to expand the group's horizons and interact with the community, not the least of which involves going on internet with a web page. If there is a better way to teach writing, a different form of publication, or a new form of electronic communication, a DWW member will find it.

Carolyn Vosburg Hall, co-editor

CUCKOLD
by Joyce Carol Oates
from Where Is Here?, Ecco Press, 1992

Oates joined DWW in 1964. She is now one of the most prolific and renowned authors in the USA with hundreds of books and short stories to her credit. She teaches at Princeton University.

That evening he arrived home at the apartment approximately thirty minutes earlier than usual but perhaps that isn't relevant.

He called her name but she wasn't in the living room.

He called her name but she wasn't in the kitchen.

He called her name but she wasn't in the bedroom.

He called her name but she wasn't in the study.

He called her name but she wasn't in the bathroom.

Calling her name, beginning now to be worried, unless he was frightened, he returned to the living room switching on all the lights and like a fool or a madman or a desperate husband he stooped to peer beneath the sofa though he knew she wouldn't be in such a place. He returned to the kitchen opening a closet door though he knew the gesture was both futile and demeaning. *Where are you ?* he called. *Where are you hiding?* switching on lights as he hurried from room to room and in the bathroom calling her name he heard an eerie echo as of the interior of a sea shell held to a child's ear for the first time, and in the bedroom he knelt peering beneath the bed though, of course, she wouldn't be in such a place, he pleaded, he threatened, he called her name like an incantatory prayer awkwardly translated from a Middle eastern tongue, he threw open the closet doors, he looked behind the book shelves, in despair he left the apartment calling her name in the hall, he knocked on neighbors doors but no one had seen her, his face now beet red, his pride in a puddle at his feet, he climbed the stairs to the roof but she wasn't on the roof, he took the elevator down eleven floors to the street but she wasn't on the street, he circled the block in the rain his heart beating like giant dice shaken violently in a cardboard cup but she wasn't there, he returned to his building and took the elevator back up stairs and let himself back in the apartment and when he stepped into the living room there she was... there restored to him ... miraculously restored to him... sitting regarding him with her lovely ironic imperturbable eyes in whose pupils he was reflected an infinitesimal fraction of an inch tall, and he whispered *Bitch! Where have you been?* and knelt to feel her pads: were they damp, were they cold, were they gritty from the street. But he couldn't tell.

MACKINNON'S MACHINE
by S.K. (Sarah) Wolf
Simon & Schuster, 1991

Wolf, a member of DWW since 1987, writes suspense and espionage novels. Of MacKinnon's Machine the New York Times review says: Action? Nonstop. Writing? Strong and Clear. Rating? Say 9 of 10.
She is a much sought after speaker and lecturer.

A. C. MacKinnon lay in bed in the dark, muffled sounds of sleep seeping through the wooden walls from the barrack room on the other side. He rose, flipped on the light, and looked at his watch. One seventeen. He turned off the light and walked to the window. High clouds had rolled in, obliterating the stars and leaving only a pale glow where the moon should be. He dressed quickly in the dark and ran his fingers through his hair as if to comb it. Then he opened the door and strode into the barrack room.

"All out! All out!" he called, flicking on lights as he went. "Dressed and outside in two minutes." At the outer door he paused and turned. "Lawrence, alert your commanding officer." Then he stepped outside.

Three minutes later they formed a ragged circle around him, Glover at the edge of it, panting and still shoving his shirt into the waist of his pants. "Two miles due north-zero-degree bearing, " MacKinnon ordered. "All speed and all stealth. Two miles ninety degrees. Return on a two-twenty-five bearing. Give me five minutes." Without further comment he slipped around the corner of the building into the dark and was gone.

"Shit," Kozlewski whispered.

"Form up and let's go," Ken Glover said quietly.

"He said five minutes," Halstead whispered.

"Yeah," Glover said, grinning in the dark. "All's fair, as they say. Let's move it." He took a bearing and pointed north, and the men moved out, walking in the slow, rolling motion that assured total silence. They all knew that MacKinnon was out there somewhere, waiting. The darkness was meant to confuse, but it protected as well. They knew silence; sixteen men walked across a graveled desert soundlessly. And they had taken a jump on the time. With luck, they would pass him in the dark, and he would never know they were there.

With luck. He had taught them about luck. "There's no such thing as luck," he had told them. "You make your own breaks. Your mind, that's your luck. Your brains. Think, men, think!"

As one, they were thinking now: he tells us five minutes, and we wait half a minute instead. Yeah, making our own luck. Yeah. MacKinnon, that's how we do it.

They moved silently through the darkness in close order, signaling one another by touch: a growth of salt grass, an escarpment, a faintly heard sound. Their heads were clear now, sleep the furthest thing from their minds. There was only one thought: beat MacKinnon. Beat him at his own game.

At the two-mile point they found the token: a white handkerchief tied around a rock, Thomasson, in the lead, picked it up and held it aloft in triumph. As one, the body turned ninety degrees and headed eastward. Yeah, MacKinnon, watch us do it.

A single shot whistled not six inches above his head, and Thomasson, without a second thought, hit the ground. Behind him, the others went down. Silence. Seipke put his head up to listen, and it was nearly blown off as automatic fire raked across the group. "Jesus H. Christ," Sullivan whispered to the man whose ear was practically in his mouth, "that's live ammo he's got."

More silence. They lay there, their faces digging into the sand and stones, waiting for the next volley, and they were greeted with silence. Halstead made a mental check of each of his body parts. Kozlewski had a sudden, unbearable urge to pee. Archie Lawrence gazed at what would have been the horizon if he had been able to see it. Fucking bloody bastard, he thought. Hasn't changed an inch. Train or I'll kill you.

Ken Glover moved his arm cautiously until he could see the lighted digits of his watch. Give you five minutes, he thought. Okay, man, this time we'll give it to you. He watched the seconds blink by in utter silence and then allowed two more minutes. Then one more. "He's gone," he whispered finally.

"You wanna be the first one up?" came a whisper close at hand.

Glover listened again and heard nothing. Slowly he raised his head off the ground, then his shoulders, then his torso. Finally he stood. Around him, one by one, the others stood. "He's definitely gone," Sullivan whispered to Kozelaski, who nodded agreement in the dark. Chastened, the group started off again. It was still awfully dark. How had he seen them? If it were possible to be quieter than silent, they were, as they moved eastward. Thomasson still held the handkerchief-covered rock in his hand, a talisman against failure.

Behind them and to their right, MacKinnon followed, a shadow slipping through the surrounding darkness, unseen, unheard.

CAPTIVE OF DESIRE
Ruth Ryan Langan
Pocket Books, April, 1990

New York Times Extended List and USA Today bestseller, Langan is the award-winning author of 50 fiction novels, both contemporary and historical, and has also co-scripted four feature-length screenplays She has appeared in radio, television and print interviews on CNN News, Good Morning America, Donahue, The Wall Street Journal, and Cosmopolitan.

Ireland - 1648

"Riders approach."

Three dozen horsemen tensed beside their mounts. For hours they had shivered in the cold rain, waiting for a command from their leader.

One man stood alone on a small rise, straining through the darkness. Though Sloan Townsend was dressed like the others, in heavy woolen cape and plumed hat, with sword at his side, something set him apart. The others stood in clusters of three or four, whispering solemnly, even laughing at times to ease the discomfort. Sloan spoke with no one. All of his energy was focused on the task before him. Though it was distasteful, it must be done. This thing must be ended once and for all.

Though born in this poor land, he had been sent to England after the death of his father, to be raised by his aristocratic mother in the court of Charles I of England. When his education was complete he had volunteered to fight with the English. Still, he thought of himself as Irish. He had returned now to Ireland to claim what was his. He touched a hand to the scar at his cheek. And to settle a score.

The O'Donnell was at death's door, no longer a warrior to fear, if rumors were true, But there was still an heir, a daughter, who must be destroyed, if there were ever to be peace in this battle-scarred land.

When he pulled himself into the saddle and unsheathed his sword the man fell silent. One by one they followed suit.

At first, all he could hear was the sound of rain falling softly. But as he became accustomed to the silence he could make out the distant thunder of horses. They were riding hard.
His fingers gripped the hilt of the sword and he felt the warmth of generations flow through him.

The men fell into line behind him, straining for a glimpse of the enemy.

He signaled to his followers, then led the charge. He would rid this world of the last O'Donnell. And then he would enjoy the fruits of this land.

* * *

While Alana's mount raced toward its destination her mind was awhirl with plans. She would nurse her father back to health. They would rebuild the faltering army of men loyal to the O'Donnells. And then they would reclaim the land to the north which had been stolen from them by the traitor, Kendall, and his sons. Black-hearted Irishmen, her father called them, who had turned their backs on the land and sought their fortunes in England.

Her thoughts were disturbed by a sudden commotion. Trapped in the midst of the horsemen she was unable to see what was happening around her. But at the shout of warning, she reined in her mount. All about her swords flashed as men and horses came together in a bloody battle. Men screamed and horses shrieked as they felt the vicious blows of the sword.

The old man, Paddy, positioned his mount in front of Alana's and lifted his sword. She watched in horrified fascination as he dodged the blade of his opponent's weapon and brought his own blade to the man's heart. As the attacker fell two more charged forward and battled the old man until he fell to the ground,

Forgetting her own peril Alana began to slide from the saddle. If she could make it to his side she could take up his sword and save her dear friend's life.

"Run, lassie," Paddy shouted hoarsely. "'Tis your only chance."

Alana paused, gripping the reins. She could not leave him,

"Go, lass. Yor father needs ye,"

Her father. She paused a moment longer, then resolutely pulled herself back into the saddle and wheeled her mount, Without a sword she was helpless to fight, She had to outrun the attackers. As her horse leaped over a fallen mount she glimpsed a swordsman lunging toward her. Deftly sliding from the saddle she clung to the side of her mount, narrowly missing the thrust of the blade. It found its way instead to her horse's throat. With a gasp the animal toppled and fell. If not for her skill Alana would have been pinned beneath the animal. At the last moment she leapt free and fell to the ground, For long minutes she lay, struggling to regain her breath.

In the gray light of dawn Alana picked her way over the bodies of men and horses and began running toward a thicket.

"The woman is mine," a man's voice called.

She heard footsteps behind her. With her heart hammering and her breath coming in short gasps she gave a last desperate burst of speed. If she could make it to the thicket, she could hide,

"So." Strong fingers grasped her shoulder, stopping her in midstride. From behind an arm locked around her throat, squeezing the breath from her.

With both hands she pried frantically at the offending arm, desperate to save herself from the suffocating grip. When at last she flung herself free of it she fell back against the trunk of a tree, taking in great gulps of air.

When she could speak she drew herself up to her full height and stared at her attacker. In the first rays of morning light he was clearly visible. He was tall, taller even then her father, the O'Donnell, His hair was thick and black, curling over the collar of his, tunic. His eyes too were dark, the color of the midnight sky. They were watching her through narrowed slits. He wore tight breeches tucked into tall boots. His tunic was a fine rich brocade, the sleeves insert with fur. The sword in his hand had a hilt of ornate gold scrolls and precious jewels.

This man was no ordinary highwayman.

"Sir, do you know that you attack an O'Donnell?"

She expected him to look surprised. Or at least contrite. He looked neither. Instead, a half-smile touched the corners of his lips.

"I do indeed."

FIRST LIGHT

by Gloria Whelan

from Playing With Shadows, University of Illinois Press, 1988

Whelan , a member of DWW since 1980, writes adult fiction and poetry, and books for children of all ages. Her most recent books are The President's Mother and The Indian School. Her most recent awards are 1998 Michigan Writer of the Year Award and American Book sellers Pick Of The List.

She hears her father snoring faintly in the bedroom next to hers like a watchman asleep on the other side of a prison door. Gail opens the window and, heady with surreptitious freedom, climbs out, stifling a giggle at the absurdity of her exit. She heads for the river and the canoe. In the moonlight the surface of the river has fractured into shards of broken light; the very act of riding upon it is astonishing.

At this midnight hour, Gail, nervous at being the only creature on earth, is relieved to see the mink cut across her path. Like herself, the mink is intent on some secret business. When she reaches the swamp, she finds a ground fog spread delicately over the water like a lace tablecloth. She slows the canoe, trying to recall where the stumps and deadheads are; it is a kind of blindman's bluff. She puts her hand into the fog and feels its bodiless chill. The canoe carries her out of the fog and between high, sandy banks that still hold something back from the river. She knows the lodge is close. She can tell from the swiftness of the current that she is gliding over the deep holes about which her father warned her, and she tightens her grip on the paddle. She knows that when she returns, working her way upstream, should she lose control of the canoe in the strong current, she won't be able to brace the paddle against the river bottom. The darkness on either side of her falls away; the bluffs are gone and there in the clearing is the lodge, its cracked walls substantial, even impressive in the weak light of the moon.

Gail pulls the canoe onto a spit of sand. As she approaches the lodge, she can see the empty rooms are carpeted with grass. She remembers a trip to Italy and a walk she and Stuart took in the Forum. She remembers the green grass against the pink and gray of the ancient stones and thinks the world is full of alluring ruins, so lovely you forget their warning.

Frosted Queen Anne's lace and silver thistles cover the clearing and have entered the lodge like pushy visitors. There is nothing depressing here; the violence and the scars are concealed by all that has happened since. She moves, from room to room, just as she remembers it. She tries to recall the childish game she played there while her father fished on the bank: it was a kind of housekeeping — setting stone tables with leaves and twigs, ordering about imaginary children. Gail feels at home in this shell that was once a house. She thinks she might write a story about the animals who live here: meadow voles, squirrels. perhaps a fox or woodchuck. She waits for some intimidating, shocking, detail to intrude on her story; none does. She remembers the blue heron starting up, sliding over her like a great gray-blue shadow, its wings beating against the air, until it had lifted itself above the trees and beyond. She is embarrassed to think how for her own purposes she has reduced the animals in her books to something, so much less than they are.

She selects a pebble, a talisman, from the crumbling walls and puts it in her pocket. She sees the lodge is the best kind of shelter, a shelter of open doors and windows.

Gail works the canoe back against the current with the open-mouthed holes lying in ambush beneath her. Should the canoe tip, the holes will swallow her up as her father has warned. An old feeling of helplessness makes her break her stroke. The canoe slips sideways and she is drifting downstream. She gouges the water with her paddle, boring through its dissolving surface, and pushes against nothing that holds. The canoe spins slowly around and around, playful while she is desperate. Downstream the dark shadow of a pine extends out from the shore. She is able to glide the wayward canoe toward the tree and reach with her paddle for its rooted stability. The canoe holds. She turns the canoe around, pushes off, and inches upstream, digging into the water with firm strokes. After she passes the high banks, she is back in shallow water. She lifts the paddle from one side of the canoe to the other, meeting the current and moving the canoe along.

Everything is familiar until she sees ahead of her in the stream a dark shape; nothing ghostly, the creature is solid, and should you rest your hand against its flank, warm. Gail slows the canoe to keep from startling the deer, which has swung its head around and is looking in her direction. Gail knows deer once went about only in the daylight. Since man has decreased their world, the deer live the freer part of their lives at night. Gail imagines them wandering nimble-footed and cautious through whatever is left over for them from the day. The deer moves across the stream, disappearing into the woods to become a shadow among other shadows.

Gail beaches the canoe at the landing and walks toward the cabin. In the morning she will tell her father what she has done. Unlike the deer, she is not content to live in the half-light of stars and moons and planets. In the east she sees the silhouettes of the pines soften and brighten and their dark shapes fall away into light.

THE BEST HOUR
by Patricia Hooper
from The Corner Of The Eye, MSU Press, 1997

On reading the morning is the best time for human procreation.

Morning: the perfect hour for making love —
when the body wakes refreshed to greet the body
stretching to meet it from its artless slumber.
Could we have been mistaken after all
these years of simply waiting it out for darkness
so we could rush upstairs? Think of the hours
we've wasted dressing quickly, eating breakfast,
before the day whisked you off. Think of the bees
coupling in broad daylight in the shrubbery
while we were pulling weeds or washing windows
to finish in time for lunch. Not that the sunset
moving across your shoulders wasn't lovely,
or the moonlight on the sheets or on the grass,
but for thirty years of thinking it accidental
that sometimes, rolling over, just at dawn,
we'd tangle with abandon, still half-dreaming,
half in the world, half out, desirous
and surprised to be so yielding quite so early.
Luckily I was in your path those mornings
you took fire like the trees the sun had touched.

BELL SONG FOR SARAH RAINES
by Bettie Cannon
Charles Scribner & Sons, New York, 1987

Cannon, a member since 1967, is the author of two young adult novels published by Charles Scribner's Sons, and All About Franklin, a Michigan Historical Society Award of Merit winner. Her short stories, poems, humor and feature articles appear in newspapers, books, and magazines.

Chapter Two

Mama packed a picnic lunch to eat in the car, did up the breakfast dishes and packed them in the last pasteboard box. Uncle Marsh took the piece of ice left in the oaken icebox and threw it into the yard. Sarah, as she emptied the drip pan into Mama's roses for the last time, watched the ice melt in the grass.

"Oughtn't we to take it over to Mrs. Drisdon?" She stared at the glittering chunk of smooth ice.

Mama agreed it was a waste but didn't ask Sarah to walk across the driveway with it.

"Marshall," Mama said instead, "if you'd been around here trying to make ends meet after two pay cuts and no job for so long, you'd be a sight more careful. Use it up, wear it out, make it do, do without." Mama quoted the words that everyone repeated over and over to each other now that times were so bad.

"Lord have mercy, Lucey, that ice isn't enough to bother with. It'll last about as long as you two could stayin' on here alone," Uncle Marsh said.

"We lasted as long as the coal held out, didn't we, Sarah?" Mama propped the icebox door open with a stick and pulled down another window blind.

"You didn't want to take any free coal from the man," Sarah said. "Not even three baskets."

"It was cannel coal, Marsh. We don't burn soft coal."

"Mama, it was better than nothing even if it does smoke things up when it burns. All we had to do was shovel it into the coal bin. The man was nice. . . ."

Mama smiled. "You should have seen her. Practically curtsied, fell all over herself thanking the *coal* man."

Sarah pictured the scene in her mind's eye. It was the week before Daddy died. 'The coal was gone and Mama didn't even know where Daddy was. He had been gone like that before, stayed away maybe two or three days at a time. Sarah never knew where he went.

But Mama knew, all right. He'd come home each time full of remorse and burdensome kindnesses. But this time it was different. This time while he was gone, Mama found the letter in the front hall closet: the letter said John Andrew Raines was on indefinite layoff until further notice. They were sorry, they said. Clipped to that letter was a notice from the Federated Motors Company closing their place of business. The letters were six months old. Daddy didn't have pay cuts, the way he said. He didn't have any pay at all.

"But he went to work every day, Mama," Sarah had said.

"Yes."

"You packed him a lunch every single day."

"I know it. You walked him up to the streetcar stop, too."

He'd had no job at all for all this time. This meant, Mama said, that they'd lose the house. There wasn't any money coming in. The bank would take the house, foreclose on the mortgage.

'They had stared at each other that day, Mama standing on a chair to reach the green box on the top shelf of the closet, Sarah looking up at her. Sarah couldn't imagine where Daddy hid himself on all those long days. Did he go to the library and read newspapers with their black headlines about hard times? Or stand in long lines to look for jobs? Maybe he went to blind pigs, those closed up, secret places where men like Daddy sat drinking whiskey out of silver-rimmed glasses. Sarah imagined ladies with low-cut dresses like movie stars seated at the Tables for Ladies and Daddy there, slim and sad, holding his cigarette between his thumb and forefinger the way he did.

Or did he eat Mama's lunches on a park bench with all the other men like those she'd seen in newsreels at the movies on Saturdays? Was he a member of the great army of unemployed FDR, President Roosevelt himself, talked about on the radio? If these things happened, why hadn't he told Mama or her? How could he have pretended that his life was one thing when it really was another? He'd gone on so long pretending, how did he know what was real? Is that why he wanted to die? Sarah didn't want to think about it all, but when Mama found the bankbook with a pattern of holes stamped through it saying that the account was closed, she had to think about it right along with Mama.

That night they had slept in Mama's and Daddy's big bed, curled together like spoons while Mama sang, "Hushabye, don't you cry. Go to sleepy, little baby." Mama sang to comfort herself, too, Sarah decided. Two days later Daddy came home, his bloody knees showing through torn trousers, a stubble beard on his face, his skin gray.

When he learned what Mama had found in the closet, that his secret had been discovered, he exploded into that last terrible rage.

But Mama wasn't singing any lullabies to Sarah now. Instead she hurried around the rooms, checking everything, taking more flotsam and jetsam, as Uncle Marsh put it, out to the car. Sarah hated the way their house looked now with tables bare, Mama's music gone from the piano, no bouquets of Mama's roses and those little flowers that looked like bells filling the air with fragrance. Sarah stood in the middle of the living room while Mama swept around her.

"Sarah. I hope," Mama said, "I hope you are not dawdling. Are you? I know you don't want to leave . . . Nancy and all, but. . . ."

Sudden tears filled Sarah's eyes. She stared down at her old-lady, navy blue leather shoes that Mama got free-for-the taking from Mrs. Drisdon. Even though the oxfords were two sizes too big for her, Sarah had to wear them anyway or go without. The shoes seemed to symbolize all that had happened and Sarah knew Mama was right. She had to leave. She didn't have to like it.

"You are not helping the situation, Miss Long-Face," Mama said and followed Sarah halfway up the stairs. "Where are you off to now? We have to get an early start." And then in a softer tone, "You know, honey, we're going to find renters. And then we'll come back when the house payments are caught up. Honey?"

Oh, hush. Quit it. You don't need to be nice. We'll never come back and you don't care. You never wanted to live here anyway. Just because your daddy owned the coal mine and Daddy was a miner.

Mama hollered up the stairs as if she could read Sarah's mind. "You'll like it, you know. Hanlon is nice. You'll make friends, maybe a boyfriend, Sarah." Sarah clenched her fists and closed her eyes. Mama was always wanting her to have a boyfriend. It was sickening. Mama went on talking.

"This place here in Detroit? It's not so grand. It's exactly like any coal camp you've ever seen. These little tacky houses here on stamp sized lawns? All alike. Just like a coal camp."

"Don't you believe it, Sarah." Uncle Marsh had come into the house from the driveway where he was packing the car. "Your Mama wouldn't know a coal camp if one rose up and smacked her in the face. Come on, Sis, tell me what you want where."

Sarah watched them go, Mama with her long auburn hair coiled in a lustrous knot on the back of her head, Uncle Marsh taller and slimmer with hair the color of pale sand curling around his ears and down into his collar. She said out loud after them, "I don't care what you say. I don't believe you. We'll never come back."

Now that they were out of the house, Sarah knew what she had to do. She moved quickly down the hall and into her room. Under the eaves in the bottom of a basket of old clothes, she found what she had hidden there the very first morning after Daddy. . . . She removed her sweater and blouse.

She pulled Daddy's white sleeveless undershirt on over her own knitted underwear, first burying her face in the redolent cloth. She had hidden it, still sweaty and unwashed, with blood spattered across the front. She would wear it now. She needed it, like those suits of armor she'd seen at the art museum, needed it to hold in that hard lump of sadness and fury inside her body. With trembling fingers, before Uncle Marsh or Mama came looking for her, she buttoned her sweater again. Her heart pounded and yet she felt a strange relief. Nothing could hurt her now.

NOBODY ELSE HAS TO KNOW

by Ingrid Tomey
Delacourt, 1999

Tomey, who joined DWW in 1983. has published four books for young adults, the latest The Queen Of Dreamland. She writes magazine articles on travel and nature.

(Synopsis of Nobody Else has To Know: An under-age teen age boy is allowed to drive by his grandfather. Momentarily distracted he runs off the road into a young girl, injuring both her and himself. He awakes to find his grandfather has taken the blame...)

He looked across the lake where a flock of geese was flying low over Marshbank Park. He waited till they had all landed on the ice before he started talking again. "You want to know something — " He stopped to wipe his nose on his jacket sleeve. "I'd rather be in the wheelchair the rest of my life if I could undo what I did to her. She's just a little kid who didn't do anything. God. I feel so bad." He shivered, feeling the cold right through his jacket to the middle of his stomach. "I feel so bad, sometimes I'd rather be dead."

His leg ached like someone had hit it with a baseball bat. He went on. "I think about you telling me to always do my best, to tell the truth, even over dumb things like a dime or something. I hated it, like when you made me tell Mrs. Wade I cut up her floor with my ice skates, stuff like that." Webb tried to laugh but it came out like a sob. "Dad'?" He bit his lip. "Why did you leave me?"

He was so cold now, his teeth were chattering. "Wh — where are you, Dad? Help me. Why don't you help me?" He hung his head and stood there silently, absorbing the cold around him, beneath him, taking it into his bones, into his blood, with a kind of resignation. Finally, he raised his head. "I don't know why I came out here." He looked over the ice toward home.

He turned and took a step back the way he had come. He could barely move, he was so stiff with the cold. The sun was sitting like a white ball on the roof of somebody's house over on the west shore. Slowly he bent one knee back and forth, then the other, did a windmill with one arm, then the other. He took, another step. Then he remembered. He wanted to lay something there, a flower or a ribbon. A little marker. He looked around on the ice. Nothing but some windblown twigs, clumps of snow. He felt in the pockets of his jacket and pulled out a used handkerchief and a bone-colored wooden button. He looked at the button. It had come off his jacket back in October and he'd been carrying it around for five months. It was all he had. He bent down and set it on the ice. When he stood up he could hardly see it. Taking off his backpack, he rummaged in it until he found his mechanical pencil. He got down on his left knee, jabbed at the ice, and poked a little hole. He jabbed again and again and again, feeling the chips fly up against his frozen hand.

Suddenly the ice cracked under his knee. In a flash, he shoved himself away, a wave of hot fear racing through his chest. "What the hell are you doing, Webber?" he said out loud. Another instant and the ice would have given way underneath him, Even in that brief moment the water had sprung up through the crack and wet his knee. He felt the numbing cold there worse than anything now. He should get off the ice. But suddenly what he was doing was more important than warmth, more important than feeling safe. He had to finish the hole. He pushed himself around to the other side of the hole on his belly and jabbed and jabbed at the ice until the hole was big enough. He reached back in his pocket and dropped the button in. It floated, a small boat in a dark little pond.

He slid back from the hole and sat up, watching the button floating in the lake. Now he could go back. He had left a marker, a memento for his father. He looked again at the lights on the shore, brighter now against the fading sky. He knew it was warmer there, but still he wasn't ready to leave. Here, on the lake, he was alone with his father: nothing of that other world could touch him. He felt almost peaceful. He thought of his mother, how upset she would be if she got home from work and he wasn't there. If she knew he had come out here after all his promises. And Grampa, who would somehow blame himself if anything happened to him. But so what? No, he wasn't ready to go back yet. He watched the little hole of dark water cradling the button.

He wondered how his father felt when he went through the ice when he hit that frigid water and sank. When he figured out that he wasn't ever going to come back up again. Did he think what a stupid thing it was that he had done, coming out to save somebody so dimwitted that he didn't know enough to stay off the ice when it was soft? Did he wish, in those few minutes, that he could do it over, that he could just stand on shore and wring his hands with the other people'? And then go home with his wife and son to eat his breakfast? While everyone thought he was such a hero, maybe he was feeling like an asshole. But it was too late by then.

"I should have done it differently," Webb said. Out on the windswept take there was only his father to hear. "After it happened

I didn't want people blaming me. I didn't want to go to jail. I wanted to just keep going along, going out with my friends, getting back to running." He sighed heavily, "Maybe I know what you felt like when you were drowning. Maybe you wish you had done it differently too. Maybe you wish you had waited for the fire trucks. But it was too late."

Webb watched the little pool of water gather the orange and pink colors of the sunset, and with the changing light, the water seemed to spread around him, across the lake. He felt like he was lifted up by the water, floating gently away in a never-ceasing current. He looked over in time to see the geese take off in one great noisy sweep. He uncurled himself, stretched out on the ice, and laid his cheek, next to the hole, It came to him then that his father had done the right thing, that he would do it all the same way again. Given the chance. But who gets second chances after they're dead? Unless you're walking around dead.

Webb lay there. The terrible cold was like a blanket of ice over his body, numbing his fingers, his toes, thickening his blood. But in his leg, deep in the bone, the small pulse fingers of pain went on and on. He stood up. He started back to shore.

WOLFE COUNTRY

by Martha Bennett Stiles

excerpt from Lonesome Road, Published by Gnomon Press, 1998, as Wolfe Country this appeared in TriQuarterly, fall 1986 and was recorded for Choice Magazine Listening, 1987

Stiles, A DWW members since 1969, has written nine books for the young, including Darkness Over The land, The Strange House At Newburyport, (a Parents' Book Club selection), Sarah The Dragon Lady, and Kate Of Still Waters. Short stories have appeared in Esquire, the New York Times, Seventeen, and others.

Lonesome Road

April frost glitters where the shadow of the mailbox and its post paints a gallows on the hard earth. A boy stands where the shadow almost touches his toes. He is considering climbing the fence that separates him from the field where a mare quietly grazes. She is due to foal soon: he would give his baseball not to be leaving her.

From the field a killdeer cries out. The boy scarcely hears it: he is listening for danger. Suddenly his head turns.

The boy imagines that the mailbox is a tree which he has planted, and that at any moment, men with axes may drive their Jeep into view over the rise where the big yellow Bourbon County bus appears at that hour every schoolday. The men will want to chop down the tree. He hears them shout first orders, then threats. He knows what they want, though they speak only Korean. When he stands resolute between them and the tree, they try to kill him. There are five of them. With his book bag he knocks their axes aside, one after another. When he gets his hands on one of these axes, the men scramble back into their Jeep.

The car that slows to a stop beside the boy is a 1980 Chevrolet with the battle flag of the Confederacy — the flag of half his great-great-grandfathers — fluttering from its antenna. The boy has stopped signaling basecamp with his walkie-talkie.

The Chevrolet's idling engine is even louder than its radio. Born to lose, the radio whines with belligerent self-pity. Despite the chill, the driver has rolled down his front windows. His car sits out at night, and he doesn't fool with wiping off the damn condensation.

The driver is in his twenties. His jaw is lean and winter reddened; it has a sullen slackness. He wears a blue shirt faded from many launderings, none recent. His sleeves are rolled up, revealing muscular forearms, their hair too light to obscure the work of the Panama City tattoo artist who was probably the only person in that country who gave him his money's worth, though he spent all that he had. He eyes the boy through kinky bangs. "Hey Lang," he asks, "you talking to the mailbox?"

Lang hasn't seen Clint Penn since Zad Thacker fired him. Before then, Clint was always riding him, asking him when he was going to learn to shoot, when he was going to learn to smoke, when he was going to stop taking orders from his mother.

"You don't have to be ashamed of talking to the mailbox," Clint tells him. "Some people talk to theirselves; some people talk to mailboxes. If a sucker don't have a friend to talk to in all this world, I sure ain't gonna laugh at him if he talks to his mailbox."

"I've got a friend. Breck Smith is my friend."

Clint swipes his bangs aside and looks slowly in every direction. "You say so, Lang, I believe you."

"He lives a little way on."

"A little way. He's your best friend, huh, but you wouldn't walk a little way to talk to him — long as you got the *mailbox* right here."

"I'm not allowed to walk on the road by myself." *Hongry chilren,* the radio mourns, *anna crop in th' feel.* The Chevy's exhaust fumes assail Lang and he would like to back away from it, but he remembers how easily Clint is offended by anything he thinks anybody might be thinking about his car.

"Can't walk on the road withouten your mama," Clint says sympathetically. Lang's veins shrink at the insult. "How 'bout a ride: your mama let you ride in a automobile withouten her? I'll carry you where your friend lives." Clint opens the passenger door.

The three right claws of the dragon on Clint's forearm grip a skull: Lang has admired this before. "No need to make that ol' schoolbus stop twicet," Clint says.

As Lang gets in, the radio commences a louder tune. Lang would like to ask Clint to lower the volume, but fears this would sound like criticism. When they get to Breck's driveway, Clint doesn't slow down. "Here," Lang says: "this is the — that was the place."

"I thought you said you wanted to go to school."

"Turn around here. You can turn around here."

Clint decelerates. "What's the matter — you forget something you want to tell the mailbox? You told me you wanted to go to school, didn't you? That's where I'm atakin' you."

Twenty miles south of Bourbon County, Lang sees a Texaco sign. He has been watching the gauge for twenty miles; it is close to empty. He edges nearer to his door and becomes very still. "Hey, Lang," Clint says softly. "Did you see where Zad Thacker had him a far?" Lang watches the Texaco sign grow larger and the stillness that has numbed his knees and elbows seems to expand like freezing water. "How do you reckon that hay shed come to catch afar like that?"

Clint is waiting for an answer. Lang flushes, mumbles, too proud to answer, too frightened to keep silent.

"I set that far, Lang." Clint spits out his window. "Zad Thacker he thinks he can run me off ... I like fars, don't you?" At the bullying sarcasm in Clint's voice, Lang feels his face heat again. The Texaco station slides past. "Zad's wasn't too good of a far; wasn't nothin' in that shed but a litter of cats, and a cat don't hardly stay around a far long enough to get warm. You take a mare, now, you set a light to her straw, she'll stay right in her stall. She might scream when her tail whooshes up, when those burnin' pieces drop on her back. She might thrash around, fall on her foal, maybe, when that smoke starts to choke her, but she'll stay right there where she thinks you're gonna keep her safe. She trusts you. She knows you won't let nothin, hurt her, long as she's in her stall. She'll scream an' her foal will scream, but they'll be right there when the coals blank out. What's left of'em."

Lang is refusing to look at Clint. He stares at a small asymmetrical hole in the Chevy floor, at his school shoes, at two empty beer cans and a piece of crumpled paper.

"I might just go back to Bourbon County, Lang. If you want me to, I might. There wasn't enough noise to suit me when Zad's shed burned." Clint pauses. "I know a barn up the road with three mares in it."

Lang will not look at Clint, but his nose is stinging; he must raise his chin or snivel. He scowls blindly out the window. "When somebody thinks they're too good for me, that's when I get to thinkin', far." Clint looks from the reflection of the Texaco pumps in the car's mirror to Lang's averted face and back with a smile to the road. "When somebody thinks they're too good for me, cuts out and leaves me, that's when I get to thinkin' what good company a good far is." Now his voice changes and the hair at the base of Lang's neck rises light and stiff as hoar frost. "If you leave me, Lang, you better stand outside your daddy's barn ever night till the rooster crows, from now on till you hear I'm dead. I'll burn your daddy's barn, Lang. I'll burn that barn with ever mare in it."

SEEING, REALLY SEEING

by Marie P. McDougal

from Chicken Soup For The Kid's Soul, Health Communications, Inc., 1998

McDougal, a DWW member since 1994, writes articles for newspapers, magazines, and guide books. She is also a poet. This story is her first effort at inspirational writing.

His nose was all smooshed looking, like maybe his mom had dropped him when he was a baby. His ears were two — maybe even two and a half-sizes too big for his head. And his eyes! His eyes bulged like they were ready to pop right out of their sockets. His clothes were nice, Tim had to admit. But he was still the homeliest kid he'd ever seen.

So why was the new kid leaning on Jennifer Lawrence's locker like they were best friends or something? She was a cheerleader and one of the coolest girls in school. And why was she smiling at him instead of twisting her nose all funny like she did when she looked at Tim? *Strange,* he thought. *Really strange.*

By lunch time, Tim had forgotten about the new kid. He sat down at his usual table — in the corner, all alone. Tim was a loner. He wasn't as ugly as the new kid — just a little on the heavy side and kind of nerdy. Nobody talked to Tim much, but he was used to it. He had adjusted.

About half-way through his peanut butter and ketchup sandwich (he put ketchup on everything), Tim looked up and saw that kid again. He was holding his lunch tray and standing over Jennifer, grinning like he'd just aced a math test. And she was grinning, too. Then she moved over and made room on the bench next to her. *Strange. Really strange.*

But even stranger was what the new kid did. Tim would have plunked into that seat so fast, his lunch bag would have been left behind, just hanging in the air. But not this new kid. He shook his head, looked around and walked straight to Tim's table.

"Mind if I join you?" he asked. Just like that. *Mind if I join you Like the entire eighth grade was fighting to sit at my table, or something,* Tim thought.

"Sure," said Tim. "I mean no. I don't mind."

So the kid sat down. And he came back, day after day, until they were friends. Real friends.

Tim had never had a real friend before, but Jeff — that was his name — invited Tim to his house, on trips with his family, and even hiking. Right — Tim hiking!

Funny thing was ... one day Tim realized he wasn't so heavy anymore. *All that hiking, I guess,* thought Tim. And kids were talking to him, nodding to him in the hallways, and even asking him questions about assignments and things. And Tim was talking back to them. He wasn't a loner anymore.

One day, when Jeff sat down at the table, Tim had to ask him. "Why did you sit with me that first day? Didn't Jen ask you to sit with her?"

"Sure, she asked. But she didn't need me."

"Need you?"

"You did."

"I did?"

Tim hoped nobody was listening. This *was a really dumb conversation,* he thought.

"You were sitting all alone," Jeff explained. "You looked lonely and scared."

"Scared?"

"Uh huh, scared. I knew that look. I used to have one, too, just like it.'

Tim couldn't believe it.

"Maybe you didn't notice, but I'm not exactly the best looking guy in school, " Jeff went on. "At my old school I sat alone. I was afraid to look up and see if anyone was laughing at me."

"You?" Tim knew he sounded stupid, but he couldn't picture Jeff by himself. He was so outgoing.

"Me. It took a friend to help me see that I wasn't alone because of my nose or my ears. I was alone because I never smiled or took an interest in other people. I was so concerned about myself that I never paid attention to anyone else. That's why I sat with you. To let you know someone cared. Jennifer already knew."

"Oh, she knows, all right," Tim said as he watched two guys fighting to sit near her. Tim and Jeff both laughed. *It felt so good to laugh and I've been doing a lot of it lately,* realized Tim.

Then Tim looked at Jeff. Really looked. *He isn't so bad looking.* thought Tim. *Oh, he's not handsome or anything like that. But he isn't homely. Jeff is my friend.*

That's when Tim realized that he was seeing Jeff for the first time. Months earlier all he had seen was a funny-looking nose and 'Dumbo' ears. Now he was seeing Jeff, *really* seeing him.

ALL MIXED UP

by Cynthia King

from The Year Of Mr. Nobody, Harper and Row, 1978

King, who joined DWW in 1977, published three books for young people, Sailing Home, In The Morning Of Time, The Year Of Mr. Nobody, and one adult Beggars And Choosers. She has been a magazine editor, writing teacher and lecturer, and director of several symposia.

Chapter Five: December

(Synopsis: In August Abbot is too short to ride on the roller coaster. Month by month, chapter by chapter he grows until he finally hits the mark.)

One day Mother took Abbot and Evan on the commuter train to the city. Abbot watched out of the dusty window as houses rushed by; trees rushed by; rocks and bridges and fences rushed by.

"Everything is in a hurry except the river," he said. "The river isn't going any place at all."

"Silly," Evan said. "The river's the only thing that *is* running. Everything else is standing still. You're all mixed up."

In the city they were supposed to look at the beautiful store windows and see Santa Claus. There were so many people that all Abbot could see were ladies' coats and pocketbooks. They stood in a long line to see a messy man with a stringy beard who, Abbot knew, couldn't be Santa Claus.

The man put a bony arm around Abbot and asked him how old he was. Abbot's voice wouldn't work. He squirmed out from under the arm.

Evan said, "He's mixed up going on not mixed up. I'm nine going on ten."

All that month the more Abbot heard about Christmas the more mixed up he got. Mother said Christmas was for children, but she made lists of grown-ups they'd send cards and presents to.

The posters in store windows showed sleighs and snow, but it was so warm he didn't need to zip his coat.

Father said it was a time of peace on earth, goodwill toward men, but Mary Jane Clancy's big brother gave Evan a bloody nose and told him to get out of his yard.

Every morning Abbot asked Father if it was Christmas yet. Every morning Father said, "No, not yet. You'll have to wait a few days more." Abbot decided the bigger he got the more he had to wait for things.

Evan said, "Look at the calendar, stupid. You can see how many days there are to wait." Abbot looked at his calendar but all he saw were squares.

One afternoon Abbot was more impatient than ever, and Mother was busier than ever. "I have a million things to do," she said. "Abbot and Sandy, get out from between my feet!"

Sitting on the kitchen stool listening to Sandy singing in the next room, Abbot thought perhaps Mother was getting younger, and all mixed up.

Then she decided that as a special treat, Evan and Abbot could walk to the village to pick out their tree. Abbot was excited. He ran to measure himself. *I must be bigger,* he thought, *or she wouldn't let me go.*

The sun was out. They met some dogs and saw some cars. At the grocery store across from the railroad station in the village they picked out the biggest tree they could find.

"It's too late to deliver it," the man said. "How will you get it home?"

"My father will drive down later," Evan said.

Abbot was proud of Evan. He acted just like a grownup. Abbot felt grown up too.

"Let's start home," Evan said.

Abbot didn't want to go. Once home he'd feel small again. Without thinking he said, "We'll carry the tree home."

"What?" Evan started to argue. But when Abbot explained how surprised Mother and Father would be, Evan agreed.

It wasn't hard to carry at first, but as they walked the tree got heavier and heavier. Finally they had to drag it. They tugged and struggled. Abbot's chest ached. His arms were sore. His feet felt so heavy he could hardly lift them.

"Hurry," Evan said. "It's late."

"Wait a minute. I want to zip my coat." An icy wind had slipped down Abbot's neck and up his sleeves. It was suddenly dark. He fumbled with the zipper.

"Are you sure this is the way? It didn't seem so far before."

"I'm sure," Evan said. "Hurry!"

Abbot wished he were home in the warm kitchen. While he worked over the zipper something strange happened. At first he didn't know what it was.

He felt it on the tip of his nose. Quietly.

Then it was something he smelled. Quietly.

There was a whisper in the trees. Quiet whisper.

When Abbot looked up he knew. And he smiled.

He held out his hand and caught a perfect snowflake.

"Look," he said to Evan. "Look." The street had a coat of white. White flecks caught in Evan's hair.

The air was soft, the cold gentle.

The birds were quiet.

And there-in sight-was the FRONT PORCH! Colored lights ran along the railing and spiraled up the columns showing the way.

"Christmas is here, isn't it?" Abbot said. "It did come after all."

"Silly," Evan said. "Of course it's here. Didn't you know this was Christmas Eve?"

"I was all mixed up," Abbot said.

RABBIT IS NEXT
co-authored by Gladys Leithauser and Lois Fromm Breitmeyer
Little Golden Books, Western Publishing Co., 1978

Jenny stood on her porch. She hugged Bradley, then carefully tucked him inside her jacket.

"You'll be better soon," she promised. "We're going to the animal hospital."

Jenny walked past two houses and turned in at the next front walk. She stopped before a big red door and read the sign: DOCTOR IS IN.

Jenny pushed open the door and stepped inside. She looked around the doctor's waiting room, which was bright and busy.

She saw a large brown dog lying at the feet of a large man. The dog's big brown eyes looked sad.

Nearby, a small, golden hamster was curled up asleep in his cage.

Then she saw another dog, but this one was very little and sat on a woman's lap.

A fluffy black cat with long white whiskers and round green eyes stared at Jenny. The old man who held it was stroking its fur.

Jenny walked carefully around a little boy sitting on the floor. He had something in his cupped hands — a tiny turtle.

Jenny sat down on a bench beside a girl who held on her shoulder something wrapped in a baby blanket. The blanket moved, and two bright eyes peeked out of a ruffled bonnet. Five little fingers reached out and pulled the girl's long hair.

"That's a funny baby." Jenny whispered to Bradley. She asked the girl, "Is your monkey sick?"

"Yes," said the girl. "She has a cold."

A door opened on the other side of the room, and Jenny saw an office with a clean, shiny table in the middle of the floor and bottles of medicine lined up on a shelf. A woman in a white coat came out of the office.

"Hello, Doctor," said the large man.

"That's the doctor," Jenny whispered to Bradley. "I'll bet *you* thought the animal doctor was an animal!'

"Rex is first," the doctor said.

The big man led the big dog into the office, and the doctor closed the door.

The little dog yapped. The fluffy cat hissed and wiggled his whiskers. The monkey covered her face with her hands. The turtle took slow steps along the floor. And the hamster only turned over in his sleep.

Soon Rex returned to the waiting room.

"He's smiling at me!" Jenny told Bradley, and she smiled back.

"The doctor took out my dog's aching tooth," said the big man. "Now he'll feel fine."

"You're next, Mrs. Stone," the doctor said to the woman. "What's wrong with little Fifi today?"

"I think she has a stomachache," the woman said. "She wouldn't eat her dog cookies this morning."

The fluffy black cat hissed and stared at the woman. The monkey frowned. The turtle drew his head inside his shell. And the hamster went on sleeping.

Little Fifi and her owner went into the office. In a few minutes they were back. The doctor was scolding. "Fifi isn't really sick she just eats too many sweets. She must eat a more balanced diet."

Jenny peeked at Bradley inside her jacket. "You're good boy. *You* never beg for treats."

"The hamster is next," the doctor said. "He looks very tired."

"Hamlet won't play on his wheel anymore," said a teen-age boy. "He's all run-down."

Jenny felt sorry for the hamster as she watched the boy carry the cage into the office.

Suddenly there was a loud *"Ee-yeow!"* and the fluffy black cat jumped down onto the floor.

"Chi-chi-chi!" the monkey chattered and leaped off the girl's shoulder.

The cat began to chase the monkey round and round the room.

"Watch out!" the little boy cried. "Don't step on my turtle!" Quickly he picked up the turtle and put him on Jenny's lap.

"Will you hold Dinky, please? They might kick him and hurt him."

"I hope Bradley isn't jealous, " Jenny thought. She patted the turtle.

The doctor, who had hurried out of her office, clapped her hands. "'Stop it! Stop that race this minute!" Then she turned to the owners. "You people simply must control your pets!"

The cat and the monkey were taken back to their places. The little boy took his turtle from Jenny's lap. The room was quiet once more.

In a little while, the boy with the hamster came back.

"Hamlet's feeling better," he said. "He took some medicine. Soon he'll be running at night the way he used to."

The doctor said, "Pip is next. Time for his shot." The old man put the fluffy black cat under his arm and followed the doctor into her office.

"That shot will keep the cat from getting sick," Jenny explained to Bradley. "You don't need a shot."

"The monkey is next," the doctor said.

Jenny watched through a crack in the door as the doctor put her stethoscope against the monkey's chest. The doctor listened.

"Here is some cough medicine," the doctor said. "Give it to her once a day, and keep her out of drafts."

The girl wrapped the blanket carefully around the monkey and waved good-bye to Jenny.

"The turtle is next," the doctor said.

Jenny heard the doctor give the little boy instructions. "Let Dinky swim around in the salt water as I told you, and his eyes will feel better." The boy and the turtle left.

Jenny waited quietly.

Soon the doctor came out, but she was not wearing her white coat. When she saw Jenny, she looked surprised.

"Oh, were you waiting for me?" asked the doctor. "I thought I had seen all the animals for today."

"Oh, please," Jenny said, "the rabbit is next!"

"The rabbit?" The doctor looked puzzled. "I don't see a rabbit." She looked around the room. She looked behind the door. She looked under the chairs. "Where's the rabbit?"

"Here he is!" cried Jenny. "His ear is hurt." A tear fell on Bradley's fur. "Can you help him?"

"I always have time for one more sick animal," the doctor said.

She sat down in a big chair with Bradley on her lap. "This is a very unusual case! " exclaimed the doctor.

She took a needle and some thread out of a black bag and began to sew up Bradley's car with neat stitches.

"He's as good as new! " said the doctor as she finished.

Jenny held out her arms for Bradley. She hugged him and put her ear close to his face. Jenny smiled a very happy smile. "Bradley says, Thank you!"

"You're welcome, Bradley," the doctor said.

And Jenny and Bradley and the doctor all went out the big red door together.

FOR ROSE AUBREY
Joyce Ferman Wells
Novelists' Ink, Vol. 8, No. 10, October, 1997

Wells, a DWW member since 1989, writes poetry, fiction, and non-fiction. Her work appears in magazines and newspapers.

This is a story about differences, about language
and old sayings, about traditions that change
and others that stick like mucilage, or cling like wet cement
hardening into concrete, about a woman taking
into her a foreign lover in a rented carriage
she yields herself, smiling and moving
in silence, her lover's mouth and eyes rounded ovals.

This is a story about parents and their deepest fears,
and of daughters who leave their houses at sixteen,
who know what they want of life, know their fate
when bleeding ceases, when bile rises up.
She cleans a chicken for the pot, holds its neck aloft,
says, "Ah, these men," a wicked gleam in her eye
for her dark-haired granddaughter, "vive la difference."

This is a story about quilting goods she bought at the ten cent store,
pastels, pinks and lavenders cut into squares in her room, sewed
stitch after stitch in flickering gas light, her lips open and moving,
unlike those of her husband whose lips closed tighter and tighter,
whose eyes grew thinner and thinner as the woman's body blossomed.
The man cursed in the dark room at the first cry, pressed his son,
newly wiped yet fragrant still of blood and birth, to his chest
and said, "Mein Gott, what have we here?"

She thinks of men living with new wives, of his living in Royal Oak
with the new wife she's never seen, knows from the name Jenny,
no dark recesses of sin color her fair skin, no murky Mediterranean
or Mohawk midnights darken their days, their rides in the Reo,
heads reflecting sun to sun. In a Grosse Pointe garret, she slides a
needle through yielding cloth, dreams of Belle Isle carriages, gambling
casinos, native sons as dark as soil. Each noble stitch confirms
differences of city and farm, dark and light, poverty, wealth,
language, food. She dreams until once again she rises to answer the
servants' bell.

BABY'S FIRST CHRISTMAS
by Barbara Arno Modrack
Seventeen Magazine, December, 1986

Modrack, a member since 1986, is a copy editor at the Flint Journal and former reporter at the Flint Journal and Oakland Press. Her short fiction has appeared in Seventeen, Sassy, and the Alaska Quarterly.

When Summer says to Loribeth late Christmas day, "What do you want to do?" it is a question that does not need an answer. Their options are: They can build a card house on the coffee table; they can paint their nails lavender with the polish Loribeth stole from the drugstore downstairs; they can watch *Rudolph the Red-Nosed Reindeer* on television; and when Loribeth's baby wakes up, they can take care of him. Nothing much requires a choice.

Summer and Loribeth are best friends from the Teen Parent class at the high school. They are sitting in Loribeth's living room on a couch they found at the curb — someone else's trash but still perfectly good.

"I don't know, " Loribeth says. "What do you want to do?" Loribeth is wrapped in a sleeping bag, flipping the pages of a fashion magazine. The last of the day comes in through the window above the street. In half an hour, the Rexall sign outside will fill the room with golden shoots of light, like a blinking Christmas tree.

There is something funny about this situation. Last year, Summer would have thought it was so cool to have a place like Loribeth's, all to themselves, no grown-ups, where they could do whatever they wanted. Now there is nothing in particular Summer wants to do. Partying is no fun lately; she quit smoking right before she was going to have the baby, and it doesn't taste good to her anymore; and she is absolutely done for good with boys.

"How was it at your mom's?" Loribeth asks. Summer spent last night and this morning at her mother's house: home for the holidays, they called it.

"It went okay," Summer says. She picks up the deck of cards and plucks two of them off the top, matching their corners and standing them on the coffee table in an inverted V.

That Christmas morning had been like so many others: opening presents in a familiar squall, her little half sisters tearing at wrappings and boxes. But it was really so different. Her presents from her mother seemed to be for someone else; they were surprisingly wrong: a sweatshirt with Garfield on it, a game of Clue, a pair of pink flannel pajamas. Summer has brought the pink pajamas to Loribeth, who is always complaining about drafts.

"I didn't get you anything," Loribeth wails when Summer gives her the box.

"It's okay. I didn't get you anything, either." Summer fishes in the box for the tag, which says "To Summer from Mom." It's a good joke. Loribeth rubs the flannel against her cheek and says, "Fluffy."

Summer's mother was there, in the hospital room last October, when Summer had the baby. She was standing over her when Summer surfaced from the anesthesia. Summer asked her what kind it was. Her mother told it was a girl, and Summer went back to sleep. The next time she woke up, her mother was gone, and at her side was Jean, her foster mother. When Summer left the hospital, her stomach flat, her arms empty, it was to go to Jean's house.

Last night, while her stepfather was out of the room, Summer's mother asked her if she thought she might come back there to live, and Summer told her she thought that was up to the court to decide; she said she didn't think that was a choice she was allowed to make. Summer didn't know how long they would let her live at Jean's. She thought it might be getting time for her to leave, maybe strike out on her own, but she wasn't sure. Maybe it wasn't that time yet at all,

Loribeth's baby sputters and cries in the bedroom, nap over. They take turns bouncing him, making shushing sounds, while his bottle warms and then cools a little. Loribeth shakes a drop of the milk on her wrist and puts the nipple in his mouth, his little hands reaching up for it as if it were a trumpet. Summer opens the refrigerator to put the formula back and asks, "Did you eat?" Loribeth's parents have not adjusted to the baby; she did not go home that day.

"I had my favorite — Lipton noodles," Loribeth says. She holds the baby over her shoulder to burp, whispering encouragement to him.

"As long as they're your favorite," Summer says.

"Hey," Loribeth says, "if you really want to give me a present, hold him while I take a shower, okay? Mick said he might stop by."

Mick is the baby's father. Summer gives Loribeth a look but takes the baby.

"Don't look at me like that," Loribeth says. "A man's got a right to see his son on Christmas."

"A man's got a right. A boy doesn't," Summer says. "But I'm not going to give you a hard time on Christmas."

While Loribeth is in the shower, Summer changes the baby's diaper, puts him in a clean sleeper, and holds him on her knees, letting him have her fingers to hold. His hair is soft and fine and smells as sweet as hay. He smiles up at her as if she is just the greatest thing. Amazing the way babies happen; a moment so quick and forgettable leaving behind something so permanent.

At her mother's house no one mentioned Summer's having had a baby. They hadn't seen her during the months it was obvious what was happening: when her middle swelled against her clothes, when her breasts were full and round. She was at Jean's then, but it wasn't possible that they had forgotten.

Before the baby was born, her mother had written her letters every day, one day advising Summer to give the baby up, the next day begging her to bring it home for her to raise. In the end, Summer made her own decision, and her mother did not try to change her mind.

What was odd was that they treated her exactly as they had before, as though she were still the same. Her mother made her waffles and syrup for dinner, thinking that was still her favorite; her stepfather still asked her to do things as if she had already refused. Last night, when Summer was in the family room watching television, her stepfather asked, "'Are you watching this?" as if it were a challenge, some test she had already failed. The funny thing was, she didn't care what she was watching and didn't care if he switched it. But falling into an old habit and disappointing herself, she didn't simply tell him to change it. Instead, she stood up and said. "If you'd just ask nice one time, it might make a difference." When she walked past the room a little later, her stepfather was sitting in the La-Z-Boy, a magazine closed on his lap, staring at the television with the sound nearly off. He had not changed the channel.

Her mother was like a bird, hovering, fluttering, trying to swoop between Summer and her stepfather, sometimes only making it worse. So much of her mother's life had been spent torn between them. Summer was starting to know she would never go back there to live. It wasn't her fault what she did to her stepfather. When he looked at her, he had to remember the way her mother was before they met: free and a little wild, conceiving a child one glorious summer when she'd run away from home to California to live with the hippies who'd gotten their picture in *Life* magazine. That's why Summer had a name like no one else she knew, a "hippie" name — although her mother was very far away from that now. Summer thought her stepfather must hate that part of her mother, and maybe that wasn't his fault, either.

Loribeth opens the bathroom door, letting a soapy mist seep into the living room. When Summer hands the baby back, he keeps hold of one of her fingers for a minute until he grabs for a strand of his mother's wet hair.

"I'd better go," Summer says.

"Okay," Loribeth says. "Hey, thanks for coming by. And thanks for the pj's. Really. They're my only present so far."

Outside it is dark, and the street is empty, the whole world gathered in living rooms, wringing the last of Christmas out of the day. Driveways are filled with cars, and squares of light from front windows spill out onto the snow in the yards. Brown, matted grass peeks out around the edges of the lawns.

By the time she got to the hospital to have the baby, the decision had been made. She never saw the baby, though one time in the hall she thought she saw the people who took her looking through the nursery window, holding on to each other as if one of them might fall.

"It was the right thing," Summer says aloud in a cloudy breath. She tries to picture her, a warm, sleeping bundle, in a nice home, maybe somewhere near here. She braces her legs and slides on a stretch of ice, stumbling just a step when she hits the sidewalk. Into the night, to the child she will never see, Summer says, "Merry Christmas."

NEVER MARRY THE BLUE-BEARDED MAN
by Tina Michelle Datsko
Genre, 1996

The walls are bleeding but do not cry out,
stretched to bursting with their secrets.
The rusty stains blossom into Roschach blots
drizzling from ceiling to floor.
She listens hard to the walls,
her breath like wings beating against the window.
She is afraid to touch either
the chalky surface or the moist splotches,
afraid of what her palms may learn
brushing against those wags.
The clay of being on her hands
would surely not wash off
but stain her palms like a Tamil dancer's.
Their henna red held up before her shouting,
I *know. I know. I know.*
There behind the wall a cavern triggers
back ten thousand years —
a thousand corpses of wives
beheaded in the moment of knowing
before the spark in the mind could
catch fire to the whole body
and limbs become a flaming, dancing cross.
He is there; the dark man possesses the house.
Its elbows will fold, closing her in, shaking her
skull to a death rattle. She opens
the door. The door is a mouth
forming the letter "0" of surprise.
She leaps through the ring of the 0
and lands running, awake,
heading toward infinity.

SMOOTH SIDEWALKS
Mary Ann Wehler
Heartlands Today Journal, 1998

Wehler, a DWW member since 1997, is a journalist and poet. She was awarded Third Prize in the Oakland Community College Poetry Contest.

The best sidewalk for skates was half-way down
the block, brand-new cement in front of two houses. I
could turn and skate backwards, knew how to stop
on my toes. I was Sonja Henie on wheels.

The Kummer boys captured me. I was caught
in the middle of a dream turn. My hands posed above my head.
They pulled me into their back yard, into their garage.
You guys are really gonna to be in trouble!

But they tied me to the chair. I looked
at the smudged window, the spider webs. I smelled
the months-old newspapers piled in the corner,
the case of brown beer bottles,

its lid flapped open to take the next empty.
One of the boys poked my stomach with his stick:
You 're the enemy
I thought of the dirt, the possibility of rat

nests. I heard the boys whisper, giggle in the corner.
Then from the back porch we heard, *Donald, Alex Kummer!*
Supper time. They untied me. *You 'll be sorry if yon tell*
We 'll get you.

It took nerve to skate down to the smooth sidewalk.
The excitement of capture, my skating became a performance.
I held my head high and twirled. Wind played in my hair,
wheels whirred on the concrete, leaves shushed In the trees

that shaded the July sidewalk. My mind whirled in fantasy.
The cool feel of the skate key that hung from my neck,
I sucked the end of it, stuck the tip of my tongue
In the square hole, pressed the shape on the skin of my arm.

OF BEGINNINGS AND ENDINGS
by Nancy Mitchell
Prime Times Magazine, 1985

Mitchell, a DWW member since 1985, is a freelance writer, editor, and speaker whose short stories and poems have appeared in Modern Maturity, Prime Times, and Alive Now!

Hannah's kitchen window framed jade buds and daffodils, but today I only saw rain slithering down the pane to crash the sill. I threw my jacket on a stool and snapped, "Young folks today give up so damn fast."

Wrapped in a bulky-knit sweater and a cloud of cigarette smoke, Hannah said, "You look awful. I'll make some tea."

Friends since grade school, Hannah and I have more yesterdays than tomorrows. Sometimes I think we're still twelve years old; when life stretched ahead like the yellow brick road to Oz. Then I see the crow's-feet, turkey necks, and parched dreams. She has more wrinkles than I because she smokes. I can hear her wheezing across the room, and that worries me.

Hannah placed a steaming cup in front of me. "Careful, it's hot. Now, tell me."

"Jack called last night. He's coming home tomorrow with a pending divorce, no job, and a 35 inch TV. Says he knows his old room is now my office so he'll sleep on the sofa."

"My Carrie got here from Texas last night — in a red Mazda stuffed with three suitcases, a woofy dog named Dexter, and a longhaired shedding cat. Wedding ring in her purse."

"Now you've got two back home. We're running out of sofas."

"Brian moved my double bed down the basement, brought the twin beds upstairs for Carrie and me, put a dresser and TV downstairs, and what more do you need in life?"

"A bathroom?"

"He put in a Portapotty and a redwood hot tub."

"There goes the hot water bill."

"Jack and Carrie have quite a history."

I nodded. "Grew up in the same church, same high school class. Friends, then lovers, then friends again."

"They can help each other get through the divorces."

"That should light a few dormant fires."

"I'll invite him for Sunday dinner."

Hannah, Carrie and I went Chinese for lunch and talked about ... what else?

I handed Carrie a menu. "Geez," she said, "your hands are cold."

"My hands and feet are always cold. Some people have big noses. Maybe that's why my ex got it on with a younger woman."

"She had a big nose?" Carrie asked.

"Hotter hands and feet. Mostly hotter between the legs."

I'll say this, we had a good laugh.

"My husband Tom drank," Carrie said suddenly, in a voice that flowed over me like cool baby oil on sunburn. "He'd hit me and I would leave and he'd call up and cry and promise and I'd go back and he'd do it all again." With a toss of ginger hair, she said, "Why did it take me so long to figure out that I wasn't the problem?"

Hannah bit her lower lip and studied her plate. It's hard to watch someone you love suffer an end.

We concentrated on the won-ton for awhile. "I went to visit my friend Sam," Hannah said softly. We leaned closer. "When he opened the door, I said, 'Want to go to bed?' and he said 'Come on in, I'll turn off the TV.' We had a great time in the shower and do you know what he did?"

"I can hardly wait," I said.

"He washed my feet. Nobody ever washed my feet before." Hannah's shoulders drooped. "He hasn't called since."

"The rat!" Carrie snapped. "Men are so threatened by liberated women."

She's too young to understand it is much more than that.

Saturday's dawn still coated the sky a pale magenta when the phone next to my bed chirped me awake. In a voice as tight as a new pair of shoes, Hannah said, "You've got to come right over."

I found her wrapped in a wooly robe, staring out the same kitchen window. "I'm going to let wildflowers take over the whole shitty backyard." Hannah pointed. "The white and pink-throated trillium will bloom next month. They last two weeks in a glass of water. Nothing lasts longer than that."

"The red Mazda is gone," I whispered.

"And Baxter ... and the suitcases ... and the wedding ring that still fits. She left the damn cat. I didn't have the heart to remind her I'm allergic."

I closed my eyes as tears gathered along my lashes.

"Tom called last night. He's got a full-time job with health benefits and regular paydays and goes to AA on Tuesdays and Fridays and said it's time for a mortgage and a baby."

I went to get a chair out of her bedroom to slump into.

Hannah blew her nose. "Carrie said, 'This is the last time I'll go back, Mom, honest. I'll join Al-Anon and we'll work on our problem together. Maybe we'll grow up enough to deserve a baby.' That's what she said."

"Did you remind her that Tom... "

"After she said, 'I love him, Mom,' I knew it wouldn't do any good to argue." Hannah deep-sucked a cigarette and let out a sigh that seemed to travel all the way from her toes.

"She's still on the yellow-brick road, dear. She'll be back."

Hannah shook her head so hard I thought her reddish hair would come loose. "I hope not! Those kids who keep coming back home... maybe part of their problem is we keep calling them kids. They give up on marriage so quickly because they've got an out; a backup home. I told Carrie if it doesn't work this time, she's on her own."

Sometimes that woman surprises the hell out of me. I said, "We had them back together, didn't we? I figured their babies would have your reddish hair and my blah-colored eyes."

"I figured they'd call you Gram and me Gramma Hanna. That has such a ring to it."

I gave her a three-dimensional grin. "Guess what? Jack has a job managing a shoe store. It pays so well he's looking for an apartment. I'm gonna miss that kid ... I mean, that young man."

"He'll be just fine, you know."

I blew my nose. Sometimes a good cry clears the head so much you can see years ahead. "So will Carrie."

"Try this one on," Hannah said. "I'm going to reactivate my real estate license, move into a small apartment and leave Brian here to wrestle with the mortgage payment and the five weekly bags of trash."

"Marvel-ose! Don't forget to leave him the sheddy cat."

"And guess what!" Hannah's eyes came alive behind the blue-hued trifocals. "I'm down to one pack a day."

She's a very commonsensical lady.

ASHES OF OLD LOVER
by Nancy Ryan
The Maverick Press, November, 1997

Ryan, who joined DWW in 1993, writes poetry, fiction, and nonfiction. She co-authored a creative writing text with the Oakland Writers Group, published by National Textbook Co., 1998.

When the power surged and the VCR whispered "Puff" before flashing "Good-bye," I remembered our last Supper at Jack's Place and how you threw ice water on my blackened chicken. I sopped up what I could with a cotton napkin, bleached as the deer skeleton we found while hiking the Allegheny Trail. You grabbed the ashtray from the nearest table. You dumped ashes on your head while the nosy young waiter commiserated. You ordered praline cream pie. I want to forget the cordless telephone's endless ringing. The purple ginger jar you brought from a New York street fair, inscribed "Ashes of Old Lovers."

That I wrote your name,
Michael,
on a piece of paper and set it afire.
That I keep you in that jar.

LOOKING FOR PAUL NEWMAN

by Gay Rubin

abridged from On A Good Day, Ridgeway Press, 1997

Rubin, a DWW member since 1974, writes fiction and poetry. She co-edited Echoes From The Moon, and lectures in various creative writing programs.

The first person here in Detroit who told me she had seen Paul Newman in person told me he was very short. My friend is not short. She is almost the same height as her first husband, who once played basketball for the Pistons. "Believe me," she said. "One thing I know, height doesn't mean a thing when you're lying down."

Did she lie down with him, I wanted to ask her, but that was the moment our daughters danced onto the stage dressed as birds and tapped the toes of their black, patent-leather shoes and sang "Glo Little Glo Worm, Glimmer, Glimmer."

"Did you?" I asked.

I'll tell you about it later," she whispered. But after our daughters flapped their wings goodbye to the audience, they tiptoed off the stage, down the aisle, and found our laps in the dark.

I asked, "What did he eat?"

"The house specialty," she whispered. She waited for a pause between acts to tell me what it was. "A divine chicken sauté with walnuts in a sherry sauce," she said. "I had it too. And for dessert he had the chocolate torte, and he drank real coffee, not decaffeinated. Believe me, I was close to him. I saw everything. I saw the ring he wore on his pinkie. A star sapphire."

"But, what did he say?" I asked.

"Call me." she said. "We'll have lunch. Maybe next week."

I didn't have to wait a week to talk about Paul Newman. The next morning my housekeeper, Althea, came in to do the laundry and showed me pictures she took of him at the Grand Prix. There were close-up, full-body shots of Paul Newman in a racing suit. There were close-up face shots of his white teeth and his blue eyes.

"Not bad," she said. "I mean the focus, don't you think?"

"The lighting, too," I said. "Back lit, hair glowing. You must have used a zoom lens."

"Uh, uh. I moved in close. I wasn't three feet away from him."

"But how?" I asked. "How did you get that close?"

"I just walked up to him," she said. "He was standing there, and I said, can I take your picture, and he said sure."

"How does he look?" I asked.

"Like that. He looks just like his picture."

"But is he tall?"

"Sort of."

Althea doesn't know anything about tall. She stands on a chair to reach the low shelf in the kitchen. Everything looks high-up to her.

"What about his eyes?" I asked.

"Just like in the picture. That lighting really is good, isn't it?"

Althea's pictures of Paul Newman were much better than the ones on the cover of *National Enquirer* the next week. Right after I didn't buy the *National Enquirer* at the grocery store, I went to my dentist's office, and that is where I saw Paul Newman get into an elevator. It was his racing jacket and his hair that I saw. So I ran to the elevator. My heels made noises like the beats of a small drum. All the people in the elevator were looking at me. Their eyes were wide and startled when I reached them. The door began to close. "Hold that elevator," I shouted. "Emergency." A man who wasn't Paul Newman, a man with brown eyes and a grey suit, grabbed the door and held it open. My necklace made music, as I squeezed myself and my big, bulky purse into the over-packed elevator. All the people pushed to the back and squeezed themselves tighter together. Some of them sighed and rolled their eyes to the ceiling, and some of them sighed and shrugged. I thought this meant that they felt inconvenienced but were understanding.

"What floor?" the man who wasn't Paul Newman asked.

"How many floors are there?" I asked.

The looks on everybody's faces changed. I won't tell you what they said. I didn't care what they said. I was looking for Paul Newman. I searched in the clutch of squashed-together people for the white hair and the red and silver racing jacket. I found the hair and the jacket, but they were on a boy. A youngster. Maybe 15 years old. There was nothing to do but ride up to the 25th floor and back down again.

After I saw my dentist, I went back to the grocery store, and I bought the *National Enquirer.* The story in the *National Enquirer* said that Paul Newman drank 92 bottles of beer at a horse show in Santa Barbara.

I called my horsey, second-cousin Sandra, who lives in California. She said his daughter was in the show; that is why Paul was there. He was watching his daughter, and he wasn't drinking beer, it was spring water. She said it wasn't even 92 bottles of spring water, but she could see why they changed it for the article. A bottle of spring water. What kind of story was that?

The next time I was at the grocery store, I bought spring water. While I was loading my cart with bottles of it, I saw my tall friend. She shouted, "I've been calling you and calling you. Where have you been?" So I pushed my cart closer to hers. "We've got to get together for lunch," she said. "I want to tell you about my dream." She moved closer to me. Almost whispered, "In my dream God spoke to me."

"What did He say?"

"Call me," she said. "We'll have lunch. I'll tell you everything."

"Just tell me one thing. Was He tall?"

"No," she said. "He looked like Paul Newman, but without hair.

I drank the spring water until there was nothing left to do but get on the plane. Then my daughter asked me why we had to meet Uncle Joe's new wife. I said, maybe we didn't. Maybe we could forget the whole thing. But it was too late. They were showing the movie that tells you what to do with your floatable seat cushion when the plane falls into an ocean. I asked the stewardess if she had any spring water. She said she had Seven-Up or club soda. I said I'd take vodka, and I drank that until we landed.

When we got off the plane, my feet were heavy, and I walked slowly. Mindy, the bird, skipped and shouted, "There they are, there they are," and there they were, a pretty woman in a red dress and my brother, Joe. Joe's new wife made a fuss over Mindy. She sat next to her in the back seat and told airplane stories all the way to the Westport Hotel. She flies all the time. She never gets tired. Not like me. I was going to rest as soon as we carried in our bags, but then Joe said he had errands to run. He said he had to pick up his shirts at the shirt laundry, and do some other things, did I want to go with him? I said no, but he said, "Sometimes I run into Paul Newman. He lives here in town, you know. He takes his shirts to the same place I do."

So of course I went. And of course I saw Paul Newman. "There he is. Look. Turning left at that light. Look at him," I shouted.

But Joe said, "Uh uh, he doesn't drive a Jag."

"What's he drive?"

"I don't know. It's small and dark."

"That Jag is small and dark."

"That's not him."

"Oh, come on, follow that car."

"It's a waste," he said, but he turned anyway, and we followed the car until it stopped in front of a white house with green shutters, and a man who was not Paul Newman got out.

Then we backtracked to the shirt laundry, and just as we parked our car, a man who looked like Paul Newman, exactly like Paul Newman, left the shirt laundry, carrying his shirts on a hanger, and got into a small dark car.

"That was him," Joe said. "We just missed him."

"My whole life is like this," I said.

Joe looked at me the way he used to when he was winning at Monopoly. "All right," he said. "We'll eat dinner at Provencino's on Sunday night. Paul Newman always eats dinner there on Sunday nights, and I'll reserve the table next to the one he reserves, and you'll see him." And Joe did what he said, and we went, all the out-of-towners, the cousins, the aunts and uncles, the nieces and nephews, to Provencino's, and Paul Newman didn't, and it didn't matter, because when I told my tall friend about it, I told her he did. I told her I couldn't help staring. I knew it was wrong, but I couldn't stop, and then he stared back. In fact our eyes locked, while we were eating spaghetti. I told her it was embarrassing, but then he took a gold pen from his breast pocket and wrote something on his napkin. Then he rolled the napkin into a ball, spit on it, and shot it under the table so it landed at my feet. I told her I went to the ladies room to read it in private.

"What did it say, what did it say?" she wanted to know. I told her it was a phone number. I said that under the phone number he had written, *Call me. Any Wednesday morning. I* told her he signed his name. She wanted to know what he said when I called him. So I told her he asked me to meet him in Manhattan at a little restaurant in the village. I did, and we had a drink. I told her I had Perrier, and he had a Heineken's Light. I told her he wore a cowboy hat, dark glasses and blue jeans, so nobody would recognize him, but people did anyway. One person came up to him and asked for his autograph, while we were drinking. "And then, and then?" she wanted to know. So I told her we went to an apartment, a large high-ceilinged place with wood floors, Indian rugs, lots of bookcases and plants and leather couches. We had another drink, and then we made love.

"You're making this up," she said.

"You're right. I didn't go to bed with him," I said. "I didn't even call him back."

"Why not?" she slapped her hand on the table, leaned forward.

I said, "Are you kidding? I don't want to end up in that position with Paul Newman. But I do like having his phone number, just in case."

LET ME DANCE
by Lila Pepper
In War With Time, Black Moss Press, 1984

Pepper, A DWW member since 1958, writes poetry, short stories, and fictional biography. Her story The Heart Has Its Reasoning appeared in New Liberty Magazine in 1952.

It was dancing always
from the very first time
I closed my eyes turning
in your arms as we circled
the floor weaving
strands of love

where is your smile
your arms to hold me?
are they wasted on air
that were my joy?
where is your strong voice
is it echoing in space?

I find it impossible
to reach you to see you
in that other dimension
you slip from me as smoke
fades on the autumn horizon
there is nothing solid of you
that I can touch or hold

I carry your essence
inside me as a memory
but I ache with longing
for the reality of your body.

how can you be spirit
who was all flesh?

HEREDITY WILL OUT

by Sally Sawyer

Michigan Playwrights reading, 1998

Sawyer, a member of DWW since 1988, is an actress, director, and playwright who specializes in children's theater. Her play, Marshmallow Dragons aired five times on Bloomfield Cable.

Characters:

Howard, Fifty years old; an engineer

Carol, his wife, about the same age, an art teacher; rather near-sighted

Aunt; Betty-Lou, 75, Southern gentlelady with thick Southern accent.

Scene: Early A.M., car parked in front of an old well-kept farm house in a mountainous countryside. Summer.

HOWARD: This is ridiculous! We've been sitting here in this car for over half an hour. What's the matter with you!

CAROL: I'm scared.

HOWARD: Of what! You talked to her on the phone didn't you?

CAROL: Yes. Twice.

HOWARD: And you wrote to her?

CAROL: Yes. Twice.

HOWARD: What the hell's your problem, Carol?

CAROL: What if she doesn't like me?

HOWARD: Oh, come on now! Why wouldn't she like you?

CAROL: It's hard for me to tell by her voice. Southerners are always polite.

HOWARD: I know one that isn't!

CAROL: Well, he's the Dixon Inn's night manager. We were late.

HOWARD: I had a guaranteed late arrival!

CAROL: Maybe they do things differently down here.

HOWARD: Eleven hours of driving all the way here from Michigan and no room! What an asshole!

CAROL: (Slight pause)I'm sorry we had to sleep in the car in Piggly Wiggly's parking lot.

HOWARD: Who slept?

CAROL: I'm sorry you didn't sleep. I didn't know.

HOWARD: Of course you wouldn't know! You were stretched out in the back seat all night!

CAROL: I offered it to you.

HOWARD: Yeah, yeah. Do you know that damn, stupid Chicken

Likin' sign kept blinking on and off all night?
Cars were screeching up there till four in the morning!

CAROL: (Giggles)

HOWARD: What're you laughing at?

CAROL: It's funny! ...(No response.)

HOWARD: (Gives her a disgusted look)

CAROL: I said I'm sorry.

HOWARD: Well ... are you going in or shall I turn around and go home!

CAROL: You wouldn't do that, would you?

HOWARD: Wanna bet?

CAROL: But I've been searching for my birth family for twenty years!

HOWARD: (Totally exasperated) Get out then! Ring the damn bell!

CAROL: No.

HOWARD: *NO?*

CAROL: I'll gather myself up in a few minutes. (Pause) Feel my hands.

HOWARD: Why?

CAROL: (Raises her voice) Just do what I ask for a change!

HOWARD: (Startled at her frantic tone, complies) Should have worn those battery heated mittens I gave you.

CAROL: Howard, it's June! It just proves I belong here in Tennessee where it's warm most of the year.

HOWARD: You are in Tennessee! It IS warm! Boy, your logic sure escapes me.
(Turns to stare at her.) You know, you really are weird!

CAROL: You say that to all the girls.

HOWARD: Well ... of all the girls, I married one who's near-sighted and has a sense of smell that's out of whack!

CAROL: I can't help it! That's the way I am! ... You can't stand onions. That's what *I* think is weird.

HOWARD: (He sighs, turns to stare out the driver's window.) Man, those mountains sure are beautiful!

CAROL: Yeah... I love it! I knew there was some good reason I can't stand flat land. Mountains are in my genes!

HOWARD: Sure...tell Mendel about that one!

CAROL: Oh come on, lighten up.

HOWARD: Lighten up! You're the one stuck to the seat!

CAROL: Just let's be quiet for a minute. Then I'll go in.

HOWARD: All right, but this is your last chance. If you don't get out in five minutes I'm turning around and going home.

CAROL: (Gives him a disgusted look; turns to look out passenger window.) Oh, look Howard! Isn't that the cutest little black and white cat you ever saw?

HOWARD: (Rises up in his seat to look past her and accidentally leans on the horn. SOUND: car horn.)
MY GOD! THAT'S A SKUNK!

CAROL: Now you've scared the poor thing and probably Aunt Betty Lou, too!

HOWARD: Look! He's turning his back on us! (Carol and Howard get out of car and run up on porch.) SHIT! HE SPRAYED! ... AUGH! THAT'S TERRIBLE!

CAROL: Can't tell it by me! (Rings bell and knocks on door.)

AUNT BETTY LOU: (Opens door to house and steps out onto porch. She has a large framed photo in one hand.)
Well, ...looky who's here! You must be Carol Anne and Howard!

CAROL: Oh, Aunt Betty Lou, this is not the way I planned to meet you! I'm so sorry about the horn and the smell! (Starts to weep.)

AUNT BETTY LOU: (Hugs Carol tenderly) I'm so happy to see you dear! What smell?

HOWARD: You mean, you can't smell that skunk either?

AUNT BETTY LOU: Thet lill ole polecat theah? No sirree. Cain't smell a thang.

HOWARD: (Does a take to the audience.) I'll be damned! Even Mendel would agree to the heredity of that one!

AUNT BETTY LOU: (Puts arm on Carol's shoulder, leads her toward the door.) Now Carol Anne, you and Howie here just come right in and I'll fix you all a real good Southern breakfast. But first, I have something ta show you. (Shows Carol the picture)

CAROL: (Is startled as she looks at picture) Wherever did you get MY picture? No ... wait. I never had clothes like *THOSE*?

AUNT BETTY LOU: Oh... (Takes picture, looks at it and hugs it) Oooweee! If you aren't the spittin' image of my pore daid sister, Sadie!

HOWARD: Well, I'll be damned!

AUNT BETTY LOU: (Smiling, opens the door and they walk in.)

STARS
Victoria Diaz
The MacGuffin, 1984

Diaz, a DWW member since 1986, specializes in arts and entertainment journalism publishing in the Observer & Eccentric, the Detroit News, the Detroit Free Press, Toledo Blade, and other area newspapers.

For as long as I can remember, Aunt El has dreamed of going to Hollywood. With this in mind, she has saved a little money over the years from her job at the sewing factory. Then, a month ago, on her 45th birthday, my father surprised her with enough money to put her "over the top," as he calls it. And now, here we sit — my mother, my father, Aunt El, and me — waiting for the train to arrive in Mundy that will take Aunt El all the way to Hollywood on her dream trip.

It is Sunday morning and there is no one else in the station except us and the woman who sits behind the counter and sells tickets.

The train is late and Aunt El is acting as if she has her mind somewhere else. Over and over again, she pulls at the edges of her handkerchief and reaches up to touch her hat — the one with the bird on top of it. Now and then she sighs, like she is real tired or something.

"Are you all right, El?" My mother — who is Aunt El's sister-looks concerned, like she thinks Aunt El might be getting sick.

Aunt El nods her head slightly and reaches up again and touches the top of her hat. She doesn't seem especially nervous or anything; she just seems to be thinking about something real hard. Every once in awhile, the bird on the top of her hat shakes a little bit.

Aunt El, you see, is absolutely crazy about movies and movie stars. If you said they were her life, you would be pretty close to right. They mean that much to her. She lives with us and I can just about swear that, every single day, if Aunt El is not actually looking at movie stars on the screen or on a magazine page, more than likely she's got them tucked away somewhere in a corner of her mind. They live and move around inside her head, just like real people.

"If I should ever *really* see Clark Gable — stand near enough to touch him, I mean — I think I would absolutely die," she has said, more than once. When she says this, she kind of folds her hands together and rolls her eyes heavenward and smiles a little and looks — almost pretty. It's kind of a strange thing, as if she's transformed or something, just thinking about it, because most people don't consider Aunt El to be especially pretty at all.

Once, last summer, while she and I were shelling peas out in the backyard under the china tree, she leaned forward suddenly and looked at me in a very serious way and said, "Can you keep a secret, Jo?"

"I swear," I said.

"I mean — not tell anybody."

"Sure — I swear." I looked her straight in the eye then and held up my right hand, just like a witness in a courtroom scene and I didn't smile at all.

"Well, all right," she said, looking at me for awhile. Then she reached down into her apron pocket and brought out a small envelope and handed it to me. "Go ahead. Look inside," she said,

On the outside of the envelope, neatly typed, was her name and address. Inside was a small black-and-white autographed picture of Clark Gable. The handwriting didn't resemble any man's handwriting I had ever seen before.

"I sent for it," she said. "It came yesterday — it was a good thing I got to the mail box before your folks did."

There was a short silence.

"I had to show it to somebody, Jo. I was about to bust — and I was afraid-well, you know — homegrown folks are — God knows, I love your Mama and Daddy and they love me, but I don't know what they'd think of a grown woman, writing to a movie star —"

"It's a nice picture," I said finally. I couldn't seem to think of anything else to say. I thought Clark Gable's moustache looked a little too neat and I thought he looked like he might even be wearing lipstick. But, of course, I never said anything to Aunt El about that.

After awhile, I handed her back the envelope and the picture and she slipped them quickly into her pocket. And we went back to shelling peas.

Now, don't you tell," she said, looking at me almost laughing. "Don't you tell nobody what a crazy woman I am!"

"I won't tell — honest — I swear it!" I said. And we both laughed then, for a long time.

"Are you sure you're all right, El?" my mother says again.

"Here she comes!" says my father suddenly, jumping up and running to the plate glass window at the front of the station and looking out. "Yes sir! Here she comes!" He is smiling like a little boy and looking as if he might start dancing up and down any minute.

"Oh my. . ." says Aunt El, and her voice, in the train station, sounds a little surprised and far away, like she's just been woke up or something. "Now, where did I put them tickets?"

"They're in your lap, Aunt El."

"Oh yes. There they are. There they are." Aunt El has a habit of saying things twice when she gets excited about something.

"Here she comes, El!" says my father, outside on the platform now.

"Oh dear," she says. "Is it really here?" And the three of us follow my father out onto the platform.

The asphalt pavement looks soft and sticky in the heat. There are no trees anywhere around the train station and the sky is yellow as butter. I can see heat ripples rise from the train as it approaches us and begins to slow down, rattling the ground underneath the platform where we stand.

When the train finally comes to a stop and two or three people get off and walk past us, the four of us just stand there for awhile, like people in a play who've forgotten their lines for a minute and aren't sure what they are supposed to say or do next.

"Well, I guess this is it," Aunt El says, finally.

"Take care of yourself," my father says. He is a real tall man and he has to bend way over to kiss Aunt El good-bye.

"You write to us, you hear," says my mother, as her and Aunt El put their arms around each other and look like they're going to cry.

"Goodbye, Aunt El. I hope you have fun in Cal-i-for-ni-a," I say. The bird on her hat is shaking as hard as before and maybe worse and it seems to me that she is looking at me — at all of us — in a real funny way.

All aboard!" the conductor shouts, and I feel a little like I'm standing somewhere outside myself, watching myself and all of us.

Aunt El turns, and picking up her small black suitcase, hesitates just for a moment. Then she starts walking away from us. But she doesn't step up on to the train. Instead, she keeps walking and walking, past the conductor and pas the train itself until she is off the platform and across the street turning the corner on the way back to our house. She never even looks back. The only time she slows down is once when she comes to a broken place in the sidewalk where some high weeds are pushing up through the cracks and she has to walk around them a little to get by.

"El!" my mother shouts, and runs to catch up with her, after she's recovered from the shock of what Aunt El has just done. "El! What's wrong? What's the matter?"

My father and I follow behind. My father says, "Well, I'll be damned" two or three times, and I don't say anything.

"Ain't nothin' wrong," says Aunt El. "It's just that today ain't the day for me to go to California. Today just ain't the day. Maybe I'll go tomorrow — or next week sometime — or maybe even next year. But today ain't the day. I just ain't — ready."

We walk on, the four of us, and none of us says a word after that; every once in awhile I can hear the change jingle in my father's pockets or the whir of a July fly here and there. But, other than that, things are real quiet. I feel like I want to cry or to get real mad, and I can't decide which. I jam my hands in my pockets and watch my shoes carry me home.

"Why didn't you go?"

The words are out before I even realize I meant to say them. It is after supper, and Aunt El and me are sitting on the front porch in the glider, watching the fireflies out at the edge of the yard.

"Why didn't you go?"

"Oh my, Jo — I can't go now — I'm just not — ready to go — not now, anyway.

"But when will you be ready? Does this mean you aren't going to go at all then?"

"Oh sure, I'm going," she says smiling. "Sure, I'm going, Jo."

"But when?"

"Someday," she says. "Someday, I'm going-for sure."

And she begins to get all dreamy-eyed then and to look very, very happy, like she was there already and having a wonderful time and everything was just exactly the way she'd dreamed it would be.

Section Five

* * * * * * * * * * *

What Women Write

FOR A LADY ON HER NINETIETH BIRTHDAY

by Florence Dolgorukov

from Cotton, Wool and Silk, the Writers' Group, Oakland Branch, AAUW, 1998

Dolgorukov joined DWW in 1979. She is a poet and fiction writer whose work has appeared in the Christian Science Monitor and other periodicals. She has published several chapbooks.

To be ninety years old is to be
like a fairy tale, full of marvels.
It is to know for sure that the individual
is truly unique, because in all
the generations you have seen
who has ever produced an exact copy?
It is to laugh at prophets,
for whatever they prophesy
is either too much or too little,
and almost certainly irrelevant.
It is to have (like a sailor) friends
on every shore of time:
the past, the present, the future;
the here, the not-here,
which is also called the hereafter.

It is to know that inside your head
Countless faces, names and past deeds exist
in living color; and that among those
gathered with you today there is perhaps
another child who will come to be
ninety or so, and remember you in the future
(not specified), and that child
will be special and full of marvels
partly because of you.

WHAT WOMEN WRITE:

WHO WE ARE

Like the main arteries to and from the core of this metropolitan area, the membership of Detroit Women Writers fans out in an ever-widening pattern. Where once all of them lived within the city boundaries, today's active members come from the northern, eastern and western suburbs, Downriver, Ann Arbor, and Canada. Backgrounds vary even more than the communities represented, for this greater metropolitan area is the American melting pot in microcosm.

Equally diverse are the writing skills, the kinds of work produced, and the publications serviced. PC's and word processors have all but obliterated the typewriter and the Internet puts the world on the screen in seconds.

Since the beginning of this century, the print market has increased enormously bringing with it an insatiable appetite for stories, poetry, plays, articles, fiction, and non-fiction. DWW members have risen to meet these challenges with skill and vigor.

In everything from internationally to locally circulated publications, specialized to more general content, it's hard to find an area of print where the members are NOT represented. DWW bylines show up on everything from gentle stories about parenting to those dealing with world issues.

In the early years of this century, the DWW voice, as expected, was predominantly female. Then, as now, the women used their own life experiences as a starting point for their work. But, there were limits to what they could achieve. The world expected them to be wives, mothers, and homemakers. Success in combining a writing career with those other three, while not impossible, was exceedingly difficult. Women didn't even win the right to vote until 1920.

Jeanne Duran remembers the first luncheon she attended as a new DWW member in 1952. Josephine Winn introduced herself and asked what she wrote. "When I told her I wrote for the confessions (magazines), she physically drew away from me. We later became good friends." What Duran didn't add was these stories supported her family. From 1959-1966 she was a fulltime *Detroit Free Press* columnist and feature writer and later a daily radio show host and lecturer.

Although there are still battles to be won, today's women have made great strides toward achieving equality and acceptance on all levels. While home and family will always be important subjects for women writers, at this juncture, the approach tends to be more universal, more applicable to the shrinking global society.

Cynthia LaFerle, one of the busiest writers in the business, builds on small incidents of family life to convey a strong value system.

In her story, "The Religion Book," Beth Aviv Greenbaum uses what happened at a committee meeting in Southfield, MI, to shed light on the complicated Israeli/Palestinian relationship. Debra Darvick writes about family life for Jewish and secular publications.

Through her collections of short stories and poetry, Pearl Kastran Ahnen, has made a significant contribution to the Greco-American oeuvre. Her most recent book is *Balancing Act*, 1997.

Mira Stefaniuk translates Ukranian prose and poetry.

Elizabeth Chiu King's demonstrations of Chinese cooking, based on her four books, promote a better understanding of her native land as well as admiration for her culinary skills.

Many members such as Marion Marzolf, Gladys Leithauser, Bradford Field, Jr. and Barry Knister, have balanced writing careers with fulltime, university level teaching.

For readers of home and interior design magazines looking for a lifestyle to which they'd like to become accustomed, Suzy Farbmen and Marge Jackson Levin provide provocative copy. Carla Schwartz, editor, packages the good life of this area in the colorful pages of *Style,* a regional magazine.

As modern-day advance scouts, writers such as Iris Sanderson Jones, Doris Scharfenberg, Mary Quinley, Carol Spicer and the versatile Mary Augusta Rodgers (Schoen), find the best places and sometimes less traveled roads for vacationers to enjoy.

In modern society's race to achieve, DWW members run at the front of the pack. Carolyn Vosburg Hall, mother, grandmother, artist and literary activist, recently published her 12th book. Margaret Hillert has published 75 books for juveniles and hundreds of poems.

Among the many in-demand DWW speakers are: poets Margo LaGattuta, Kathleen Leo, and Naomi Long Madgett; fiction writers, Ingrid Tomey, Ruth Ryan Langan and Sarah Wolf; and historian Annick Hivert-Carthew.

For members such as poet Judith Goran (now retired clinical psychologist) and poet and fiction writer and Aline Soules, librarian, writing is a second, but not necessarily a secondary career.

Elizabeth Kane Buzzelli's love of the beauty of Michigan's more remote areas is evident in many of her stories. No better example of that than her essay published here in which the beaver's actions become a metaphor for living.

Julie Candler, found the national spotlight with her column, "Woman at the Wheel," that ran in every issue of *Woman's Day* magazine from 1964-1982. She now writes regularly for several national business publications on technical subjects

Darlene House, advertising copywriter and public relations specialist, is firmly established in the business field as a writer of many articles as well as a leader of corporate training seminars.

Still, even at the millennium, in a technically-oriented society, some things never change. Women balance home and family responsibilities with their desire to write. It may happen in an office, at a kitchen table while the baby naps and dinner cooks, late at night while the household sleeps, or on a shady back porch while the kids shoot hoops. But, somewhere, somehow it happens.

Like the legions of American women who made quilts to satisfy their practical and creative spirits, women writers start with scraps from life. But their scraps are experiences, glimpses, and memories. These coupled with a driving urge to communicate and a love of reading and writing set the stage for the magic of the printed word.

From such scraps and desires, even a person whose life is largely family-centered may produce intriguing fiction, fantasy, or morality tales that touch on harsh realities. For a good writer is a committed reader and an apt listener. And in any neighborhood, on any street, in any family there are stories about what happens when things turn ugly, or strange — or wonderful.

From the time she first began, nobody did a better job with this than Joyce Carol Oates, a member of Detroit Women Writers in the 1960's. She speaks about her love of writing in the Afterword to her book, titled, *Where Are You Going, Where Have You Been?*

"My lifelong love of writing is underlaid by a great love of reading, itself rooted in childhood."

The excitment that grabs and will not let go emanates from that moment when the story takes over and the writer becomes the vehicle for relating it.

It is the shared experience of such a moment of creation and the urge to keep repeating and improving upon it, that lights the fire and fuels the friendship among writers.

That is what unites the diverse personalities that have in the past and continue to make up the membership of Detroit Women Writers.

Corinne Abatt, co-editor

CHECK OUT HOW YOU AGE AT THE SUPERMARKET
by Corinne Abatt
Detroit News, 1998

As editor of the arts section for the Observer and Eccentric Newspapers, Abatt won the Governor's Media Honor Roll Award in 1990. She joined DWW in 1992 and, since her retirement, her freelance articles and stories have appeared in local, regional, and national publications.

While supermarkets and hardware stores aren't the most romantic places to mark the passing of time, they happen to be my choice for several reasons.

For one thing they are where I've been hanging out for several hours each week for decades. Sure, I know the great and talented are far more sophisticated about how they take measure of their years.

Truth is another reason not to take these places too lightly. You may kid yourself when you look in a mirror. Your friends and family may lie to keep you happy. But without a lot of plastic surgery, you can't fake reactions of strangers in the dairy or plumbing departments.

And believe me, reactions change. At the supermarket, when I had a baby and a couple of toddlers in tow, lone men gave me plenty of space — like you could have the whole cereal aisle to yourself if the kids were really wired. Only other mothers with a batch of crying kids would invade your space, mostly because that truism about misery loving company still goes.

A decade or so later, there was the Saturday night I went grocery shopping after dropping the kids off at the Teen Center. Nobody told me the produce department was known as a great place for picking up more than fruit and veggies.

Anyway, this guy siddles up behind me saying how much he digs really ripe tomatoes and would I help him pick some out. In those days before Anita Hill took a stand on sexual harassment, you didn't scream for the manager, you either told the guy he belonged in aisle two with the canned corn or you pushed your cart over his foot and left. I chose the latter.

Then there was the Sunday morning when the kids were long gone from the fold, and the only thing in my basket was a couple of single portion frozen dinners. A distinguished looking, older man asked me which bran cereal I preferred. Our discussion moved from Kelloggs All-Bran to granola on Spain's Costa del Sol before a frantic, surprisingly young woman came barreling down the aisle with a cart full of Gerber jars and a crying baby. "I said you were to find diapers.

We don't need cereal." He disappeared like snow in late April, but not without a smile of longing.

Just the other day, I was reminded of that incident with a wave of nostalgia. A guy nosing along the baking supply shelf where I was checking prices on brown sugar for cookies for my grandkids almost bumped into me. He looked up and complained loudly that cornmeal wasn't where it was supposed to be. I wanted to tell him that after a certain age, nothing is where it's supposed to be. Instead I pointed to a package of cornbread mix. His disdain for that suggestion immediately established a bond between us. He later came back to tell me the real cornmeal was on aisle five in case I needed some.

This time, safety registered in every line of face. If the attractive woman behind him in line was his wife, I am certain she will brag to her neighbors about how kind her husband is to little old ladies in Reeboks.

My big, recent thrill happened in the hardware store. On the checkout counter was an ugly toy spaceman emitting tinkly sounds. I was hoping the thing wasn't on my grandson's birthday list when the guy in front turns, gives me a quick smile and says, "John Williams plays it in a different key."

Not only did he assume I knew who John Williams is, which I do, he assumed I knew the notes were from Williams' composition, "Star Wars," which finally hit me on the drive home. In either case, his assumptions provided a moment of satisfaction. While I no longer look like pick-up fodder, I don't look completely stupid either.

This surprising non-threatening persona, which appears about the mid 60's, comes as a bonus. People want to talk to you. Sometimes you get a whole life story, as I once did, while waiting for a price check at T.J. Maxx. I think one woman made up her mind to divorce her husband while we chatted waiting for a seat at the deli.

It's heart-warming to finally be welcomed as a non threatening member of the human race — definitely worth the wait.

BACK PORCH

Aline Soules

Michigan Poets, Citizens Insurance Company of America, 1997

Soules, a member of DWW since 1995, writes poetry and short fiction.

A back porch is honest.
Old rambling roses
you planted when you moved in
crawl untended up its poles
and trail over the roof.
The wooden planks are cracked
and the flaking paint is splotched
with green and red
from your children's paintbox.

Slouched on an old chair
no longer good enough
for the living room,
you don't worry about
offending sensibilities
with old work clothes or dirty boots.
You relax with a cup of tea,
leave a wet ring on the sloping floor
and smell the roses with the chicken
roasting for dinner in the kitchen beyond.

Leaning back, you think
about nothing and everything —
when your son is due back
from hockey, the light
through the rose petals, the diet
you'll never start, the last time
you made love.

As the sun slants deeper,
shadows lengthen across the floor
mingle against the sides
of the house — roses, the chair,
the poles that connect
the railings to the roof,
and you.

A PHILOSOPHICAL DEBATE WITH A BEAVER

by Elizabeth Kane Buzzelli
Traverse Magazine, 1995

Buzzelli, a DWW member since 1978, writes short stories, novels (Gift Of Evil), nonfiction, newspaper and magazine articles. She is a sought-after teacher and lecturer at conferences and with the Creative Writers In The School Program. She was awarded an Art Serve/Michigan grant in 1998 to finish her book, "Simple Things; An Up North Life.."

The pond is a quiet, magical pool formed at the base of steep glacial-cut hills. Not very large, quite overgrown, maybe it doesn't even deserve the name "pond" but it is a body of still water, not swampy. You can walk down to the edge in most places without sinking. I think it's only been a pond since the beginning of this century. Before a road was built between the pond and Starvation Lake, the water drained right down to the lake without interference. The stream bed it cut is still visible.

The road was made by men erecting a long embankment. To build it across this low spot they dug a series of deep holes, transferred the sand to the new roadbed and left the water to collect, one end of the pond still stretching out toward the lake, but foiled now, trapped.

I don't know how deep the pond is. I got waders to get out there with a measuring pole but haven't had the guts to actually step off the edge yet. A long branch, stuck down at water's edge shows it to be two feet in some spots, three and more in others — where the muskrats excavated. I have no idea how deep the center is, but I suspect it's shallow straight across.

The pond is home to a hundred or more painted turtles and any number of different species of frog and salamander, not to mention skating bugs, mosquitoes, dragonflies, and ducks. A very busy place.

When we first came here I vowed the pond would stay just as it was, that I wouldn't tear up trees or bushes, plant things, and make it different. Everything was perfectly balanced. Who was I to tamper with it, to tame it, to make it into something other than it was? I vowed to be ecologically correct.

Then the beaver moved in.

It was June. Before I saw him, I saw his work. Trees were down, as if in windfalls. Three long, grass-flattened slides appeared on the hillsides, all ending at the water's edge. One morning I came on a freshly downed tree gnawed into perfect lengths as if the beaver were fitted with a measuring tape. He must have planned to move his lumber that night, sliding his logs down to the pond's bottom.

By July I still hadn't seen the beaver, but as more and more trees fell I began to wish fervently that he'd go away. Who knew what he'd do to the careful balance the turtles and frogs had achieved? And worse than anything else was the hole he was tearing in the curtain of green protecting my pond from the road that ran along its upper rim.

I couldn't bear what was happening, but what could I do? Consider a live trap? Take him someplace else? Where? And did I have the right? I was stuck with my own non-intervention vow.

One evening in late July I went to sit by the pond just at dusk. Everything was absolutely still, bathed with that wonderful mauve light that comes only at sunset. There wasn't a rustle in the trees. No movement in the grass. It was one of the most perfect evenings I've ever experienced. In that place, beside the pond, not even a mosquito broke the quiet.

Suddenly there came a loud explosion of sound. Water rose in geysers as if someone had thrown a rock into the pond. I leaped up, scared to death. There came another explosion of sound and water. Then stillness. My nemesis, the beaver, swam at the far end. On seeing me, and obviously not wanting to be disturbed, he had slammed his big tail against the surface of the water, sending jets high into the air and me scrambling for safety.

After a while, when no more explosions came, I gathered my dignity and sat back down on the bench. The beaver and I watched each other. He swam in large concentric circles calculated as snubs of his nose at me. I refused to budge. After another 20 minutes I got up and, with a lot of noise of my own (throat clearing and finger snapping and foot stomping), I turned my back on him and walked to the house, chin just slightly in the air as if to show him who was afraid of whom.

By September over a hundred trees of varying sizes — from very small to sizable — were down and a hovel of twigs was growing in the pond. He wasn't going to go away and obviously I wasn't going to do anything about it so some rethinking was in order.

This upstart beaver knocked my sentimental philosophy of a static rural idyll all to pieces. The pond wasn't going to remain unchanged — despite me. Nature is definitely not the sweet state of endless stasis I had imagined. It is flux and constant upheaval. It is growth. It is destruction and renewal; and not to be interfered with by any single idea I had formed. In fact, I guess I'm not in charge of the pond at all. Like every other living thing, I'm only a part of the whole — turtles, frogs, skating bugs, beaver — and me.

So now I'm considering a few iris around the shore, like Monet's pond at Giverny. This spring there will be new pools of sunshine along the slopes (thanks to the beaver), perfect for a few crabapple trees; maybe a couple of mountain ash. It could be beautiful, this new pond. Different than I had intended, but then, who am I to look a gift beaver in the mouth?

PACK RAT
by Naomi Long Madgett
from Exits and Exits, Lotus Press, 1988

My trouble is
I always try to save
everything

old clocks and calendars
expired words buried
in open graves

But hoarded grains of sand
keep shifting as rivers
redefine boundaries and seasons

lengths of old string
rolled into neat balls
neither measure nor bind

nor do shelves laden with rancid sweets
preserve
what ants continually nibble away

Love should be eaten
while it is ripe
and then the pits discarded

Lord give me the last
one cracked bowl holding
absolutely nothing

CALL OF THE WILD
by Cynthia La Ferle
Cleveland Plain Dealer Sunday Magazine, 1996

LaFerle, a DWW member since 1987, writes a weekly column for the Daily Tribune of Royal Oak. She has published numerous pieces in local and national publications. She lectures and teaches creative writing.

Thanks to my previous career as a travel editor, I know how to rate a mattress and what constitutes an immaculate motel bathroom. I'm blissfully at home in a wicker rocker on the porch of a New England country inn, sipping an iced tea while watching the sun dip behind a mountain range.

But until my son joined Cub Scouts two years ago, my getaways did not include wilderness adventures. To me, communing with nature meant reading Thoreau and occasionally potting begonias. So spending a weekend in the woods — with a chorus of bullfrogs, sundry snakes, two dozen little boys and their suburban mothers — didn't sound like my idea of a good time.

Like most parents, however, I've learned to adapt.

And while I am not exactly what you'd call a happy camper, the Scouts have taught me to appreciate the Great Outdoors. In fact, this month I'll embark on my third annual "Mom & Me" camping weekend with my son's pack. These weekends were devised to encourage mother-and-son bonding, and to refute the theory that women will not sleep with bugs.

I've also learned that the experienced travel writer's motto ("Always pack light") doesn't apply to camping. On our first outing, for instance, my son fell into a bog within 15 minutes of our arrival at the campsite. He had to borrow my hiking boots until his own dried out the next day. Meanwhile, I had no choice but to tour the swamp in soggy tennis shoes.

"This weekend is an endurance test for parents," one mom confided, half-seriously.

The following year, I stuffed a half-dozen pairs of boots into the back of our Jeep but forgot my own raincoat. Of course, that was the weekend it poured and poured ... and poured.

I'll never forget the sight of six devoted mothers building a campfire, in the evening drizzle. (We were determined to do this thing right: We were going to roast every hot dog and melt every marshmallow we'd hauled along with our Duraflame logs.) Our boys, however, were smart enough to get out of the rain. When we tried to coax them to the camp fire, we found them in one of the cabins. They were hunkered around "Life," the board game of the moment.

"Bring the hot dogs in here," one 9-year-old demanded as he scooted his car-shaped marker across the board. "I'm getting ready to sell one of my houses and I'm having a midlife crisis!"

If we're very lucky, the hike to the public restrooms is only 13 minutes (uphill) from our campsite. The trick, I found, is to keep a spare flashlight in your sleeping bag so that you can grab it quickly if nature calls at 2 a.m.

Nobody sleeps much on these weekends. The kids are buzzing on caffeine, having consumed several gallons of Pepsi and Mountain Dew. The moms, smelling like a bonfire and desperately wishing for one hot shower, toss fitfully in their sleeping bags while the boys play flashlight games and tell ghost stories.

"Did you hear the one about the one-eyed man who went berserk in the northwoods and *was NEVER FOUND?"*

After two nights like these, the groggy drive back home on Sunday is tolerable only with a mug of instant coffee and the promise of a warm bath. Completely exhausted, my son and I usually are too tired to rehash the highlights of our trip.

But last year, on the way home, he mumbled, "Thanks for the weekend, Mom. Great weekend." It was a rare moment of sincere, unprompted gratitude.

Catching a glimpse of myself in the rearview mirror, I remembered I wasn't wearing makeup. My eyes looked older, and in an instant I saw the years racing past me like the cars on the expressway. My boy looked older, too, his lanky body slouched on the seat next to me.

Suddenly, that weekend — my endurance test — seemed awfully short. I was proud of myself for building fires and touching frogs.

THE BEAR FACTS: THE FIRST TEDDY BEAR
by Carolyn Vosburg Hall,
from The Teddy Bear Craft Book, Prentice Hall Press, 1983

Hall, a DWW member since 1976, is an artist and author of 12 books published by Double Day, Prentice Hall, Van Nostrand Reinhold and others. She has won awards for art work and writing, and was a newspaper art critic for 10 years. Her full-color Sewing For Your Garden was published in 1999.

Everybody loves a winner, so it's no surprise that more than one person claimed to be the inventor of the teddy bear. Nobody knows who made the first toy bear, but we do know who made the first one named "Teddy Bear."

In 1902 President Teddy Roosevelt went hunting in the South. His hunting companions caught a bedraggled adult bear, perhaps singed by a forest fire, and roped him to a tree for Roosevelt to shoot. Sportsman Roosevelt refused. Clifford Berryman, a political cartoonist, coupled this event with a current political incident concerning a border dispute between Mississippi and Louisiana. He portrayed Roosevelt refusing to "Draw... the line in Mississippi."

Berryman's first cartoon showing an angry, stubborn bear appeared in the *Washington Post* on November 16, 1902. A subsequent, more familiar, version of the cartoon appeared in the *Evening Star* with a more appealing shivering bear cub. The public loved Berryman's bears, which were reprinted literally millions of times and became the standard symbol of the Roosevelt Republicans.

It was probably the *Evening Star* cartoon that inspired Morris Michtom to create two small toy bears. Michtom, a Russian immigrant, had played with carved wooden toys in his childhood. He, like his countrymen, knew hundreds of folk tales about Russia's most famous bear, Mishka.

Michtom was always on the lookout for new ideas for his novelty and stationery store in Brooklyn. Both he and his wife, Rose, often made small playthings to sell. In the shop window, Michtom displayed the small bears he and Rose made using Berryman's cartoon as a model.

They did not have long to wait for public reaction. Five minutes later, a customer walked in to buy one of the bears. Orders for 12 bears came in that historic first day.

Overwhelmed by success, Michtom decided he should ask President Roosevelt's permission to name the bears after him. Michtom made a special bear and mailed it off to Washington. Roosevelt's famous reply arrived quickly. "Dear Mr. Michtom, I don't think my name is likely to be worth much in the toy bear business, but you are welcome to use it."

Before the end of the next year, Michtom established the Ideal Toy and Novelty Company (now Ideal Toy) and manufactured teddy bears by the hundreds. Michtom's son, later head of the company, maintained that nearly all bears produced in the United States between 1903 and 1906 came from Ideal, but since they couldn't patent the name at the time, many companies soon turned out teddy bears.

At the same time, the teddy bear was "invented" by Margarete Steiff and her nephew in Germany. Crippled by polio as a child, Margarete earned her living by making stuffed toys. Her little felt elephants delighted neighborhood children so much that she created other animals — a donkey, a pig, a horse, and a camel.

Descendants of Margarete Steiff describe her invention of the teddy bear as follows. By 1897, her business had grown to include several family members, among them her nephew Richard Steiff. As a student artist, he spent hours observing and sketching bears at the zoo. In 1902 he designed a fluffy mohair bear with movable head and limbs. Margarete doubted the plump bear made from expensive fabric would sell. It did not — until the following year at the Leipzig Toy Fair. An American buyer delighted with the cuddly bear ordered 3000!

Both the Steiff Company and the Ideal Toy Company began to sell hundreds of teddy bears, then millions! Innumerable bear objects followed: coloring and story books, postcards, paper dolls, clothing for bears, mechanical bears, bear decorations on dishes, and more. This fad passed, but teddy bears didn't fade away. Today, millions of teddy bears are sold each year.

TIGHT BEDS
by Margo LaGattuta
from Everywhere is Someplace Else, PlainView Press, 1998

LaGattuta joined DWW in 1980. She is Midwest editor for the PlainView Press in Texas. She edits poetry collections and is associate editor and writer for Suburban Lifestyles. She hosts a weekly radio program, Art In The Air.

My mother makes them with
hospital corners. *They should be*
tight, she says, *like envelopes*
that you slip into at night,
mail yourself straight through
till morning, and you'll come out
folded and clean as percale.

But I never dream that flat
or smooth anymore. I twist
a comforter till it rides up,
holds me tight as I fly into
my night journeys. I learned

to sleep tight from my ex-
husband, who kept climbing
invisible stairs at right
angles to my own. Our
dozing bodies had the look
of two frenzied egrets running
up and down opposite skyways.

But our son Adam had the wildest
bed of them all. His rose up high and
flew right through his bedroom door.
He was out-of-body, cruising the ceiling,
yet still in his own twin bed. He took a
sharp left at the front hallway.

Now he's flown all the way out
to Chicago; he's even held on tight
to his patched-up crazy quilt
for a loop de loop around L.A.
While here in his empty room,

the child he was still calls for
one more drink of water, for
another wild story of how we
used to live, and for one more
frantic chance to be tucked in tight.

UP AN UNFAMILIAR TRAIL
by Margo LaGattuta
Someplace Else, PlainView Press, 1998

I see tiny hairs on the back of my
idea stand up. Wind combs through them
as if pushing curtains back, and I see
various trees and a sly mountain.

The mountain is what I don't know.
It stands over me, ominous sometimes
in its silent snow, has a trail for goats
to wander up, a ragged trail full of
potholes and a cool, dancing river.

The river runs right through what I
don't know, invites me in for a dip.
One toe, another, and a shiver goes
up my back. What I don't know is
getting deep now, and by nightfall I
might be afraid. But still I walk in,

knowing I'll never see the full
view in this waking world.

Ah, but the water, the buoyancy
when I stop resisting the flow.
The river in what I don't know
holds me up, prepares me
for the complicated climb.

EVENING: A WATERCOLOR
by Gladys Garner Leithauser
The Christian Science Monitor, 1959

Only a few of us rode
in the gathering dark.
On the glistening pavement,
lights mirrored themselves in a chain,
Linked-gold, where the bus swung wide
to circle the park,
Blue-green, where the factory windows
started again.

Nobody spoke, but the way
did not seem at all long.
The sibilant tires reassured us
in thrumming refrain,
And the bus driver whistled
the cool little flakes of a song
That hovered a moment like snow
and were lost in the rain.

MUSEUM PIECE NO. 16228
by Elaine Watson
Ball state University Forum, 1980,
reprinted in Anthology of Magazine Verse & Yearbook of American Poetry, 1981

You lie there, with your line of stiff red griffens
dissolving into linen colorless with age:
a scrap of history pressed beneath some glass.
The museum card says "circa 1550."

Whose body-warmth enhanced your gaudy threads
and made those griffens prance
and dance with sixteenth century flesh
now long dispersed and lost

but for this little scrap that says
"Remember me?

SOLITARY TIMES
by Lynne Meredith Cohn
from the Advocate, 1977

Cohn, a member of DWW since 1997, is a poet and journalist with work in the Detroit News, The Jewish News, Woman's Own, and New York Newsday. Her poetry book, Driving Off The Horizon, was published by IM Press. She teaches adult and children's writing workshops.

Some days,
I pour blueberries into a bowl
and watch the sky move.
Small furry animals run races across the yard.
The crocuses in the garden open
like fists unfolding. I think of kissing you
and close my eyes, wrap an open
palm around a mug of hot tea,
the heat crawling inside
my skin like you did,
curl into the bent pages
of a book I've read before
and put a pot of water to boil for noodles.
These days are invitations,
quiet streams running over rocks.
The trees stretch into children
hanging from a jungle gym
and I record it all wordlessly,
the way the night sneaks
into the mailbox
and waits.

SHARING THE ROAD WITH A TRUCK

by Julie Candler

from Woman at The Wheel, 1964 (reprinted several times)

Candler, a DWW member since 1961, has written hundreds of magazine articles. She was the first woman in the nation to write an automotive column for the major women's magazine, Woman's Day, appearing there monthly for 18 years. She is now contributing editor for Nation's Business and Corp! magazines.

It was a truck driver's wife who suggested that "Woman at the Wheel, could help drivers by giving them a look at traffic from the trucker's point of view. Mrs. Jacqueline McCreesh, of Victoria, British Columbia, wrote to say she thinks information about the 17 million trucks on our highways should be included in the manuals given every new driver.

"A truck is not a car and cannot do the same things a car can do," says Mrs. McCreesh. She adds that because many drivers are not aware of this, she hears story after story from her husband about accidents and near-accidents involving trucks.

To learn firsthand from truckers how drivers can share the road with them in the safest way possible, I attended last January's winter-driving tests conducted by the National Safety Council in Stevens Point, Wisconsin. I even drove a twelve-ton Mack truck to see firsthand how the freight haulers view the problem. Here's what I learned:

Trucks Need More Distance for Stopping

One of Mrs. McCreesh's stories is about the vegetable man who made a left-hand turn in front of her husband's truck. "The man stopped and signaled at the same time, giving the driver behind him no warning, so away my husband merrily bumped across a ditch and into an empty field." The vegetable man was not aware that a truck, especially a loaded one, needs more stopping distance than a car.

"Roughly, the stopping distance increases with the size and weight of the truck," says winter-driving tester Lewis Kibbee, director of engineering for the American Trucking Association. The Safety Council estimates that a passenger car's braking distance on dry pavement at twenty miles per hour averages twenty feet.

The moral: Never pull out into a lane of traffic a short distance ahead of a truck. If you pass him, don't cut back in too soon. Wait until you see the front of his cab in your rearview mirror. Always slow down for a turn, and never stop suddenly in front of a truck.

Trucks May Stop Quickly

A somewhat different situation develops at high speeds, when a car lacks the stability to stop quickly and jamming on the brakes may throw it out of control. Lewis Kibbee points out that trucks have greater stability and bigger brakes. "Don't follow closely, because if he has to make a panic stop at high speeds, you can't possibly stop as fast as he can. You will run right under him." Truckers advise sticking to one car length for every ten miles of speed.

Trucks Need Cornering Room

When you see the driver of a big trailer truck signaling for a turn, watch for the possibility that he will move slightly in the opposite direction before making the turn. Without going left first to make plenty of room for the trailer to come around, it might run off the road. At a city intersection, the trailer could climb the curb.

So when you see a truck driver veer slightly left, watch his turn signals. They may indicate he is getting ready to turn right. Whatever you do, don't try to pass to his right. If he is making a ninety degree right turn, you may get caught in a squeeze play between trailer and curb.

Truckers Always Want an Out

The trucker has been trained always to leave himself an out — someplace to go for an escape route in case of an emergency. He prefers not to have you driving alongside him in the next lane because it leaves him nowhere to go if trouble pops up on the other side. Once they are committed, drivers should go on around, unless they see trouble ahead. In that case, they should fall back behind the truck.

Truckers Depend on Their Outside Rearview Mirrors

At night, never turn your headlights to bright when a truck is within their range ahead. Your brights reflecting off the big outside rearview mirrors on the left and right of the cab can be blinding to a driver. He must watch those mirrors constantly, day and night to check his load, the tires and the traffic behind and on either side.

Some Trucks Have Blind Spots on the Right

Never pass a long trailer truck to the right, because the driver may not see you. Many trucks have blind spots that make it impossible to see everything happening in that direction. Most of the big cabs are equipped with convex mirrors to give them a good picture of what is happening alongside them on their right. But don't depend on it.

There's one exception to the rule. You may pass on the right on a multiple lane freeway, but only; after communicating your intention to the driver. He will know you are planning to pass him if you blink your headlights or give him a quick tap on the horn. If a big truck is hogging a left-hand lane, the driver is not following the truckers' rules.

Trucks Are Jolted by Turbulence Too

Brace yourself for a sudden gust of wind and momentary difficulty in steering if you pass a truck at high speed. Whether the trucker is traveling in the same or in the opposite direction, he too will feel the turbulence created by the breakup of air resistance between the two vehicles. You can lessen the force of the turbulence by slowing down and pulling over and he will try to do the same. The wider the gap between your car and the truck, the less turbulence you will feel.

Truckers Dread Jackknifing

"Under wet conditions, when the brakes on a truck are slammed on, the truck will very likely start to skid," warns trucker's wife Jacqueline McCreesh. "It takes a lot of experience to handle the emergency." The rear axle of the tractor may skid sideways or the rear of its big trailer may skid around and the two will end up at a jackknife angle to one another. On wet or icy highways, be especially careful to give truckers room to maneuver.

Truckers Want to Help You

"If you have trouble on the road," says Lewis Kibbee, "a truck driver is a good person to have come up and offer to help. These fellows are good in emergencies. They can get their flares out or signal for somebody to send for help. Local trucks are radio-equipped and can call their dispatcher to telephone for an ambulance.

The truckers usually know the area and the location of the wreckers and the police. If you get stuck in snow in below-freezing weather, no truck driver will leave you."

In a bad snowstorm, get behind a big truck and the driver will help you by breaking the road open for you. If there is a big drift someplace, chances are that his big diesel engine can get him through.

A truck ahead can also guide you in a bad rainstorm, but it may splash puddles of rainwater over your windshield. Conscientious truckers avoid this possibility by using mud flaps behind their wheels. But when it comes to the blinding spurts of water that hit you as you pass a truck in wet weather, the truckers cannot help. Advises Kibbee, "You get the splash when you are right alongside the wheels, so just don't stay there. Go right on through. But when you get up to the next set of wheels, there will be more splash."

Trucks Cannot Signal You to Pass

Truck drivers are instructed not to signal other motorists. They are forbidden by federal law from using turn signals for any purpose other than signaling turns. Fleet safety experts tell them to use headlights only for illumination, never for assuming the responsibility for another driver's safety by telling him that it is safe to pass.

You may notice a trucker who blinks his headlights at you, day or night, just after you pass. "If that happens," says Robert Purcell of the National Safety Council's fleet safety-training division, "he's just saying that he knows you are there and that you are going to pull in."

Truckers Are Proud of Their Records

Truck drivers are proud of records that show they have a far lower accident rate than passenger-car drivers. If you see a driver who is bullying and bad-mannered, or doing something dangerous, take down the number of the cab and the number of the trailer, as well as the name of the company. Call or write them, giving them the numbers, plus the time and place of the incident. Your complaint will become part of that driver's record and will remind him to be more courteous in the future.

A trucker is a businessman with a big responsibility: safe delivery of huge loads of valuable freight. Respect him.

As Mrs. Lewis Kibbee said, "I think if drivers take the attitude that the truckers are their friends and not their enemies, they will find the truckers courteous and good friends on the road."

THREE POEMS
by Gerry Tamm
Wall Street Journal

Tamm, a DWW member since 1986, publishes poems in the McGuffin, The Bridge, and Mobius, She has appeared in Highlights For Children and the Wall Street Journal.

NETWORKING, TECH TYPE

Improved communication
Is merely an illusion.
We've gone from office grapevine
To terminal confusion.
4/11/89

NO PRETTY PACKAGE

When future archaeologists
Engage in history mapping,
They'll find the 1980s
Encased in plastic wrapping.
12/19/89

MAN-MADE TERMS?

The neighborhood ladies chat every day,
Or kaffeeklatsch if you prefer,
A practice reserved for the female sex;
The men at the office *confer!*
9/21/89

PRIME TIME POWER PLAY
By Marj Levin
Detroit Free Press, 1986

Levin, a DWW members since 1956, is editor of Detroit Cigar Lifestyles. She co-founded the National Organization For Women (NOW) in Michigan. She freelances for many publications, hosted a weekly show on Channel 56, A Woman's Place, and reported for the Detroit Free Press for 13 years.

Day is done. The dishwasher's swishing. The kids are in bed. If this is Tuesday, it must be "Moonlighting." Your one-and-only plops beside you on the couch and zaps the remote control.

Ah, there's Maddie on the screen wearing white to work again, and David nursing another hangover. You love it until the first commercial break. Click, goes the remote and another commercial flashes on the screen. Click, click, click - three stations later he locates a basketball game.

You hold your tongue for 90 seconds. "Turn it back, the commercial's over!"

"OK, OK, just a minute."

"Come on, I want to see it."

"OK. OK!"

Click, click, click - back to Maddie and David. Why is he screaming about a pigeon in a green hat? It's three minutes into the scene and you've lost the thread.

Another battle in the remote control war is being fought.

In the last half of the 20th century, women have won the right to work as telephone linemen, drive long distance trailers, and sit on the bench of the Supreme Court. But they have yet to share, let alone control, the channel changer.

Granted, few American women would be reckless enough to reach for it during the sacrosanct Super Bowl, but what about the rest of the year? Why are women still second-class citizens in the land of television — relegated to the second set, the black -and-white portable, the one without remote control?

Their frustration has led more than one wife to declare that if there was ever a divorce in the family it would be because of television. To investigate this fomenting crisis, the *Free Press* interviewed dozens of women, a few men, and several professionals in the field of mediation.

Many women, even those who work as many hours as their husbands, have to wrestle for their television rights.

Don and Jean Verslype of Birmingham have been married 29 years, and Jean says it's a confrontation every night. She is a secretary in a real estate office: he works at Ford Motor Co. Instead of relaxing after dinner, Jean says, "the clicker drives me wacko."

Verslype says her husband will find a Red Wings game, then click to a talk show. "If he doesn't like what he hears, he'll click it back to the game. That's what we do half the evening. I had to fight to watch 'Matlock' last night. I said, quit clicking that thing all night long and give me a chance."

Many women who don't have the stamina just give up. Some rationalize their surrender by saying he watches more television (sports and newscasts) than she does, so she "lets" him have it.

Possession *is* nine-tenths of the law, Eunice Stone of Birmingham reminds us. Stone says that when the remote device appeared, women automatically turned it, as well as the written directions, over to their husbands. "And they never retrieved it," says Stone, who says she now reads all directions herself.

Some women survive life with a channel hopper by watching another set. Amelie Harvey of Detroit says her husband, Allen, watches sports; she watches movies. "But we have two televisions with remote control, one in the den and one in the bedroom, so I go there."

Most families do not have two separate but equal sets. Even those who do may not find watching solo much fun. Betty Forman of Detroit has a friend who has two sets, "but she'd rather sit in misery with her husband than watch alone."

Forman says her ex-husband's television habits weren't the sole reason for her divorce, "but the remote control did drive me nuts. I'd just get up and leave the room. I've never been happier than I am now - without a television on."

Some wives have learned to grin and bear it. Bill Schoen of Birmingham readily admits that his wife, Mary Augusta, "hates like hell to have the channels changed. She'd love to get rid of the clicker, but then I'd have to get up to change channels, because I get bored with commercials."

"It's one of those problems that has no solution — short of maybe murder," says Mary Augusta Schoen. "To avoid commercials he'll switch to a program about Star Wars, then to Miami Vice, then to something else, it's surrealistic, like a Fellini movie."

She thinks impatience is an inborn trait in men and leads to channel-switching: "Women are used to putting up with things, waiting it out. Men take it as a personal affront if they get bored."

One fact clearly emerges: Controlling the remote depends on gender, not marital status. Lester Van Maele, who lives with his mother and brother in Warren, says, "I control the remote because it was my idea to get it. My mother watches what I watch and so does my brother. My brother has to, because I'm stronger in body and mind than he is."

When young siblings fight among themselves for the remote, it can irritate parents, but when they become teenagers the conflict can become a parent-child issue. Fathers and sons think of the remote control as a symbol of power and authority and sometimes grapple for it. One Birmingham father bought a newer, universal remote for himself on which he's programmed all the television sets in the house.

And whoever controls the universal remote controls the home. Some family members may have to take adult education courses in remote control programming to stay equal to the competition.

Carolyn Capkowski of East Lansing says her roommate's boyfriend is king of the couch potatoes. "He just sits in front of the TV in our apartment and flips it all day long. He doesn't watch, just switches," Capkowski says. "And it's not even his home. It's not even his TV set. It's mine, and it drives me crazy. My roommate worries about what will happen when they get married."

Having two different sets with remote control helps work out differences for couples who can afford it and enjoy some solitude, says Southfield marital and family therapist, Ann Katz. But having only one remote control and a man who keeps a firm grasp on it can indicate something else.

"It's hard for men to give up certain positions," says Katz. "They have to have some sense of remaining head of the household and TV may be the last stronghold. Holding on to the remote is probably a vestige of the old image of the father sitting in the one big easy chair, holding down the fort."

If the wife wants an equal share of TV time, compromises have to be negotiated. He likes to watch sports, she prefers sitcoms, but if she says, "I'll be willing to sit with you, if you're willing to sit with me," they may be able to work out an equitable schedule, Katz says.

Learning how to communicate and resolve television differences could extend to other areas of the marriage, says Katz. The ultimate sharing of each other's interests would enhance the total relationship, "if the caring is there."

Detroit labor relations attorney, Linn Hynds advises that "the first maxim in negotiation is to do it from a position of strength."

With so many women already weak in this arena, how would they gather their resources?

"The ultimate is the power of a strike. The wife has to make that known, that she's prepared to strike!" She could stop performing many household tasks, "things she does every day," says Hynds.

Management then has three choices, he says. "They might try to perform the tasks themselves. Or they could hire replacements, but that could become sticky and probably illegal. Thirdly, they could just not get the job done."

Eventually the two sides would have to sit down and bargain.

If one fails to live up to the agreement, they then enter the arena of labor relations grievances, says Hynds.

"If one becomes dissatisfied under the contract he could go to an independent to review the merits of the case to make a dispassionate ruling. This might involve the children or other family members."

Its worth a try... any day after Super Bowl Sunday.

BAT

by Vivian DeGain

from Variations on The Ordinary, PlainView Press, 1995

Insomnia hangs from the rafters,
a tiny velvet umbrella
that folds up into itself.
Its eyes, blue glacial ice,
accuse me of sloth,
of being lazy and disorganized.
Like echolocation,
I throw it out and it comes back again,
amplified mosquitoes
that murmur lists of chores and more.

Its pointy ears of silk and fur,
are cupped for sonar,
hear my heart's longings
for a day with nothing to do,
for an afternoon in the park
watching clouds,
or a group of college boys in tight jeans.
Instead of being forty with three kids,
I'm eighteen and have a Frisbee,
which I throw into the air.

I hear the saucer whir in the dark overhead.
I feel the whirl by my face.
It's silky and black,
a small soaring boomerang the size of my hand.
Wings of webbed skin,
its fingers brush a line across my lips
and sail in the moonlight.

Sleep would be a blessing,
but the bat circles in the night.
It glides through the murky fog
and sniffs the smells of salt and blood
and nags and nags to feed on me.

CHICKEN ON SKEWERS

by Elizabeth Chiu King and Donna H. Dean

from A Wok A Week, China Books and Periodicals, 1998

King, a DWW member since 1988, writes Chinese cook books. She has appeared on many TV and radio programs, and writes for newspapers.

This communal dish gets everyone involved in the preparation, cooking *and* eating! Ideal for Summer — or anytime you fancy chicken — this low-calorie and tasty dish can be served as an appetizer or entree. The whiskey in the marinade adds zip, but dry white wine is a good, while less tasty, substitute.

1 medium chicken breast, skinned, boned and partially frozen

24 to 28 8-inch bamboo skewers

MARINADE

1 teaspoon cornstarch	1 tablespoon ketchup
1/2 teaspoon sugar	1 tablespoon oyster flavored sauce
1/2 teaspoon baking soda	1 tablespoon whiskey
1/8 teaspoon white pepper	1 teaspoon grated ginger root
1 tablespoon hoisin sauce	1 teaspoon minced garlic

1. In a large bowl, mix the marinade ingredients until smooth. Set aside.
2. Trim the fat and cut the breast into very thin slices, about 3 inches long and 1 inch wide. You should get about 25 slices. Add the sliced chicken to the marinade. Mix well, let stand for 30 minutes or longer.
3. Prepare the outdoor grill or preheat the oven on broil for 5 minutes. If cooking indoors, line a rimmed cookie sheet with aluminum foil.
4. After the chicken has marinated for at least 30 minutes, weave a skewer like a needle through the center of each slice. If slices are short, combine two or more on one skewer. Place the skewers side by side on the cookie sheet for inside broiling or on a platter to take outside to the grill. Mix the remaining marinade with 1/4 cup of cold water and pour over the skewers.
5. Cook about 4 inches from the heat for 8 minutes on the first side and 7 minutes on the second. Serve hot.

Preparation Time: 25-30 minutes	Marinating time: 30 minutes
Cooking Time: 15 minutes	Serves 8

Each serving: 52 Calories/ 8 Calories from Fat/ 15% Calories from Fat

CHINESE INGREDIENTS

Many Chinese ingredients are now common items on supermarket shelves: soy sauce, canned water chestnuts, wonton wrappers, curry powder, Maggi Seasoning, and sesame seeds. Those listed below are carried in some supermarkets and all Chinese or Oriental markets.

Chinese Dried Black Mushrooms (Dried Shitake Mushrooms): Before slicing or cooking, soak these dried mushrooms in warm water. Though expensive, they weigh little — so you get a lot for your money — and they add a unique flavor to the dish. They store indefinitely in a refrigerated, tightly covered container.

Chinese Broccoli (Gailay): A luscious, crunchy hybrid of broccoli and kale. Great fiber and flavor.

Five-spice powder: A reddish-brown powder made from ground cinnamon, cloves, fennel, dried peppercorn and star anise. Keeps indefinitely on the shelf.

Glassy Noodles (Mung Bean Thread): Packaged in dry bundles, these noodles must soak in cold water before cooking. During soaking the noodles become transparent. Dry noodles keep indefinitely.

Hoisen Sauce: A thick reddish-brown sweet sauce made from wheat flour, soy beans, sugar, garlic, chili paste, and vinegar. Hoisin sauce is a delicious seasoning and dipping sauce. Stores for months in a tightly-covered, refrigerated bottle or jar.

Hunan Chili Paste: A fiery and pungent condiment made from soy beans, red hot chili, garlic, and other spices. Hunan Chili Paste is both a seasoning and a dip. Stores for months in a tightly-covered, refrigerated bottle or jar.

Jasmine Rice: So named because of its fragrant aroma, this rice cooks just like regular white rice.

Oyster Flavored Sauce: A dark-brown, thick sauce made from soy sauce, corn starch, and other seasonings. Oyster-flavored sauce blends and enriches food flavors and imparts a velvety texture to the finished dish. Stores indefinitely in the bottle when refrigerated.

Pepper Corns (Dried Sichuan Peppercorns): Products of the Sichuan region of China, these reddish-brown peppercorns are highly aromatic and mildly hot. The Chinese usually combine them with whole star anise for a special and favorite seasoning. They store indefinitely on the shelf in covered containers.

Sesame Seed Oil: Made from toasted sesame seeds, this oil serves as an ingredient in salad dressings and as a flavoring agent. It is seldom used as a cooking oil because it is expensive and smokes at a lower temperature. Stores indefinitely in a tightly covered bottle.

Straw Mushrooms: Cultivated in beds of straw and usually sold canned, these delightful wee fellows add a delicate flavor to any dish. Leftover portions keep for about a week when stored in water, covered, and refrigerated.

THE WOMAN WITH MELON BREASTS
Lorene Erickson
from the MacGuffin, 1989

The woman had a chest like a breakfast table. Fried eggs. Burnt toast. Crisped bacon. Formica.

The woman wanted melon breasts. Ripe, round, full of smell and juice. Sweet to serve with prosciutto. In *European Life and Travel* she'd seen a picture of melons, chilled on a glass plate with raspberry sherbet. Served on a plank table. The table on the lawn in front of the eight hundred year old farmhouse. The family, ruddy-cheeked, dressed in layers of linens, the woman with full breasts, the daughters with potential in their eyes, the man and boys tousled and flushed with the power of fecundity.

The sure happiness of those people was more than she could bear. She turned her back on her kitchen and drove west to Howell, home of the Honeyrock melon with ropy veins and lush meat.

The woman stopped at a road-side stand. Melons spilled out of peck baskets and bushel baskets. Fields of melons rolled out like carpet behind the house which was behind the stand. Too many melons. They would rot in the harvest sun, their overripe melon smell rising like smoke over the fences toward the highway. Rotted egg yolks. A glut of seeds.

The round young girls running the stand lifted dollars from outstretched hands. The woman became confused. Which ones to choose? They looked the same; elliptical with honey skins and tight green navels.

She hafted and turned and examined first one, then another and another and another. She pressed each blossom end. Her chest ached with expectation. Somewhere in the universe of melons was her own perfect pair. When she found them, she could feed the world.

When she found them, she would plant them in pockets stitched on the insides of all her blouses. She would carry her melons high. Friends would gather and stare and ask: "May we see the scars?" Children would want to nuzzle between her melon breasts. Her husband would sit at the table and smile, one hand reaching for the spoon. There would be no waste here.

THE TEST OF LOVE
by Barry Knister
Detroit Free Press Magazine, June 2, 1991

Knister, who joined DWW in 1998, has published a novel, The Dating Service (Jove), and short stories in Magazine of Fantasy and Science Fiction. His travel pieces appear in Michigan Woman and the Detroit Free Press. He has just retired from teaching English at Lawrence Technological Institute.

"We call this one the pot roast of sea vegetables," my wife Barbara says as she passes me another bowl. "It's very substantial."

"Good." I take it from her. "I like pot roast."

We're eating in the kitchen again tonight. That's one of several changes in our daily routine that has resulted from our newly-emptied nest. With both girls away at college, the dining room now seems too big, full of shadows and echoes we never noticed before.

"You like pot roast too much," Barbara says.

She's looking across the table with a certain sternness, a school-marm vigilance. We eat in the kitchen these days also because of her macrobiotic cooking class. That too has to do with our down-sized family. The class helps to take up the slack left by Beth and Nancy, who used to shop with their mom a lot.

I smile across the table. This simple exchange with my wife is full of meaning. Take the word "substantial." In the lexicon of strange dishes from obscure places I will never visit, "substantial" represents an important euphemism. Its purpose is to avert questions related to, say, flavor. "Wholesome" is another such word.

Or "You like it too much," Barbara's reference to my stubborn allegiance to animal protein. These days, here in our empty nest, eating meat gets grouped with Saddam Hussein's war crimes. Since she started her class, I sometimes think Barbara holds me vaguely responsible for the girls' absence: Maybe it wasn't the demands of college, but rather meat on my breath that drove them away.

"And this one's basmati rice," she says, pointing to another bowl. "Very special."

"Don't tell me, I know," I say reaching for it. "The Cadillac of rice, to go with the Louis Vuitton of legumes."

"We wouldn't use such materialistic comparisons," she says. The "We" is intended to isolate me in the West, that awful seat of brutal technology, the rape of nature, and the origin of most of the world's cholesterol.

But I'm trying to be more tolerant in the girls' absence, more sensitive. So I just keep smiling my millet farmer's smile, the happy peasant look I associate with a vegetarian orientation.

"So how does this work?" I ask, bowl suspended. "Does the burdock go in the miso soup, or on top of the daikon mushoom?" (As far as I can tell, boiled burdock belongs to the same food group as cedar shingles. Daikon mushrooms have a lot in common with rubber washers.)

"You have it wrong, but that is OK," she says.

Wrong? I've got my millet, my basmati, my miso soup...

"The order's wrong," she says. "You're supposed to alternate. First yin, then yang. You took all the yang at once."

"So what will happen?"

"It's cumulative. Nothing happens today, or tomorrow. It gathers. If you learn how to eat this way, it's part of a whole vision of life."

I love Barbara. I'm grateful she never says things like "life-style." Vision of life is much better, more human. That's another reason why I'll do my best during this transition period to cooperate with her latest project — however loony it may be.

"I like eating this way in the kitchen," she says. "It's cozy."

I nod and keep chewing supportively. I don't mention that the kitchen is "cozy" partly because of a 200 percent humidity produced by four cauldrons still wheezing on the stove. I always assumed people in Asia ate quietly and decorously as a matter of custom.

I was wrong. Barbara's cooking class has taught me better. Silence during these meals has to do with thermal dynamics, not custom. People don't talk in saunas. Besides, in a macrobiotic household, you can't sustain life if you stop chewing to talk.

"Next week, we're making a type of taro pie," Barbara says. "So, what do you think?"

The moment has come for me to ante up with an assessment of tonight's meal. I nod again, chewing, buying time. This is one of those small but significant tests in marriage. Such tests are more important these days, now that our nest is empty: There are no daughters for my wife to retreat to if the pot roast barbarian across the table proves disloyal.

But the truth is that Barbara has no serious interest in what I think about these new recipes. What she *is* interested in is the degree of my love, as revealed by the imagination I can bring to the lies I'm going to invent here.

"Well—" I'm still nodding, employing the blank expression I use to suggest care in choosing my words. "It's very different — and by that I mean subtle."

"Subtle," she says, pouring herself more twig tea. "You mean delicate?"

Another probe of my loyalty. There isn't a hint of delicacy in these concoctions. Barbara knows this. Self-deception has a short half-life with her. It's also useful that she too had a firm relation to pot roast up to the time the nest emptied and she signed up for this course.

"No, Honey, it's not delicate exactly." More chewing and middle-distance reflection from me. "I'd call it a kind of . . alien simplicity."

I look over at Barbara to see how this is going down. Her eyes are closed, she's chewing — kale, I think, judging from the yang squeak.

Happily, I know that this latest filler-in for girls away at school is not going to last much longer. Soon, we'll be able to move on to other things—flea markets, perhaps, or courses at Pewabic pottery.

THE TALISMAN
by Hope Morritt
from Strong Winds Anthology, 1997

i found your watch today
tucked into a corner
of the dresser drawer — a talisman
for me to wear like a charm
luring memories —
you spotlighted on the stage
thanking the president
of the company for the
gold piece — twenty years
of safe driving through
sleet & rain & snow
a canvas of lonely miles
now all gone —

i hold the talisman
in my warm palm
& feel your presence
keenly defined

DANCIN'

by Gerry Tamm

from Variations On The Ordinary,
PlainView Press, 1995

My husband hates it
when I lead,
no problem when we
dance free.
He feels the rhythm
moves with it,
takes me with him.
But we do rounds now
choreography to
   rumbas
   waltzes
   cha-chas
   two-steps
   tangos and
   jive.
A man who doesn't like
   to be told
   to conform
   to count steps,
who likes to
   show off
   improvise
has learned the
   two step
   vine
   and hitch,
   the scissors
   diamond turn
   and twinkle,
loves the showy
   serpenté
   peek-a-boo chase.

But when it comes to
the solo left-turning box
he fakes it.

AUTOCHTHON
by Florence Dolgorukov
The Literary Review, Spring, 1982

(Editor's Note: Autochthon (Latin from Greek):One sprung from the ground which he inhabits.)

I inherited this great house
and have never yet seen it all.
Sometimes visitors have been in distant rooms,
and described marvels to me.

Sometimes I find other creatures
making their homes under this roof,
and often strangers walk through
as if they lived here.

I have always thought it was my house.
My parents died here, and their parents too;
but I have lost track
of the place they were buried,
and forgotten their legends.

I can't find the deed, either,
and sometimes I'm afraid
I may be evicted.

Detroit Women Writers Membership

100 YEARS OF MEMBERSHIP IN DETROIT WOMEN WRITERS
Length of membership dates are incomplete and approximate.
About 500 members in all
*Past President s starred
Charter member in bold type

	Year Joined
Abatt. Corinne	1992
Adams, Margaret	1930
*Adams, Myrtle	1923
*Ahnen, Pearl	1981
Alden, Margaret H.	1913
Alpern, Marge	1977
Anderson, Aristine	**1900**
Anderson, Kim	1991
Angeli, Mary Louise	1979
Arbor, Lynn (Schoettle)	1977
Arnold, Jackie Smith	1991
Arnoldussen, Barbara	1974
Ashbaugh, Delphine Dodge	1913
Avery, Berniece	1974
Avery, Helen Duke	1951
Ayers, Mabel, L.	**1900**
Bacon, Lilly B.	1922
Baldwin, Martha	1904
Barr, Jean	1900
Bartell, Linda Lang	1983
**********Bartlett, Alice C.**	**1900**
Bassett, Eda M.	1900
*Bather, Della H.	1913
Bechtel, Lenore	1963
Becker, Therese	1980
Beech, Joan	1994
Bell, Helen Jane	1965
Bell, Louie M.	1921
Bellemare, Joan	1991
Bemis, Marion Holden	1953
Bennet, Kathleen	1928
Bennett, Kathleen	1971
Benson, Linda, R.	1981
Bentley, Donna	1991
Bentley, Elizabeth	1921
Bergman, Emma	1935
Bird, Hazel K.	1920
Blankenship, Sharon	1991
Bloomer, Gertrude	1937
Bordman, Patricia	1980
Bow, Marion	1937
Bowser, Pauline	1930
Boyer, Peg	1968
Brand, Dorothy Clark	1942
Brandes, Anne Little	1923
Brazer, Marjorie	1981
Breene, Bessie Springer	1921
Breitenbach, Louise	1913
Breitmeyer, Lois	1964
Broner, Esther	1963
Brooks, May Belle	1918
Brown, Isabelle Craig	1925
Brown, Susan	1980
Bryant, Barbara	1964
Buchanan, Myra	1951
Bunge, Nancy	1991
Burns, Virginia Law	1960
*Buzzelli, Elizabeth Kane	1978
Cadieux, Leontine Keane	1965
Cahn, Mabel A. (Or: May)	1925
Cain, Ruth	1994
Calnon, Florence E.	1902
Campau, Celia	1900
Candler, Julie	1961
*Cannon, Bettie	1967
Carey, Valerie Scho	1984
Carroll, Ann	1930
Carrow, Alda V.	1944
Cash, Mercy	1935
Champney, Stella	1920
Chandler, Sally	1998
Chapman, Grace L.	1904
Childs, Dorothy	1961
Chisholm, Jean	1966
Church, Mary	1974
Cinguemani, Kate (also see: Breitenbach)	1920
*Clancey, Mrs. Louie	1925
Clayton, Mrs. Laurel Barnes	1929
Clift, Eliza Denham	1931
Clough, Ethlyn T.	1913
Coan, Mabel	1927
Coffin, Lyn	1996
Cohn, Lynne M.	1997
Colle, Cate	1978
Comstock, Deborah	1981
Cook, Dr. Emma D.	1900
Cooper, Virginia	1960
Cory, Lillian	1947

Crawford, June Crosson	1989
Crawford, Mabel	1920
Creager, Ellen C.	1997
*Crook, Bette J.	1945
Cummins, Rene	1956
Curtis, Mrs.	1904
Cutler, Gladys	1951
Darvick, Debra B.	1993
Daoust, Mary P.	1983
Datsko, Tina Michelle	1982
Davies, Florence	1921
Davis, Beulah Bailey	1933
Davis, Mary Kay	1981
Davis, Mrs. Nellie (Paulson)	1937
Dayton, Willard L.	1927
DeGain, Vivian	1994
DePuy, E. Cora	1903
DeRan, Edna Smith	1922
DeView, Lucille	1981
Diack, Helen M.	1937
Diaz, Victoria	1986
Dickinson, Margaret	1964
Dickson, Doris	1965
Dibble, Gladys Gage	1951
Dingman, Isabel	1947
Dipboye, Marilyn	1979
Doeren, Madeleine	1937
Dolgorukov, Florence	1979
Donaldson, Lou Robb	1945
Dorr, Jane	1984
Douglas, Eveline	1981
Douglas, Thelma	1965
Dowling, Elizabeth	1937
Drake, Barbara	1977
Dreyer, Merta M.	1929
Dubin, Kitty	1983
Duda, Margaret	1969
*Dudley, Cecil Rives	1927
*Dunbar, Edith	1977
Duran, Jeanne	1952
Durr, Mrs. Kenneth	1947
Dywasuk, Colette	1973
Dyar, Clara E.	1913
Eastman, Mrs. Frank	1914
Eberle, Carole	1980
Edmonds, Adelaide	1922
Elliott, Bernice	1924
Elwart, Joan	1962
Embry, Edith	1954
Erickson, Lorene	1980
Eskridge, Ann E.	1995
Eveleth, Edith	1944
Falzone, Theresa Attard	1996
Farbman, Suzy	1968
Farmiloe, Dorothy	1968
Field, Jr., Bradford	1994
Field, Ellyce R.	1988
*Fitz, Julia Grice	1969
Figmic, Mrs. J.A.	1931
*FitzPatrick, Aileen	1958
Flaherty, Nellie L.	1929
Fletcher, Grace Nies	1930
Fleenor, Juliann Evans	1985
Floren, Leola	1998
Foster, Linda Nemac	1980
Franson, Carol	1970
Freeman, Wanda	1992
Frohme, LucilleValaska	1947
Gale, Ella	1967
Gale, Frances	1917
Gamber, G ıla	1 934
Garavaglia, Anne	1964
Gehagan, Nellie	1900
Gentry, Winalee	1959
German, Eleanor	1957
*Gibbons, Ann	1954
Gilbert, Edith	1960
Gillett, Mary Jo Firth	1992
Gillette, Virginia	1976
Gilmartin, Andrina Iveison	1958
Goodwin, Isabel Pitts	1943
Gordon, Winnifred S.	1915
Gore, Emily English	1952
Goren, Dr. Judith	1970
Graham, Elizabeth G.	1966
Gray, Dr. Anna B.	1924
Green, Phyllis	1970
Greenbaum, Beth Aviv	1981
Greenway, Wilma	1947
Greenwood, May	1924
*Grigg, Mona	1982
Gruneck, Grace	1947
Guest, Judith	1977
Guy, Anne	1940
Guysi, Olive V.	1904
Hadsitts, Irma	1900
Hagan, Cathleen	1998
*Hall, Carolyn Vosburg	1976
Hall-Balduf, Susan	1988
Halsey, Margaret	1968
Hampton, S. Emma (Stark)	1900
Harben, Lıllian	1958
Harrow, Katherine	1915
Harvey, Marion	1920
Hatch, Helen Louise	1930
Hatchigan, Jessica	1985
Hay, Jessica M.	1937
Heck, Margaret	1937
Heck-Rabi, Louise	1977
Heller, Pauline	1921
Hellie, Ann	1967
Hendrix, Margaret	1961
*Henley, Bessie (Betty)	1928
Henry, Vera T.	1951
Henshall, Jeanette, F.	1921
Hicks, June	1976
Hildenbrand, Barbara Anne	1973
Hillert, Margaret	1962
Hills, Constance	1944
Hivert-Carthew, Annick	1994

Hobart, Ethel	1927
Hoffman, Jo Ann	1977
*Holden, Sheila	1942
Hollands, Hulda T.	1900
Hollister, Lillian	1900
Holmes, Kennerly	1942
Holt, Gilberte	1913
Hooper, Patricia	1985
*House, Darlene	1989
Howard, Dorothy	1963
Hurd, Muriel Jeffries	1933
Hutchinson, Anne	1998
Jackman, Diane	1989
Jackson, Almeda M.	1980
Jackson, Priscilla	1953
Jacques, Mary R.	1921
Jaznowski, Eileen	1964
Jenkin, Mabel	1947
Jenkins, Grace J. (Mrs. Carl)	1900
*Johnson, Grace Jenkins (also: Jenkins, Grace J.)	1900
Johnson, Gwen-Kirsten	1994
*Johnson, Mrs. J. Carl	1934
Johnson, Mary A.	1980
Johnston, Mary M.	1900
Johnston, Nora Bethel	1960
Jones, Judy	1976
*Jones, Iris Sanderson	1963
Jones, Kate Harbin	1930
*Jorgensen, Mary West	1937
Kallmeier, Helen B.	1920
Kania, Karin	1979
Karow, Mabel Veider	1926
Katz, Carol	1983
Katzenmeyer, Carol	1962
Kavanagh-Patrick, Bridget	1994
Kay, Peg	1971
Keane, Leontine Cadieux	1966
Kelsey, Maude F.	1922
Kicknosway, Faye	1980
Kincaid, Mary	1977
King, Carolyn	1958
*King, Cynthia (Toni)	1977
King, Elizabeth Chiu	1988
King, Peggy Cameron,	1959
Knight, Allison	1991
Knight, Mary	1984
Knister, Barry	1998
Knoppow, Susan	1995
Korn, Claire	1985
Kraus, Carolyn Wells	1985
Krause, Margaret	1920
Krieger, Martha	1990
*Kubacka, Marian	1951
*Kurth, Emma B.	1918
Labbitt, Myrtle	1964
Lambert, Marion	1935
Lanagan, Frederica	1900
LaFerle, Cynthia	1987
LaGattuta, Margo	1980

Langan, Ruth Ryan	1983
LaTour, Sarah J.	**1900**
Leggett, Lucy A. Honorary President	**1900**
Leithauser, Gladys G.	1965
Lemkie, Annie Stearnes	1900
*Leo, Kathleen Ripley	1978
*Levin, Marjory Jackson	1956
Ling , Katherine G.	1924
*Littell, Mrs. L.B.	1913
Lockwood, Hazel	1937
Long, Agnes	1920
Loud, Marion	1920
Lucier, Clara, M	1944
Luckow-Healy, Lisa	1998
Lull, Ella	1932
*Lyman, Marilyn	1958
MacDonald, Beatrice	1925
MacIntosh, Emily S.	1902
Mackinnon, Wanda	1955
MacLean, Kay	1943
Madgett, Naomi Long	1967
McArthur, Barbara	1981
McCarthy, Jane White	1998
McCormick, Ann duMais	1989
McDaniel, Natalie	1947
McDougal, Marie	1994
McCaslin, Mattie	1913
McCorkle, Helen	1920
McDonald, Jean	1903
McFarland, Virginia	1969
McGerty, Maureen	1998
McGraw, Carole	1998
McGuire, Alice	1919
McNair, Mary	1993
McVeigh, Amy	1991
*McWood, Dorothy	1948
Mammel, Phyllis	1949
Manthey, Betty H.	1922
Mantyla, Wilma	1943
Marker, Mary McSherry	1960
Marlett, Melba	1968
Marshall, Yvonne	1944
Martz, Jean B.	
*Marzolf, Marion	1980
Martin, Mabel	1922
Mather, Bobbie	1967
Melrose, Fern	1968
*Michelson, Mollie	1936
Milios, Rita	1988
Miller, Helen Janet (Schuler)	1930
Miller, Mabel L.	1920
Mills, Maud E.	1900
Milner, Florence	1913
Mitchell, Nancy	1985
Mizner, Elizabeth Howard	1952
Modrack, Barbara	1986
Moll, Martha	1913
Montgomery, Frances T.	1923
Montle, Wilma	1996

Montwori, Deborah	1981
Moore, Eileen Stubb	1940
Morand, Rose	1998
Morneau, Cecilia	1976
Morritt, Hope	1998
Morse, Susan	1980
Munson-Benson, T.	1976
*Munson, Floy Tefft	1935
Murray, Ethel	1900
Nagle, Geraldine	1992
Nardiella, Patricia A. Moed	1995
Naughton, Louise E.	1971
*Needles, Mrs. G.W.	1914
Nelson, Nancy Owen	1998
Neuhoff, Betty Wardell	1931
Newell, E.M.	1923
***Nichols, Mrs. Franc**	**1900**
Nielsen, Anne-Marie	1967
Nisbett, Susan Isaacs	1980
Oakley, Barbara A.	1998
Oates, Joyce Carol (Smith)	1964
*Oestreich, Anna L.	1930
Opsahl, Polly	1998
Oram, Lily Maud	1930
Overman, Ione S.	1927
Paetz, Catherine I.	1927
Page, Beulah Bailey	1936
Palmer, Carol A.	1937
Parker, Bonnie	1964
*Parker, Helen Pitts	1925
*Parker, Virginia Bailey	1991
Parks, Marion F.	1979
Parnie, Elaine Helmer	1951
Paul, Jeanne	1980
Paulson, Nellie Davis	1928
Pearson, Kathy	1967
Pawlowski, Diane R.	1980
Pepper, Leila	1958
Peterson, Margaret Williamson	1950
Pierce, Violet Monroe	1927
Pitchford, Theodus Carroll	1984
*Pitrone, Jean	1960
Plumb, Beatrice	1972
Pobujewski, Sally	1988
Pollard, Elizabeth	1913
Porter, Monica	1967
Portnoy, Maida	1983
Powels, Bernice Ireland	1925
Potter, Amelia	1929
Prescott, Eleanor Manning	1921
Prescott, Helen	1980
Price, Elsie	1968
Price, Zella Varian	1946
Pritchard, Sheila	1948
Putnam, Leona, S.	1945
Quinley, Mary	1992
Radgens, Joyce	1984
Ranck, Helen	1970
Randall, Harriet	1983
Randall, Nellie	1976
Randall, Virginia	1970
Ransom, Jeanie Franz	1988
Rasey, Dr. Marie	1935
Rathbone, Violet	1935
Regan, Patricia	1944
Reindel, Arlene	1983
Reith, Alma Carmichael	1973
Remick, Grace	1913
Renko, Dorothy	1979
Reynaud, Karen Chortney	1998
Rhines, Margaret	1920
Rice, Patty C.	1980
Richardson, Deborah	1976
Richart, Mary	1952
Rippier, Marie Olliver	1925
Ritchie, Virginia	1964
Robb, Kathryn	1951
*Roberts, Mary	1947
Roberts, Sheila	1980
Rogers, Elyse	1965
*Ronan, Eileen	1959
Rooksby, Ellen	1913
Rose, Elinor K.	1957
*Rubin, Gay	1974
Rubin, Linda Stern	1979
Rugenstein, Carole	1985
Ryan, Nancy	1993
St. Barnard, Helen	1931
Salie, Jean	1981
Sanford, Marcelline Hemingway	1953
Sawyer, Sally	1988
Scaffetti, Sandra	1981
Schaal, Mrs. Kenneth S.	1922
*Scharfenberg, Doris	1967
Schoen, Mary Augusta Rodgers	1958
Schoettle, Lynn	1974
Schwartz, Carla Jean	1986
*Secrist, Margaret	1949
Seese, Ethel Gray	1969
Seiden, Virginia	1959
*Sellers, Susan	1913
Sheetz, Wealthy	1920
***Sherman, Pruella J.**	**1900**
Shock, H. Buteau	1941
Sienkiewicz, Linda	1998
Skoglund, Renee M.	1994
***Sleeper, Hattie C.**	**1900**
Smell, Priscilla	1934
Smith, Belle M. Michael	1925
*Smith, Catherine (Kay)	1951
Smith, Ella Gordon	1944
Smith, Ethel M.	1937
Smith, Joyce Carol Oates	1964
Smith, Julie Dean	1992
Smith, Mary Beth	1987
Smith, Pearl	1920
Sparks, Beatrice Harreld	1940

Smits, Anna Mary Wells	1942
Solak, Nancy	1987
Soules, Aline	1995
Sparrow, Laura	1985
Sprague, Esther Bryant	1951
Spicer, Carol	1965
Spinning, Hester J.	**1900**
Stachurski, Elizabeth	1987
Starrette,Sandra	1988
Starkey, Jennie O.	1903
Stefaniuk, Mira	1988
Stern-Heiden, Margaret	1929
Stewart, Bernice	1922
Stiles, Martha Bennet	1969
*Stocking, Elizabeth L.	1903
Stoddard, Jennie	1901
Stovel, Margaret	1904
Strauss, Freddie R.	1923
Streeter, Mrs. Claude F.	1922
Suczek, Charity deVigue	1951
Suhler, Margaret	1920
Sulzburger, Elsie R.	1920
Sutes , Della T.	1902
Tait, Kate	1913
Tamm, Geraldine	1986
Taylor, Amie L.	1989
Taylor, Lucy A.	1990
Taylor, Polly B.	1937
Tefft, Bess Hojamen	1965
Tessler, Sandra	1980
Than, Mona Bardwin	1932
Thompson, Cora (or Floris)	1928
Thompson, Elaine	1940
Tomey, Ingrid	1983
Tompert, Ann	1978
Torosian, Jeanne Wylie	1936
Travis, Katherine	1942
Troutman, Jacquelyn D.	1995
Twogood, Ethel M.	1924
Unger, Joan	1970
Uram, Sue	1995
VanBuskirk, Selma	1948
*Vandermede, Gail E.	1940
Vanderveer, Vesta H.	1925
Van Dyk, M. Patricia	1988
Van Tuyl, Mary C.	1958
Voss, Josephine	**1900**
Wagner, Linda	1968
Wagner, Mary L.	1997
***Wain, Ida F.**	**1900**
Walker, Dorothy Howells	1929
Walker, Pat	1976
Ware, Gail	1994
Warner, Mrs. Harry	1925
Warsaw, Irene	1954
Warren,Mrs. Wadsworth	1930
Warrington, Lynn P.	1992
Waterworth, Florence W.	1913
Watson, Elaine	1969
Webber, Mrs. Frank	1924
Weberman, Patricia McArthur-Dunn	1979
Wehler, Mary Ann	1997
Weinman, Rose Barlow	1920
Welch, Susan	1989
Weller, Patricia J.	1992
Wells, Joyce Ferman	1989
Wheat, Marie Moss	1920
Wheatley, Evelyn Stephenson	1954
Whelan, Gloria	1980
White, Jane May	1930
Whitney, Charlotte	1987
White, Gertrude Mason	1954
White, June (or Jane)	1925
Wiberg, Dorothy	
Wilkes, Florence E.	1924
Williams, Calla	1937
Willman, Marianne	1987
Wilson, Mrs. C.R.	1920
Wilson, Etta	1903
*Winn, Josephine	1951
Workman, Helen Chaffee	1930
Wolf, Sarah Shoemaker	1987
Woodhouse, Mrs. John	1920
Worth, Stephanie	1993
Wrenn, Sharon	1989
Wunsch, Josephine	1963
Wylie, Miss Jeanne (Torosian)	1940
Yost, Jessie V.	1932

List of DWW Presidents: 1900-2000

1900-02	Alice Elinor Bartlett
1902-03	Ida F. Wain
1903-04	Pruella Janet Sherman
1904-05	Ida F. Wain
1905-06	Aruella Janet Sherman
1906-07	Alice Elinor Bartlett
1907-08	Mrs. Franc M. Nichols
1908-11	Hattie C. Sleeper
1911-13	Alice Elinor Bartlett
1913-15	Eizabeth Stocking
1915-16	Mrs. L. B. Littell
1916-17	Mrs. Delphine Dodge Ashbaug
1917-18	Susan Sellers
1918-20	Alice Elinor Bartlett
1920-22	Mrs. Karl F. Kurth
1922-25	Mrs. Frank A. (Della H.) Bather
1925-26	Mrs. Louie B. Clancey
1926-28	Mrs. Anna L. Oestreich
1928-30	Mrs. Emma Everett Needles
1930-32	Vesta Hardy Vandeveer
1932-34	Mrs. Cecil Rives Dudley
1934-36	Mrs. J. Carl Johnson
1936-37	Mrs. Frederick T. Munson
1937-38	Mrs. Arthur M. Parker
1937-39	Mrs. Hayden Henley
1939-41	Mrs. Olaf N. Michelson
1941-43	Mrs. Arthur M. Parker
1943-45	Mrs. J. Gordon Adams
1945-47	Mary West Jorgensen
1947-48	Gail Vandermede
1948-51	Mrs. J. C. Roberts
1951-53	Sheila Holden
1953-55	Margaret Secrist
1955-57	Bette Crook
1957-59	Ann Gibbons
1959-60	Dorothy McWood
1960-61	Mrs. J. E. Kubacka
1961-62	Aileen Fitzpatrick
1962-64	Josephine Winn
1964-65	Eileen Ronan
1965-67	Kay Smith
1967-69	Marilyn Lyman
1969-71	Iris Jones
1971-72	Marjory Levin
1972-73	Doris Scharfenberg
1973-75	Bettie Cannon
1975-77	Julia Grice
1977-79	Jean Pitrone
1979-81	Cynthia King
1981-83	Carolyn Vosburg Hall
1983-85	Elizabeth Kane Buzzelli
1985-86	Gay Rubin
1987-89	Mona Grigg
1989-91	Pearl Ahnen
1991-93	Edith Dunbar
1993-95	Marion Marzolf
1995-97	Virginia Bailey Parker
1997-99	Kathleen Ripley Leo
1999-2001	Darlene House